D1528994

Meaning and Being in Myth

Meaning and Being
in Myth

Norman Austin

The Pennsylvania State University Press
University Park and London

Library of Congress Cataloging-in-Publication Data

Austin, Norman.
  Meaning and being in myth / Norman Austin.
     p. cm.
  Bibliography: p.
  Includes index.
  ISBN 0-271-00681-1
  1. Myth.   I. Title.
 BL304.A97   1990
 291.1′3—dc20   89-34186
                                              CIP

Humbly our old poets knew to make
wanderings into

homecomings of a sort—harbor, palace, temple, all
having been quarried out of those blue foothills
no further off, these last clear autumn
days, than infancy.
—James Merrill, "Losing the Marbles"

TO THE THREE GRACES

Adele Barker
Pamela Hopkins
Gail Larrick

Contents

Preface

In 1974, with my study of Homer's *Odyssey* in the hands of the editors at the University of California Press, I took a sabbatical leave, intending to write another book on Homer, having, as I thought, sufficient material left over from my research on the *Odyssey* to fill another volume. But my research in that sabbatical year followed its own wayward course. I trust that John S. Guggenheim, whose generous provisions funded my leave of absence, will not take it amiss, should reports of our world reach his, that the projected book on Homer has shrunk down to a few slim pages in this present study.

In addition to the Guggenheim Foundation, I would like to thank my colleagues at the University of California at Los Angeles, and at the University of Arizona, for sabbatical leaves, which forwarded this project immeasurably, and the American Council of Learned Societies for a grant-in-aid, which enabled me to read more extensively the literature on modern psychoanalytic theory.

A project so long in gestation owes a debt to many besides those whose names find their way into the Notes. I am grateful to many colleagues whose conversations and published papers have made important, if subliminal, contributions to the thinking from which this study has grown. I am grateful also to Jane Brown, with whom I studied dance during my sabbatical year in 1974. At a time when I was nearly inundated by the welter of signifiers issuing from our modern academies, Jane Brown's studio in Oakland was a haven where I learned, through movement, a deeper integration of thought and being. To William Mullen I owe special thanks, a colleague and friend who has followed this project from its conception with an encouragement and a credence surpassing collegial bonds. The many students too, enrolled in the myth and literature courses, where I first articulated the ideas in this study, have been points of light on my path. Two I have named in the Notes for their specific contributions in my chapter on *The Stranger,* but countless others remain in my memory as living presences whose enthusiasm and perception have had a decisive influence on my thinking.

"Hamlet's Hungry Ghost" was first published in *Shenandoah,* vol. 37 (1987); the original essay has been modified somewhat to bring it into alignment with the other chapters in this present study. I would like to acknowledge here the kindness of the late editor of *Shenandoah,* James Boatwright, for allowing me several occasions to develop my personal cosmology in the pages of that hardy little magazine. "The Case of the Missing Self," published in volume 33 (1982) of the magazine, and "Homer's Icons," published in volume 34 (1983), were preliminary exercises for the chapter on Homer's gods.

The gods sent me three mentors in my youth, whose influence on my career I would like to acknowledge here: Mr. Gordon Martin, my first Latin master, whose first class in beginning Latin remains vivid in my memory almost forty years after the event; Mr. R. M. H. Shepherd, my first professor of Greek at the University of Toronto, whose sense of the vitality of Greek made even the memorizing of paradigms seem a worthwhile exercise; and Mr. Robert Halliday, a retired missionary when I knew him, who brushed the dust off his old classical texts so that he could coach me through first-year Greek. The dedication of these three scholars to classical culture so profoundly affected my life at critical moments of decision that it is unlikely that this study would have come to fruition without their guidance in my formative years.

While this book was in progress, I joked that I would include a special tribute to the staff at the various coffee shops where the manuscript grew, night by night, on lined foolscap. But it was no jest. The twenty-four-hour coffee shops in Tucson are a great boon to the writer, thinker, or observer of human nature. Since this study was wholly composed in coffee shops, I would like to thank the staff of the Terrace Lounge at the University, where I spent many productive mornings, and the staff at the several coffee shops around town, who watched over the manuscript's progress on the night shift. They were truly angels, perhaps even *boddhisatvas,* coming and going with ready smiles, words of encouragement, and countless refills of my coffee cup.

A scholar who undertakes to study myth experiences a curious ambivalence, wondering whether the material is directed primarily to children, or whether it is too sophisticated for children. The squabbles on Mt. Olympos may seem quite infantile, but what of the castration of Ouranos? The scholar, taking such material into the classroom, faces the same ambiguity on another level. Are the students, for whom the scholar elucidates the material, children or adults? Of course the answer is that they are both. Myths appeal to the juvenile in us, but to survive into literature they must also satisfy adult reason. Thus the treatment of myth calls for a certain nimble movement back and forth between infancy and adulthood. I have tried to be faithful to both poles, but if my colleagues in the field find some of my observations commonplace, I trust that they will be sympathetic, remembering the polarities inherent in myth, and that they will find, among the commonplaces, speculation worthy of a scholar.

James Merrill has given his kind permission for me to quote from his two masterpieces, "Losing the Marbles" and "The Parnassians," both included in his most recent book of poems, *The Inner Room,* published by Alfred A. Knopf (1988). I am grateful to Mr. Merrill and his publishers for their courtesy.

Finally, my acknowledgments would be incomplete without a special thanks to the editorial board, the senior editor, and the staff of the Pennsylvania State University Press for their confidence in this study, and their encouragement.

Introduction

The gods belong to the field of the real.
—Jacques Lacan[1]

Several years ago, when I was asked to teach the departmental mythology course, I accepted the assignment with some misgivings, uncertain where I should find the golden bough to illuminate my way either into the great forest of myth or through the thicket of modern theories on ancient myth. Frazer's dying and rising corn god, the solar hero, myth as allegory, myth as a disease of language—each theory seemed cogent in its time, until a newer theorist arose to discount the more simplistic theories of his predecessors. Was it an adequate service to myth merely to enumerate the theories, without taking a stand on any of them?

But as I began teaching the course the myths took hold of me as living presences, insisting on their meaning even when they eluded adequate explanations of that meaning. The numinous force of myths both intimidated the search for their meaning and made the search more imperative. Like our private dreams, myths drift into shape from who knows what depths of our genetic history, but when they impinge upon our consciousness we are faced with two alternatives: either to dismiss them as quaint superstitions or to receive them as the distillates of our ancestors' wisdom.

Myths, protean themselves, demand a like agility in their students. I was compelled, like every serious student of myth, to expand my research on several different fronts—into modern psychological theory, anthropology, philosophy, hermeneutics, semiotics, and finally, even into science. It came as a surprise to discover that the atom of the ancient atomists was as much a mythical concept as the Olympian gods. Like the Olympians, the atom was eternal, indestructible, and transcended sense perception; like them, it could be apprehended by intuition alone. When the Olympians were revealed as too transparently human to stand as the ultimate Ground of Being, the imagination took another leap, and replaced one order of mythical powers with another. If myth is, as the mind's search for the absolute, a primitive science, science at its farthest reach circles around again to myth.

Myth purports to offer an adequate explanation for everything—for the elements and laws of nature, for social structures, ethics, and the dynamics of the individual psyche. The student of myth must, sooner or later, become a cosmologist since every myth both presupposes and illustrates a cosmology, as every fact presupposes a complete theoretical system. Thus this study, which began as a meditation on the social and psychological constructs that gave rise to specific classical Greek myths, grew into a full-blown cosmology, drawing eclectically from many sources.

I have appropriated terminology freely from diverse thinkers: the I-Thou relations from Buber; Being and non-Being from the German philosophers; self and Other from Hegel; the id, ego, and superego from Freud; the archetypes and the Self from Jung; signifiers and the subject from Lacan. A thinker's thoughts, once coined, become common currency. Abstract terms, especially those referring to the domain of the psyche, resist succinct definition, but I trust that my uses of such terms will be intelligible from their context; further, that my movement between one set of terms and another will find acceptance not only for the intrinsic value of the terms but as an indication of the overlap between one thinker's theoretical system and another's.

It is only fair for me to state the primary intuitions underlying the cosmology to which myth has led me. The first is that myth, though determined in its form by its immediate historical context, transcends any historical moment, being at the fundamental level the quest for the self. But the self is the most problematic of terms, which proliferates in all directions, cloaks itself in manifold disguises, and creates a multitude of images to fascinate or deceive the hunter. The myth of Narcissus is the central myth in human thought, though the fate of Narcissus, to drown in his own reflections, is not the only solution.[2]

The self cannot, as Dewey remarked, find its unity in itself alone, but must achieve this unity only in transcending itself. Or, in Hegel's terms, the self cannot achieve self-consciousness without the consciousness of the Other. Lacan put the problem in another way: the individual self must find itself through the network of signifiers, which, being already culturally determined, are in the field of the Other. Thus the self discovers itself only in alienation. Even Narcissus, who imagines that he can find himself without hazarding himself in the field of the Other, is doomed to find only empty images of himself, and on the very face of the Other that he had shunned.

The self searches for the authentic subject, but this subject lies hidden in the alien field of the Other. Seeing intimations of the subject everywhere, but finding the subject nowhere, the self projects another and larger self as the subject; that is, the gods, through whom it can envision and realize itself. The gods of myth and religion, who enjoy the fullness of Being, suffering neither the hazards of time nor the anguish of self-consciousness, are at the first level the signifiers of that absolute Other, inscrutable and inaccessible. Like the superego in Freud's psychic cosmology, the gods stand guard to prohibit the ego from trespassing its limits, and thus mark the ego's terrible alienation from Being. But the function of the gods is not only punitive. The gods also are the signifiers that bridge the chasm between the self and the Other. Standing in the field of the Other, the gods are the sympathetic witnesses to the self's travail as it moves from object-consciousness, at the first level of consciousness, to full self-consciousness.

If the quest of the human mind is to achieve an absolute unity, and even an identity, with the world, we can track the same process from the opposite direction. The second intuition underlying this study, which is but the primary intuition seen from the reverse, is that the world strives to manifest itself in consciousness. The world does not impinge upon us in a merely deterministic way; it informs us in the fullest sense, not only shaping us but guiding and, as Buber puts it, addressing us.

Even the simplest biological organism does more than react blindly to external stimuli; organisms *use* nature to regenerate and reproduce themselves. Biology, arresting entropy if only provisionally, introduces teleology into the world. Inanimate matter has only a history, but even the humblest biological organism has a destiny. The mythologist can discern in the amoeba's probings the first intimations of the self tenuously realizing itself in the field of the Other.

The sockeye salmon, leaping upstream, is a more magnificent paradigm of biology's imperative of self-realization in the field of the Other. We might argue that the smolt are swept downstream mindlessly, carried by the force of gravity. But on its return run, three years later, the mature salmon is no longer flotsam at the mercy of the elements. It must use the principles of hydrodynamics, and the downward thrust of gravity, to propel its body, now of much greater mass and resistance, three hundred miles upward against the current, until it reaches the inland pool where it was spawned. Is the ancient hero's quest for self-realization so very different from the salmon's ecstatic ascent to its birthplace, which, once achieved, becomes its burial ground? If we admire Achilles more than the salmon, it is because we can penetrate deeper into the mind of Achilles, and sympathize with the anguish of an animal netted in his own signifiers and discovering, too late, the missing subject.

The salmon's feat of engineering we call instinct, because here the form and function are so closely synchronized as to allow almost no interval, as Bergson puts it, between representation and act.[3] But as instinct shades into intellect a breach opens up between form and function, which allows for the larger play of representations we call consciousness. *Homo sapiens* gave up an instinct finely tuned to its immediate environment for an intellect capable of imagining any number of possible environments. We exchanged, in short, the animal's instinctual here and now for a problematic past and a problematic future.

The human organism uses all the forces of nature instinctively, as other organisms do, but in that breach between representation and act the human mind has created a second body; that is, a body of signifiers, designed at first merely to follow after and mirror back to the material body its own image in its relations with the other images in nature; but then, by happy accident, or inspiration, schooled to transcend the body of nature.

Language was at first, no doubt, a tool like any other for working more efficiently on matter. But humans then found in their signifiers a thought-plasm, as it were, from which to fashion the metaphysical self, that gymnast balanced on the highwire between intellect and instinct.[4] The impulse of the lowest organisms shades into instinct in more complex organisms; instinct shades into conscious intention in a body possessed of, and by, its signifiers. If Achilles drives himself headlong to his death, as the salmon does, he must in addition reflect on that movement, and make biological necessity his conscious intention.

Thus, in the human mind, gravity itself arises into consciousness, appearing first in myth as the density and inertia of the earth element, and by slow degrees revealing itself in its most abstract form, as a property of mass. As humans arrive at consciousness only through participation in the world, so nature too moves toward consciousness through its participation in the development of the human mind.

Seeing myth as the medium for the articulation of our experience in the world and for the world's revelation of its own inner dynamic to the human mind, I find myself drawn to terms like Plato's Forms or Jung's archetypes, while mindful that such terms may raise as many questions as they answer. Though Freud's hypotheses have been very influential on my thought—who, after reading Freud, can avoid seeing the dynamic conflict of ego, superego, and id in the relations of the ancient heroes to their gods?—yet I cannot believe that the icons of myth derive only from our individual, postnatal experiences. Each of our cells is a descendant of the first living cell, and even after millions of years of evolutionary brachiation, human cells are still near-cousins to the cells of plant and tree. The memories complexly coded in the nucleus of our cells reach back almost to infinity, and memory must, in some mysterious way, stretch even into the future, if memory is a biological mechanism for recording past uses in order to guide future uses. Our eyes remembered seeing even when they lay closed in the darkness of the womb. Platonists will recognize here Plato's doctrine of learning as recollection. The infant's first sight of the world is an act of remembering.

I use the term archetype to mean primordial forms. Since we grow from infancy to adulthood within a social context, it is only reasonable that the first projections of these forms should be clothed in a personal dress. Thus we can talk of the Father archetype, the Mother, the Puer, the Senex, and other such terms as real presences in every human psyche. Since we are also sexualized beings, I also have no difficulty in accepting Jung's terms Animus and Anima, as symbolic terms representing our projections of the archetypal masculine and feminine in the human psyche. But gravity also is an archetype, and the other modern abstractions—space, time, energy. We can express such forces or laws of nature in the cryptic equations of science, but there is more to gravity than its mathematical formula. We experience gravity; it impinges on our consciousness every day in manifold ways. Just as the physics of light does not express our experience of light, so Newton's laws cannot give us our experience of gravity. For our experience of the forces of nature we turn to art, religion, and myth. The abstractions of modern science rest still on primary intuitions of a reality that, like Jung's archetypes or the Platonic Forms, transcends all intellectual articulations.

As long as we continue to be sentient beings we shall continue to need myth, since myth is the primary ground on which we articulate our experience of ourselves in our social and natural environment. The imagination, a plastic medium, receives impressions from the archetypal forms of nature, and by an active force realizes those impressions in its own forms, as images, symbols, and ideas. The imagination projects, for our contemplation, the archetypal images of our human experience in the world; in addition, like a transformer, it translates the ineffable forms of nature into structures and images so that the ineffable may become articulated in consciousness. Myth I take as the ground of the numinous archetypes, the screen, as it were, through which the imagination perceives the forms of nature, and onto which it projects the forms of its own experience. The gods I take to be the numinous powers that inhabit, and rule, this field. It follows that every numinous presence is divine—here I follow the practice of the Romans, for whom the numinous was synonymous with the divine.

The great religions concur that the god that can be named is not God. The numinous archetypes are the ground of all Being, but the gods are their images, mere icons at best. To mistake the icon for the archetype is to confuse the figure with the ground, the signifier with the signified. Maturity consists in learning to distinguish the icon from the archetype, but even so the archetype does not disappear: the iconic representation becomes larger and more inclusive.

The gods are at the first level the representations of the forces of nature, autonomous and arbitrary. But the gods of myth, who wear human faces, despite all prohibitions against seeing or naming them, are also projections of our idealized selves, which, like all ideals, are as intimidating as they are hortatory. I understand these gods as Soleri does, who calls them "a pursued hypothesis." We project onto the eternal plane an imagined order of beings in whose will our destiny has its proper place, to validate the mysterious windings of that destiny and guide them forward into an uncertain future. On one hand inscrutable, as the signifiers of absolute Being, the gods are yet archetypes of our own selves—projections to account for the inexplicable, problematic, or demonic in our own behavior; and also exemplars of our higher self, that self that regards all our faltering experiments in Being with tenderness and admiration. Building on the primary narcissism of the infant, we project a world of eternal Being, which we can love because it loves us.

In this study I have attempted to explicate myths both as social constructs, as in my analysis of Hesiod's myth of Pandora, and as the imagination's intuition of the most abstract principles, as in my interpretation of Hesiod's primal elements—Chaos, Gaia, and Eros—as intimations arising into the forms we now recognize as space, matter, and energy. It is an error, in my view, to draw a rigid distinction between myth and science, and to dismiss the archaic Greeks as prescientific, while priding ourselves on our escape from mythical thinking. Myth and science lie on a continuum, which I have attempted to illustrate in my chapter on the serpent.

The serpent has been archetypal symbol of evil throughout our Western history. Laid under a curse by Jahweh in the Garden of Eden, it has been declared a monstrosity of Creation. Yet the ancient celestial gods, who were no less zealous than Jahweh in extirpating the serpent, had also their chthonic serpentine forms or cults; even today the serpent, coiled around the caduceus of Asclepius, serves as the symbol of the healing profession. The serpent is the signifier of what is most alien, yet this horrifying Other is at the same time most near and most desirable. The Oriental theories of the kundalini and our modern theories of the tripartite brain converge to intimate that the mythical combat between the serpent and the Olympian patriarch may well be the representation of the conflict deep within ourselves, between the old brain and the new, dating perhaps from the time when vertebrates parted company with reptiles and insects, and the one party took the path toward instinct; the other, toward intellect.

When I first read the Book of Job in the light of myth, I was struck by the obvious mythical elements in the drama—the sons of God presenting themselves before the Lord, in disregard for monotheistic orthodoxy; Satan, the Adversary, conversing with the Lord; the two of them wagering with each other for a human soul; and the twofold plane of the poem, with numinous archetypes negotiating in the invisible realm, and manifesting their wills on the material plane as catastrophes of nature. Attuned also to the primary significance of tabus in mythology, I was led to meditate more deeply on the tabu against blasphemy, around which the drama revolves, the greatest of all tabus in religion and myth.

The poem slowly revealed an even deeper stratum of mythical thought than the obvious folktale motifs in the drama. The voice in the whirlwind invokes Rahab, Behemoth, Leviathan, various names for the primordial antagonist. We have, in the Book of Job, a philosophical exploration of the common myth of the hero's combat with the ancient chaos demon. Here, however, Behemoth and Leviathan, though acknowledged as the primordial Adversary, are not stigmatized, but celebrated as chief among the works of the Creator. The serpent, who was cursed in the Garden of Eden for seducing our first parents into consciousness, is here rehabilitated as Lucifer, the bright and morning star. Satan, with whom Job wrestles, and Leviathan are one and the same: the archetypal symbol of the Other. As long as the serpent remains under the curse, and excluded from Creation, consciousness remains arrested at object-consciousness. Self-consciousness requires that the Adversary be realized as chief among the sons of God.

The high status of the primal serpent in this myth and the tabu against blaspheming the Almighty are intimately connected. No one is tempted to blasphemy in times of prosperity; the temptation arises only when the Adversary intrudes upon our ease and cleaves the world into self and Other. The tabu against blasphemy was instituted to prevent a short circuit in the self's progress toward full self-consciousness. To blaspheme the Almighty when the Almighty manifests itself as the Other is to risk fixation at the stage of primary narcissism. Job's wife, in exhorting Job to blasphemy, chooses narcissism, but Job, holding to his own integrity and to the integrity of the Almighty, chooses the path of self-consciousness, which is to wrestle with the Adversary through duality to the discovery that God and the Adversary are one.

I have included an essay on *Hamlet* and another on Camus' *The Stranger* in this study to illustrate the primacy of mythical archetypes even in modern literature, where the field has been cleared of the ancient gods. *Hamlet* stands midway, in this respect, between ancient literary works, which employ the machinery of myth without embarrassment, and an existentialist novel like *The Stranger,* from which the machinery has been rigorously excluded. No gods watch over Hamlet's career, either to inhibit or to encourage his action. The human mind has here been emancipated from the terrible gaze of the Almighty, which had once discovered Adam and Eve in their nakedness. But the emancipation brings no peace. Hamlet is troubled still by a ghost, a faded copy, as it were, of the Ancient of Days, but a numinous presence nevertheless, exerting its will on Hamlet from beyond the reach of his conscious mind. Liberated from the gods, the human mind is still haunted by ghosts— and this may be a worse condition. The general approval given to the ghost in scholarly criticism of the play, and the findings of modern psychoanalysis, convince me that the ghost of Hamlet's father is as potent today as he was when the play was first performed.

Even ghosts have vanished from Meursault's world in Camus' *The Stranger.* Hamlet is a guilty hero, harried by a ghost, whose very function is to induce guilt. But Meursault, emancipated even from such vestiges of the mythical powers, knows no guilt. With neither gods nor ghosts to trouble his conscience, we would expect Meursault to be supremely happy. Far from it; Meursault is the unhappiest of men. Deposing the ancient gods is no guarantee of happiness. It can be argued, in fact, that Meursault's alienation, the vacuity at the center of his being, is a more terrible fate than the fate of the ancient tragic heroes who, even in the abyss, did not sever their I-Thou relations with the world.

I was struck by the presence of a myth embedded even in this novel, which repudiates the mythical or metaphysical plane of being. Meursault's encounter with the sun, when the heat and glare befuddle his mind, is the modern version of the hero's fatal encounter with the numinous powers. Though not anthropomorphized, the sun here is as numinous in its force as the ancient Olympians were when a mortal trespassed into their territory. And the meaning is the same, even if the myth be cast in modern existentialist terms: the hero's death, when he transgresses into the field of the numinous, is the story of the grandiose ego destroyed by its presumption.

If Meursault's fatal encounter with the sun is the overt myth in the novel, reminiscent of the fall of Icarus or Phaethon, the novel is haunted by yet another myth, which justifies the novel's inclusion in a set of readings on myth. That is the myth of Narcissus. Meursault demonstrates many of the traits of narcissistic disorder: a grandiose ego, an inability to form real attachments to any thing or person, a refusal to accept responsibility for any action or to feel guilt, a great ennui coupled with contempt for those who find any meaning in their lives.[5] The narcissism is well camouflaged until Meursault reveals, in his final confession, that he has created an inhuman cosmology to validate the vacuum in his own feelings, an unconscious universe to mirror back to him his own curse upon his consciousness. Meursault's trajectory in this novel, which ends with his wish that jeering spectators should curse him as they witness his execution, betrays a narcissism so absolute, yet so desperate, that it will contrive first murder, and then suicide, to pierce through to a real experience of itself in the world.

The Book of Job and Camus' *The Stranger* are counterbalanced in a profound symmetry of opposition. Job, engulfed in the vortex of the Other, will not betray his I-Thou covenant with the world. Meursault, finding in the Other only alienation, tramples the covenant underfoot, and is left a prisoner of his own fear and anger. Great indeed is the temptation to curse the Ground of Being. Consciousness is a small voice swallowed up in a void indifferent, it seems, to consciousness. But consciousness can no more be disavowed than the abyss of unconsciousness that surrounds it. Narcissism at one extreme and Hegelian self-consciousness at the other: *The Stranger* and the Book of Job stand as the two poles in the process of self-realization, which I take to be the true quest of myth.

1

The Numinous Ground

It is a universal experience that the world presents itself to us in two modes, which are opposed yet, in mysterious ways, related to each other. Ancient or modern, monists or dualists, we concur that the world is fundamentally duplicitous. The world both is and is not what it seems. This duplicity in the very nature of things has led people to posit two separate worlds. The world of phenomena is opposed to the world variously called supernatural or metaphysical; change and appearance are opposed to the eternal absolutes. In modern times we have come to recognize in the two worlds two modes of knowing and relating to the world, which Langer identifies as two different schemas of symbolic thought, the "discursive" and the "representational."[1] Her two schemas correspond to Milton's "reason discursive, or intuitive."[2]

The discursive mode—"ordinary consciousness," Barfield calls it—presents the world as a system of facts.[3] Through sense perception and deductive reason, by calculation and experiment, this mode generates a world marked by regularity and predictability. Here cause and effect are known, or presumed to be knowable, given the appropriate instruments. This mode, industrious to a fault, weaves on the loom of logic the seamless fabric that, in ordinary conversation, we call the world. It proclaims itself the Logos, lord of syntax and semantics. Ayer states the claims for this mode in the most unequivocal way when he describes the task of philosophy as simply to determine "whether a sentence expresses a genuine proposition about a matter of fact." [4]

No sooner has the objective mode pronounced its principles, however, than it begins to undermine its own authority. Ayer gives his criterion for empirical verifiability, only to hedge it around with qualifications. Acknowledging that conclusive verifiability is impossible, Ayer opts for "the 'weak' sense of the term 'verifiable,'" thus begging the argument from the beginning. [5] Ayer's criterion grows more ambiguous with every qualification, until he admits that it yields propositions whose "truth can never become more than highly probable." [6] Objective certainty dissolves into probability, and even the empirical philosopher is condemned by his own logic to nonsense utterances, as such philosophers like to call nonfactual statements.

The flaw in the empirical argument is that we live not in a world of facts but in a field of signifiers. A fact, in and of itself, has no significance. "Every proposition proposing a fact," Whitehead writes, "must, in its complete analysis, propose the general character of the universe required for the fact." [7] Facts derive significance by entering into the experience of a subject. "There is nothing in the real world which is merely an inert fact," Whitehead continues; "every reality is there for feeling; it promotes feeling; and it is felt." [8] The subject must then translate the feeling into signifiers, which alone grant significance. True philosophy leads us away from objects and facts into the domain of significance, and here the real problem begins.

Lacan diagrams the problem by drawing two circles, which overlap but do not coincide. [9] The one circle he labels "Being (the subject)," and the other, "Meaning (the other)." The overlap of the circles Lacan marks as the field of "non-meaning," because we are faced with the choice of meaning or being, being or meaning, but not both equally and simultaneously. "If we choose being," Lacan writes, "the subject disappears, it eludes us, it falls into non-meaning. If we choose meaning, the meaning survives only deprived of that part of non-meaning that is, strictly speaking, that which constitutes in the realization of the subject, the unconscious. In other words, it is of the nature of this meaning, as it emerges in the field of the Other, to be, in a large part of its field, eclipsed by the disappearance of being, induced by the very function of the signifier." [10] Meaning eclipses being; being eclipses meaning; and alienation, Lacan points out, is the inevitable effect. A philosophy that concerns itself only with statements of empirical fact, remaining within the circle of objective thought, not only suppresses being as the price of its objectivity, but happily ignores the problem of its own alienation.

Langer's term, "presentational," for the alternate mode of thought restores to us one of the most fundamental aspects of our experience of the world.

The world *presents* itself to us; it addresses us, as Buber puts it.[11] The world, conversing with us, directs us into the domain of the subject. In Langer's presentational mode (Milton's "intuitive reason"), we apprehend the world as subject, and experience ourselves acting in the world; indeed, summoned to act, as the subject. In this mode the world presents itself as mysteriously opaque; it resists knowing, yet demands to be known. This mode too asserts cause and effect, yet the connection between them is elusive, as if there were a disjunction between them. Much as certain subatomic particles seem to vanish into nothingness enroute from one point to another, in the intuitive mode cause vanishes, to appear as effect in some unexpected location, or in some unpredicted form. Objective philosophy slides over the gap between cause and effect, but psychoanalysis discovered here the abyss.[12]

The intuitive mode erupts into consciousness, intruding into the calculations of the objective mode like an emanation from another order of reality. It startles us; it takes possession of us, as if by an alien power. Events in this mode seem to defy the laws operating in the objective mode. Where the objective mode presents the world as homogenous and continuous, in which the same laws act uniformly throughout, the intuitive mode discloses a world that seems disjunctive, random, even catastrophic. This mode arouses in us feelings of the uncanny, the terrifying, the sublime, and compels us to invent vocabularies of the paranormal or the supernatural to explain its effects on our consciousness. "Archetypes," Jung writes, "are complexes of experience that come upon us like fate."[13]

Every event in the intuitive mode is an epiphany. The objective mode moves quickly to cast its veil of continuity over the tear in the fabric by labeling the epiphany an optical illusion, a merely subjective experience. But the intuitive mode is forceful; if refused entrance at one gate, it will make for itself a passage somewhere else. The intuitive mode insists on its presence with such authority that the world it presents seems more real than the world of empirical fact.

The intuitive mode has its language too, but a language that seems to be governed by a different syntax than the syntax we use in discursive logic. It does not so much speak as intimate, revealing itself obliquely in dreams, intuitions, improbable coincidences. It is glimpsed by peripheral vision, but when the central focus turns toward the phenomenon, the phenomenon vanishes. "The god who has his oracle at Delphi," Heraclitus said, "neither conceals or reveals; he speaks in signs."[14] The intuitive mode is oracular. It cannot be diagrammed, as we might draw a figure in mathematics to represent an object by point-for-point correspondence. The intuitive mode addresses us in evocative icons, signifiers that point to *that-which-is-to-be-signified*.[15] Elusive, paradoxical, indifferent to the constraints of time and space, indestructible, this mode yet declares itself to be the true Logos, which was in the beginning, both the source and the end of all significance.

Psychoanalysis recognizes in these two modes the distinction between the conscious and the unconscious, terms that are as problematic as any other. Freudians look with some condescension on the oceanic unconscious of the Jungians, and the Jungians take the restriction of Freudian theory to the personal unconscious as something akin to a fixation. Even Freudians, if we are to believe Lacan, have played fast and loose with the definition of the personal unconscious, which Freud took such care to delineate. We should not be surprised at this dissension, since the unconscious, whatever the register in which it is inscribed, is precisely that which resists registration; it is the unknown and the unknowable. Whether we accept the specific theories, we can hardly dismiss the findings of psychoanalysis that something in the human psyche (personal or collective), which is unknown, struggles to make itself known to the conscious mind. This latent unknown, lying, it seems, just below the threshold of the conscious mind, discloses itself as impediment, disturbance, or absence, and disrupts the organization of the conscious mind.[16]

We cannot but admit that this latent force or content, though it may be ignored for long periods with apparent success, in some subtle way undermines the certainties of the conscious mind. The Cartesian *cogito,* as Lacan elucidates it, is founded on doubt, the doubt that reason brings to bear on the very procedures that reason uses to certify itself. Lacan rewrites the Cartesian formula: *"By virtue of the fact that I doubt, I am sure that I think."*[17] Reason, even while granting validity to no rules but its own, yet searches elsewhere for some guarantor not simply of its rules, but of its own being. The unconscious inscribes its "colophon of doubt," as Lacan calls it, in the margin of every text.

The contribution of psychoanalysis (of whatever school) has been to elucidate the anxiety lying at the heart of Cartesian certitude. The objective mode, in itself, is always incomplete. The missing element is the subject, about which objective reason has nothing to say, restricted, by its own confession, only to matters of fact. The subject is at home in the intuitive mode, and for this reason the intuitive mode has been taken for the merely subjective, and suppressed more rigorously in modern times than in antiquity. But what is suppressed returns with greater force, and in less healthy forms. The archetypes, which the ancients respected as signifiers of the subject, have become, as Jung points out, clinical symptoms of psychosomatic disorder.

The gravitational pull of myth, for young and old alike, is the presence within myth of the subject.[18] The common theory that primitive peoples invent myths to explain natural phenomena mistakes the incidental for the essence of myth. Even primitive peoples can think in logical sequences of cause and effect, when it comes to plowing a furrow in the soil, hunting the prey, or building a house to withstand the elements. For the sailor, guiding his rudder and sail according to the play of wind and water currents, Poseidon is a superfluous explanation. Belief in Poseidon in itself never made a man a sailor. Science has extended our understanding of secondary causes, but primitive peoples, working within their own technology, know as much of secondary and tertiary causes as we. Myth projects a Poseidon precisely be- cause Poseidon is a superfluous cause, from the perspective of the discursive mode.[19] Poseidon, master of the storm, is the First Cause; not the hypotheti- cal final term in a series of causes, but the very principle of causality, enclos- ing all secondary causes within its field. The First Cause, which myth in- vokes, is the subject.

In ordinary consciousness objects function according to mechanical rules, and we become virtually automatons ourselves in our relations with such objects. Mythical consciousness, however, restores to us the living presence of the subject. The anthropomorphism of myth is the expression of the living relations that people in myth-oriented cultures experience with the world. Anthropomorphism addresses the world, responding to the world's urgent summons to enter into the I-Thou covenant with the world. "This envisage- ment of the world as a realm of living forces," Langer writes, "each a being with desires and purposes that bring it into conflict with other teleologically directed powers, is really the key idea of all mythical interpretations: the idea of the Spirit World."[20] Personification, far from being an inferior mode of knowledge, is, as Hillman writes, "an epistemology of the heart."[21]

The presentational mode, from which all myth arises, is numinous, the locus of the *numen*. We translate the Latin word *numen* (like the *mana* of the Polynesians) all too lightly as some kind of mysterious or occult power that primitive peoples attribute to a place, or to a person in authority, such as the priest or king. They invest, we say, some element in objective reality with an aura that arises, in fact, out of their purely subjective experience. To attribute mana or numen to places or phenomena we take as evidence of magical think- ing. But what is magic? Magic is the power possessed by autonomous beings, and autonomy is the defining characteristic of the subject. Objects of them- selves can never possess the numen, since they are not autonomous, but merely functions at the effect of some other cause. If an object emanates the numen, it is the locus of a living presence. *Numen* (from the root *nu*—) is the nod by which the gods assert, by consent or refusal, their autonomous will. The numinous, wherever it occurs, and whatever the form, marks the encounter with the real. Hillman, in his discussion of the nightmare, writes: "Its numinous power requires a commensurately overwhelming idea: through the nightmare the reality of the natural God is revealed."[22]

Since we have suppressed the intuitive in favor of the objective mode, in which we think meaning alone resides, we are compelled, to a large degree, to enter the world of our private dreams for that encounter with the real, which the ancients encoded in their collective myths. It is amusing to read, with our post-Freudian consciousness, of the consternation of the nineteenth-century missionaries when they discovered that native peoples took their dreams for real.[23] Dreams may not always be truthful, but they are incontrovertibly real. If we need objective evidence, perspiration, a change in breathing, or an acceleration of the pulse, testify that in the dream state the dreamer experienced something real.

In dreams we encounter the Spirit World, as Langer calls the world of myth. The dream knows nothing of objects. What passes for an object in a dream is always an autonomous being, inscrutable and unpredictable. The pistol in the man's hand may change into a bird, the carpet into a whirlpool, the elevator compact into an oubliette. When we awake, the objective mode reasserts its authority and declares the dream a fantasy, but no such criticisms intrude upon the dream state. While we are in the dream state nothing is more authentic than the events of the dream.[24]

Lévy-Bruhl gives several illuminating examples of the confusion that resulted when the belief system of the missionaries collided with the beliefs of the pagans. In one such story a Reverend Grubb, missionary to the Lenguas in Grand Chaco, relates that an Indian, from a village some 150 miles distant, presented himself at Mr. Grubb's door to demand compensation for some pumpkins that Mr. Grubb had stolen.[25] The good missionary expostulated that he could not have stolen the pumpkins, since he had not visited the man's village for a long time. Whereupon the Indian admitted that the missionary had not stolen the pumpkins in the body, yet he insisted on compensation for the stolen pumpkins all the same.

It transpired in further argument that the Indian based his accusation on a dream, in which he had seen the missionary enter his garden and carry off three of his pumpkins. The compensation, which the Indian demanded, was for the three dream pumpkins. No argument or persuasion could convince the Indian that his dream pumpkins were not real pumpkins. The bewildering element in the story was the Indian's willingness to concede that Mr. Grubb had not entered his garden in the body, nor had he stolen empirical pumpkins; nevertheless, Mr. Grubb had really stolen the pumpkins, the Indian insisted, and the stolen pumpkins were indubitably real. The dream pumpkins took priority, in the Indian's consciousness, over the empirical pumpkins, which alone held any reality in Mr. Grubb's world.

It is a sad irony that the missionary, fixated on the objective mode, was incapable of recognizing the spirit world, even when it spoke to him directly. "He recognizes," Lévy-Bruhl writes, "that the Indian maintains that he has met Mr. Grubb's soul in his garden."[26] But alas, Mr. Grubb could not accept the reality of the soul, and even Lévy-Bruhl, sympathetic as he is to mythical thinking, confuses the issue by talking of logical incongruity, and the "pre-logical" mentality of primitive people. From our present perspective the Indian's dream and his interpretation seem eminently logical, and undoubtedly the subsequent history of the relations between the missionaries and the Indians of Grand Chaco has confirmed all too accurately the Indian's prophetic vision. Had he been better versed in the affairs of the soul, the missionary might have recognized himself as, indeed, the trespasser in the garden, and understood that the dream arose from the Indian's anxiety that the missionaries had come to steal not just his livelihood but his signifiers, which are more valuable than pumpkins.

"If we look for 'speculative thought' in the documents of the ancients," Frankfort writes, "we shall be forced to admit that there is very little indeed in our written records which deserves the name of 'thought' in the strict sense of that term. There are very few passages which show the discipline, the cogency of reasoning, which we associate with thinking. The thought of the Near East appears wrapped in imagination." [27] While sympathetic to the mythical worldview, Frankfort sees the I-Thou relations, which underlie mythical thinking, as essentially passive. In the subject-object mode (which I take to be Buber's "I-it" mode of cognition) a person is active, Frankfort writes, but "in 'understanding' a fellow-creature, on the other hand, a man or an animal is essentially passive, whatever his subsequent action may turn out to be. For at first he receives an impression. This knowledge is therefore direct, emotional, and inarticulate." [28] Cassirer expresses the same belief: "Myth lacks any means of extending the moment beyond itself. . . . Instead of the dialectical movement of thought, we have here a mere subjection to the impression itself and its momentary 'presence.' " [29] Both scholars voice the common prejudice, which believes that only the manipulation of the object can be called authentic thought.

To cull one fragment or another, here or there, from a whole system of mythical thought, as Frankfort does in support of his argument, may lead us to smile with him at "the charming inconsequentiality" of mythical explanations. [30] But even so, the Egyptian vision of the god of heaven (to use one of Frankfort's examples) "as a gigantic falcon hovering over the earth with outstretched wings, the coloured clouds of sunset and sunrise being his speckled breast and the sun and moon his eyes," hardly expresses an unmediated sense-impression. The icon of Horus, as Frankfort describes him, contains the wonder, the mystery, the bold correspondences of the imagination, and the speculative vigor that mark the encounter of human consciousness with the true subject.

When we turn from a single, isolated icon to a sustained opus of mythical symbolism, such as Hesiod's *Theogony,* the modern criticism of myth as passive intuition is completely untenable. A dialectical movement informs the

Theogony throughout. Earth and sky, mother and father, man and woman, father and son, god and human, are the most salient terms in the dialectic, but beneath the various specific polarities the serious dialectic of the poem is the movement of desire between the poles of Being and non-Being. The question to which the *Theogony* addresses itself with the greatest urgency is: How is it that human beings must live at the very center of the polarities of earth and sky, suffering between the desire for celestial immortality, which can never be fulfilled, and the gravitational pull of the earth toward extinction? Was the castration of Ouranos the moment of the rupture, when polarity sprang into being? Was it the moment when father Kronos ingested his swarming brood? Or was it when his son Zeus offered his father a stone, and tricked the father into releasing his stranglehold on the next generation? Was it the moment when Prometheus discovered the fire of intelligence, and threw all Olympos into consternation? Was it, perhaps, when woman was first created, to lure innocent men with the thread of desire into the world of the senses, and far beyond the senses, into a field that made nonsense of the senses? The problem of the relations between meaning and Being is so pressing that the *Theogony* brings forth one possible explanation after another to account for the fact of human alienation. The problem informs Homer's *Iliad* too, where it bursts into the open in the *Iliad* with all the rage of an adolescent who discovers that he has been cheated not of honor alone, but of life and honor.[31] If speculative thought is speculation about the nature of Being, myth is pure speculation and, conversely, every speculation about Being is, in essence, mythical.

The unconscious, by its power to penetrate the defenses of the conscious mind and to speak its own enigmatic oracles, suggests a wholeness beyond consciousness. But this oneness too may be another illusion. "The *one* that is introduced by the experience of the unconscious," Lacan argues, "is the one of the split, of the stroke, of rupture."[32] This other world, which Freud was to designate as the unconscious, presents itself not so much as a completeness in itself, but as something that demands to be completed. It manifests itself by absence, yet this is a strange absence, which stains everything in the objective mode with its presence. The Freudian unconscious manifests itself as something in suspense in the area, Lacan suggests, "of the *unborn*."[33] This Freudian unconscious, which stumbles into the affairs of our personal consciousness, is not far removed from the *deus absconditus* of medieval theology, the god who reveals himself by his absence.

Myth, voicing the thoughts of the unconscious, leads us into the field of the subject; yet, when we enter the field, the subject disappears. Semele's fate, to be consumed in flames by the vision of Zeus in his glory, states the problem in its simplest form. The empirical ego cannot endure the vision of the pure subject without being eradicated, since the subject, in its full autonomous power, is also the utterly Other, which transcends all signifiers. Semele can survive, as an independent subject as it were, only when the absolute subject remains at a distance, as the *deus absconditus*. Eurydice tells the story in another way. If Orpheus sees Eurydice, he cannot bring her back into the light. If he leads her into the light, he cannot see her. If he sees her, he loses her; if he loses her, he sees her. If myth were only an allegorical account of natural phenomena, it would scarcely warrant our attention, since science has proven more useful than allegory for investigating the laws of nature. Yet myth continues to fascinate us because every myth is a variation on the song Orpheus sang for Eurydice, which enchanted even the rocks and the wild animals, and drove the Thracian women mad with desire.

In dreams and myths all roads lead to the subject, yet the subject is nowhere to be seen. The biological organism grows by cellular replication and differentiation, and an analogous principle operates in the growth of the psyche. The embryo's original symbiosis becomes differentiated at birth, according to the specifications of the senses. The newborn must search now, by touch, taste, smell, sound, and sight, for the nurturing that flowed automatically while the embryo lay in the umbilical state. The biological will to life is translated now into desire (the Freudian libido). Desire itself is differentiated into an increasing complex of drives (in the Freudian sense of the term), but each of them, as Lacan reminds us, is only a partial drive, since no single drive can fully express the sheer life force that we loosely call instinct.

This desire is, as Lacan frequently repeats, the desire for the Other. The newborn, physically helpless, dependent on the external environment to supply the necessary nutrition, must first articulate needs into desires, and then project those desires outward to draw the satisfactions of its needs in from the field of the Other. Each drive must find its (more or less adequate) match in the field of the Other. But the field of the Other being a grid of signifiers, the newborn must translate needs into signifiers corresponding to the signifiers already culturally determined. Thus the inarticulate subject becomes articulate only by delivering its being over to signifiers, which signify the being of, and for, another subject.

With the differentiation of the drives, the self multiplies itself. One self suckles, while another self excretes. One self listens, while another self babbles. One self sees, while yet another self sees itself being seen. How does this much-multiplied self ever find the certainty that it truly exists? Because it is sustained in the gaze of the subject, which, alas, is the Other. The field of signifiers becomes a hall of mirrors, which reflect reflections of the subject, while the subject remains always elsewhere.[34] "Inseparable, incomparable, irreducible, now, happening only once," Buber writes of his personal, concrete reality, "it gazes upon me with a horrifying look."[35]

Other biological organisms have differentiated senses and drives; they too

inhabit a world of mirrors, and even they fall for the fatal delusion of appearances. But they seem not to vex themselves over the question of Being and
non-Being. Even here, however, we should speak only provisionally, since
modern research into primate behavior suggests that the human anxiety regarding identity and status can be found almost anywhere else among the
social species. Whatever the degree or prevalence of alienation among the
other animals, however, alienation has certainly figured as the central problem of the great cosmogonic myths since the beginning of recorded history.
Gilgamesh, the *Iliad,* the Book of Genesis, indeed the whole Old Testament,
Hesiod's *Theogony,* or his *Works and Days*—wherever we look in the ancient
documents from our Old European tradition, we find alienation at the heart
of the human experience of the world.

Adam and Eve choose the freedom of their own being, and in doing so
choose alienation, since there is no escape from the gaze of the subject. Hesiod's myth of Prometheus and Pandora tells the same story. Prometheus, to
assert the freedom of consciousness, deceives Zeus, but the subject cannot
be deceived, and the consequence of this deception is that humans are forever
deceived by Pandora, the phantom of their desire. In Homer's *Iliad* Achilles,
alienated from his community, searches for a personal integrity independent
of community values, but the freedom he chooses is his self-destruction.

The Old Testament story of the tower of Babel is a textbook paradigm of
the alienation of the subject. At one time, the story goes, "the whole earth
was of one language, and of one speech."[36] The people decide to build a city,
and a tower, whose top would reach heaven; "and let us make a name, they
said, lest we be scattered abroad on the face of the whole earth" (verse 4).
But the Lord, seeing the people building the tower, said, "Behold . . . now
nothing will be restrained from them, which they have imagined to do. Go
to, let us go down, and there confound their language, that they may not
understand one another's speech. . . . Therefore is the name of it called Babel; because the Lord did there confound the language of all the earth" (verses
6–7, 9).

This myth is an allomorph of Hesiod's myth of Prometheus and Pandora.
The earth was of one language in the primordial time before the rupture,
whether between the conscious and the unconscious or between the self and
the Other. Hesiod's myth of Pandora opens in this same primordial moment,
the time when gods and humans are feasting together, before gods and humans have been polarized, and humans have not yet been polarized into desiring men and their desired women. Consciousness discovers this primordial
moment, when everyone could speak and understand everyone else's language, only in the discovery of the ego that it cannot speak the language of
the Other.

Why did Promethean intelligence disrupt the feast, in Hesiod's myth, and set the human and divine orders at odds with each other? Why did the people in the Genesis myth need to leave a name for themselves? For whom would they inscribe their name, if not for someone who would not understand the sign? And what was the name they expected to make? As the myth tells it, the people needed the tower of Babel as their sign, in case they should be scattered, and no longer homogenous; in case difference should at some time arise. Yet the tower of Babel is the signifier that creates difference.

The imagination (to borrow from the Lord's vocabulary in the King James version) needs to make a name only because the name is not within its power, but already lies in the field of the Other. The very tower, which the people build to be their monument and name, creates the decisive schism, which sets the subject forever at a distance, and delivers the signifier forever into the power of the absolutely Other, God. The tower was intended as a bridge to the Other, but the Other became the Other only through the building of the bridge. The higher the tower reaches toward the subject, the greater the schism between the ego and the subject, and the more firmly the Other asserts its authority over the name. "Go to," says the Lord, "let us go down, and there confound their language, that they may not understand one another's speech." The ruined tower of Babel is the monument to the incompatibility of the signifier and the subject.[37]

The tower of Babel, the signifier that confounds language, and Pandora, the signifier that confuses men's desire with false images, refer to the same alienation. Desire occludes the subject by its very search to locate that subject, and confounds the system of signifiers. Language becomes a system for miscomprehension, since no one possesses the power of the name, except the subject, who will not reveal himself.

The ancient myths locate the alienation of the mind within the mind itself. Consciousness wills its own freedom, only to find itself in the snare of the unconscious. Adam and Eve, eating of the tree of the knowledge of good and evil, become conscious of their own nakedness. Nakedness is the mythical image of that rupture, which our first parents willed, between themselves and nature, when what they thought was freedom was, in fact, to be directly exposed to the baneful gaze of the Other. In the state of nature Adam and Eve were not naked, since there was nothing to be covered or uncovered. But once they had eaten of the fruit of knowledge, something needed to be covered up. A part of the body must be marked as the locus of the secret that, because it is a secret, is now shameful, and because it is shameful, must be uncovered. Adam and Eve were naked when they discovered themselves in the gaze of the subject, who became the ineffable and the invisible Other only when Adam and Eve discovered their nakedness.

Meaning eclipses being: the theme runs as much through our ancient myths as through modern philosophy. At some point in history, the myths tell us, thinking intervened and disrupted the course of nature, and every advance in thinking only aggravated the world's duplicity. Promethean intelligence severs the I-Thou bond between gods and humans, and instates Pandora as the perverted illusion of reality, who confounds men with hopeless desire. Being retreats into the secret places as meaning expands its domain, and whatever meaning brings to the surface is not Being, but the idol of Being, fashioned and manipulated by desire. The rupture between gods and humans, and the confusion between the orders, results from a sacrifice in Hesiod's myth. But what was sacrificed? And who was the beneficiary of the Promethean intervention in this sacrifice?

The misogynist rage, which the figure of Pandora provokes in Hesiod, reveals the depth of his alienation. If the gods are the subject, and Pandora their signifier, sacrifices to the subject only distance the subject still farther, until it retires from human sight altogether, leaving only Pandora as the utterly Other, an idol in every respect; the false image first of the gods, and then of man himself, which he pursues in the form of woman, who is the hopelessly Other. Pandora is situated exactly in that overlap of meaning and Being, which Lacan names "the field of non-meaning." Lacan has exactly caught Hesiod's frustration, who believes himself frustrated by the deceptive Pandora (or woman), whereas, in fact, Pandora is the phantom by which Hesiod can keep himself ever more frustrated, at the effect of his desire: "The subject sustains himself as desiring in relation to an ever more complex signifying ensemble."[38]

Pandora, who holds out for men the lure of pleasure, only to protract and exasperate desire, stands as the great signifier of the subject in both Hesiod's cosmological poems. Embodying the powers and attributes of the gods, she is Being translated into meaning, but the translation is corrupt; thanks to the clever "foresight" of Prometheus, Pandora is the simulacrum of Being. As the Being of woman, Pandora is corrupt on the human level also, since she seduces men's desire for meaning with a meaning that is meaningless. "The subject, *in initio,* begins in the locus of the Other, in so far as it is there that the first signifier emerges."[39] Small wonder that hope, in Hesiod's myth, is so hopelessly confused.

Like the fig leaves, which Adam and Eve made for themselves to reveal what they must conceal, myth circles around the secret place, hiding the trauma even while marking its hiding place. The fig leaves, which Adam and Eve wore, were not to cover a part of the body, since humans can tolerate the sight of the genitals of other animals. Only human genitals are the *pudenda,* as our Latin dictionaries name them—not "the shameful things," but "the things that must induce shame." Adam and Eve named the animals, the old story tells us, but this was not yet language. Language began with the fig leaf, which was their first signifier. The fig leaf marked the tabu locus, but the function of a tabu is to create desire. The tabu object is marked as that which must be desired. The genitals are not the shameful, but the signifiers of the shameful. Desire is the shameful, and therefore more to be desired.

Throughout all generations many have been satisfied to take a passive comfort in myth, and myth is skillful in promoting itself as the comfortable lie. Indeed, this is myth's proud claim, that its function is to keep the secret hidden. Listening passively to the myth, even when the myth tells of mutilations and terrible punishments, people can leave the theater cleansed of their fear and terror, sanitized by the myth. As long as Oedipus is the protagonist on the stage, we are not Oedipus. Let his terrible secret be exposed to the whole world, provided we can leave the theater with our secret intact. Myth is a powerful hypnotic, in which cultures inscribe their own ideology, and the mythologist's task is certainly to discover the little secrets that one ideology or another hides away in the folds of a myth.[40]

But myth also reveals that which was to be concealed. Like our dreams, which seem to disguise our secrets to protect our sleep, myth keeps confessing the very secrets that it was constructed to conceal. With a chorus of signifiers it circles around the traumatic rupture, where the subject vanished into the field of the Other.

The ancient myths are as pessimistic about the possibility of reconciliations between the two orders, the human and the divine, as modern psychoanalysis is about the reconciliation between the conscious and the unconscious. If the problem of consciousness is that Being is eclipsed by meaning, then indeed the situation seems as hopeless as Pandora declares it to be. Yet something, lying just beyond the threshold of consciousness, by its fugitive epiphanies continues to call attention to itself as the real. This fugitive, which makes itself felt in our dreams and myths, in our philosophies and religions, and in all works of poetic vision, is the presence of the subject, even if it is the subject-to-be-realized. Modern psychoanalytic theory (of whatever affiliation) corroborates the intimations of the great cosmological myths of antiquity, that the alienation occurred when consciousness discovered itself in the split between the self and the Other.

If the mind is the cause of its own alienation, the mind must also have within itself the remedy for the disease. Antiquity had, in addition to the pessimistic myths of a world forever escaping meaning, other myths and rituals, which spoke of healing and reconciliation. Sacrifice was one such ritual, but sacrifice is a problematic therapy, as Hesiod's myth of Prometheus and Pandora shows, since sacrifice, far from closing the gap, drives the wedge even deeper. In the *Iliad* the Trojan women offered a Sidonian robe to Athena, with a prayer for Athena's favor. Athena accepted the offering, but "turned her head aside," as Homer puts it.[41] Athena declined to reveal her numen. Sacrifice confirms the master in his superiority, and the slave in his servitude.

The Other becomes more other, and the self more alienated.[42]

The more significant alternative to sacrifice, in classical antiquity, were the rituals of the mystery cults. Sacrifice is a hoped-for reconciliation, but initiates in the Eleusinian mysteries reenacted reconciliation through a rebirth from Demeter, the mother. But the mother in this myth was also Persephone, consort of Hades, the invisible one. Such a ritual, which, as a rebirth from the mother, was also a redemption from the law of the father, is almost unknown in our public rituals, since the mother is now more rigorously excluded than in antiquity. We can only surmise the effect of the mystery on the initiates from our private, inner encounters with the mother. The initiates would say only that they had seen Persephone, who is the queen of the realm where all signifiers and distinctions end. The death, through which the initiates passed, was no metaphor. Someone, or something, died in that initiation. We can surmise that, in that encounter with death, the initiates experienced the limit of the ego and its desire, and emerged from the grave transformed, at peace with the paradox of meaning and Being.

Initiation into the Eleusinian mysteries was a sacrament. A sacrament, as an act that spans the disjunction between the alienating mode of object-consciousness and the mode of the numinous subject, restores the subject to its place in the self. Religions prescribe rituals to induce the sacrament by mimesis, but mimesis and prescriptions alone are insufficient. The essential element in the sacrament is grace, which cannot be commanded, since it descends from the autonomous subject.

The meal, which Achilles and Priam share in Achilles' tent, is a sacrament. Only by the grace of the gods could Achilles and Priam forego each his own anger, and see in the other himself. Achilles may win honor from his comrades for killing Hector, but killing Hector gives him no honor in the gods' eyes. Killing Hector is an act of vengeance, an attempt by the self to achieve its autonomy by annihilating the Other. But to kill the Other is a spurious strategy, which only imprisons the self in its own alienation. Achilles, in desecrating Hector's corpse, "disgraces the earth," as Apollo puts it, and thus distances himself still farther from both the Olympians and the chthonic powers.[43] Achilles wins his honor from the gods when he surrenders the corpse of his enemy to the dead man's family.[44] By some alchemical process, which transcends his alienation, Achilles sees, for a moment at least, that his life has meaning by being held in the gaze of the gods, even if it is a meaning that eludes him.

Much of modern psychological theory, with its talk of object relations, and its fascination with mirrors that reflect more or less spurious images, suggests, by implication at least, that our alienation is inexorable. The world as the Other can never reflect back to us a meaning adequate to our being. But the mirrors that surround us from birth, and shape our identity in the world, are not flat surfaces, nor are we flat surfaces that passively mirror whatever lies within our environment. The mirroring that goes on between us and the world is a dynamic process, since every mirror is itself the locus of the subject. The claims of the objective mode are powerful, and the Other so much more visible than the self; yet the sacramental I-Thou relations, of which Buber writes with such eloquence, are not so rare that they are accessible only to mystics, philosophers, or neurotics. Despite the alienation of language and culture, we have all experienced the sacramental moment, when the subject was fully realized in us, as we in it. In such moments, when difference is not so much dissolved as recognized and transcended, the subject beholds itself, not alienated, but realized in the gaze of the Other. We experience, in Whitehead's eloquent phrase, "the unison of immediacy."[45]

Vergil gives a homely example of this sacrament in the conclusion of his Fourth Eclogue, the so-called Messianic Eclogue. The occasion of the poem is the consulship of Vergil's friend and benefactor, Pollio, and the birth of a child, whom Vergil leaves unidentified, whether from political or poetic tact. Vergil chooses to celebrate, in the child's birth, the birth of the new Golden Age. Though affecting the modest aspirations of the bucolic genre, the poem opens onto the largest cosmic vision. The newborn *puer,* celebrated in the poem, will be a second Achilles, whose heroism will bring wars, civil discord, and even commerce to an end. This *puer,* Vergil dares to claim, is the offspring of Jupiter himself. Proving his heroic mettle in life, he will join the gods at his death. The whole world—earth, sea, and sky—nods assent to this messianic birth.

Soaring in his cosmic vision, Vergil boasts that Pan, the shepherd-musician of the old Arcadia, will relinquish his place of honor to Vergil, the shepherd-poet of the new dispensation. As if he had soared beyond propriety, Vergil abruptly descends from his cosmic flight to the little boy in the cradle, and concludes his poem with an admonition to the infant to smile at his mother, both as a recompense for her weary pregnancy and to ensure his ultimate elevation to the company of the gods (lines 60–63):

incipe, parve puer, risu cognoscere matrem;
matri longa decem tulerunt fastidia menses.
incipe, parve puer: qui non risere parenti
nec deus hunc mensa, dea nec dignata cubili est.

Begin, little lad, to recognize mother with a smile.
Ten months have brought a great weariness to mother.
Begin, little lad. Who has not smiled for his parent
The god does not deem worthy of his table, nor the goddess of her couch.

Who are the god and goddess, whose bed and board the lad may expect to enjoy if he produces a winsome smile for his mother? Commentaries remind us of Herakles, elevated after his death to Mt. Olympos, where, in Homer's words, "he takes pleasure in feasting with the deathless gods, and has fair-ankled Hebe for his consort."[46] The *puer* of Vergil's poem will be a latter-day Herakles, like Herakles elevated to godhood—"he will see heroes mingling with the gods, and he himself will be seen of them" (lines 15–16). But what has a baby's first smile to do with apotheosis? It took more than smiles to win Herakles his immortality on Olympos.

One editor confesses himself baffled by the passage, though he finds some sense in the baby's smile, as the mother's reward for her pregnancy and as a good omen.[47] That will do for a start. Omens are signifiers, signifying to object-consciousness the presence of the numinous subject. In this sense the whole poem is an omen, a prophetic utterance to bring into existence the messianic age that it prophesies. All the homely images in the poem—cradle, pasture, garden—direct us to an archetypal landscape of the imagination, where Vergil situates us in the opening lines of the poem: the final age of the Sibylline oracles has come; the great cycle of time begins anew; the Virgin returns, and the rule of Saturn; with the birth of this *puer* the iron race will disappear, and throughout the world a golden race will arise.

The child's biological mother appears only in the coda of the poem. But the poem as a whole is alive with the presence of the archetypal mother. Nature, in this poem, is a bountiful mother, who smiles to witness the birth of her latest child. The earth pours forth her abundance for her darling; the baby's cradle blossoms with flowers; even the spiked acanthus laughs to see this newborn child. In the new dispensation commerce will no longer be necessary, nor agriculture, since Nature everywhere will produce everything of her own accord. Dyes will become obsolete; of their own accord the sheep will produce wool of all colors—purple, yellow, vermilion. We smile at this fanciful image of polychromatic sheep, and so we should. Mother Nature, in this poem, indulges the child in all of us.

As the mother in this poem is both a specific human mother and the archetypal Mother, so the child is both a historical child and the archetypal *Puer aeternus* of Jungian psychology, the ageless being who descends from the fields of light, "trailing clouds of glory," as Wordsworth expresses it in his "Intimations of Immortality."[48] Epiphanius's account of the pagan feast of the Virgin at Alexandria (quoted by Jung) identifies Vergil's *puer* more exactly.[49] On the night of the Epiphany (January 5/6) the pagans would celebrate their great Festival of the Virgin (the *Korion*) with great revelry. They would bring a carved wooden statue up from a subterranean sanctuary, and carry it around the temple precinct seven times, to the sound of flutes and tambourines. When they had completed the procession, they would carry the image back down into the crypt. When asked the meaning of this rite, the Alexandrians would reply: "Today, at this hour, the *Kore,* that is to say the Virgin, has given birth to the Aeon." The *puer* in Vergil's prophetic Eclogue is this same Aeon, time itself reborn.

Every birth is a new creation and simultaneously the re-creation of the archetypes in time. The smile between mother and child in the coda of Vergil's Eclogue is a mimesis of the archetypal smile with which Nature greets this birth, when she spreads flowers around the cradle, pours forth her "little gifts" (*munuscula*) for the child, scents the air with Oriental fragrances, yellows the fields with ripening grain, and grows polychromatic sheep to delight a child's eye. If we too do not smile as we read this poem, we have missed the lesson, for all Nature works, in this poem, to coax a smile as much from the child in us as from the child who is the subject of the poem.

What mother does not work to elicit a baby's smile? Why is this slight motor response in the baby's facial muscles a signifier of such import that it engages a mother's intense concentration, and is treasured forever in her memory? Our entry into consciousness is traumatic. Leaving the comforts of the womb, we are suddenly assaulted by rude mishandlings, helpless against the alien intrusion. Nature equips the infant with one power, which, feeble as it is, is sufficient to coax even the Olympians into its service. The newborn is endowed with charm. Greatest of wizards, the master of the cradle discovers that he can charm his way into the hearts of the giants hovering over his cradle, not only melting their ferocity but even compelling them to forage for his Majesty.[50] The baby's first smile marks the baby's discovery of its own power. O crafty innocence!

What conscious being would consent to leave the numinous fields of the subject for Plato's Cave of Shadows, the world of difference and otherness? How has consciousness agreed to accept its presence, frail, absurd, alienating as it is, in the cosmic design? Nature casts the infant out into a world that seems, on balance, more dangerous to biology than hospitable, yet Nature continues her experiment in biology generation after generation. Nature must seduce consciousness to consent to this absurd experiment. We give our consent by falling in love. We fall in love with the world through the seduction of the senses, of course, but there is more to love than sensual delight. Nature practices her seduction through the imagination, "the living power and prime agent of all human perception," as Coleridge describes it, and the "repetition in the finite mind of the eternal act of creation in the infinite I AM."[51] Nature's creatures take themselves for the creator. This is Nature's one compensation for translating pleasure into desire.

Humans have two gestations, two wombs, two mothers. We are all, like Dionysos, the twice-born. For the first nine months of our lives we are cradled in the womb of our biological mother. But we are still fetuses when we issue from the womb, and continue neurologically in the fetal state, biologists speculate, for as long as a year or eighteen months after birth.[52] Thus we continue through a second gestation, when our biological mother becomes our wet-nurse, providing us with the necessary security and nutrition while our neurons are sprouting and differentiating in response to the external stimuli. The world is, literally, our second womb. In this second womb we exchange the umbilical symbiosis with our biological mother for a symbiosis with the larger world, differentiated according to the senses, and made conscious by the imagination.

Nature provides her creatures with a bonding mechanism to ensure the transition from the unconscious symbiosis of the first gestation to the conscious symbiosis of the second gestation. At the simplest biological level, bonding substitutes for the severed umbilicus, directing the original symbiosis toward specified targets. On the psychological level, this bonding translates into transference and identification. Nature smiles to see the infant's smile, because it signifies that the bonding mechanism is functioning at both levels, physiological and psychological. A baby who cannot or will not smile may survive in spite of all hazards, but its pilgrimage through the world of signifiers will be so much the harder.

My colleague, Richard Frank, tells of a time when he and his wife were visiting a museum in Budapest. The woman taking the tickets at the door asked if they would leave their baby with her while they toured the museum. They agreed, and when they had completed their tour, they returned to find the woman, with two other women, insistently crooning a single word over the baby—"igen." When the Franks asked the meaning of the word, they were told it was the Hungarian word for "yes." The three mothers were crooning over the baby like the three Fates, hypnotizing the baby into saying yes to life.

The smile that Vergil, the young rustic, attempts to coax from the baby is the sign that biological bonding has successfully entered the field of the imagination. In responding to his mother's smile, the baby discovers himself as the signifier, both sign and sign-maker, for his mother. *I am amused to discover that I am the smile on the face of that other person.* The exchange of smiles between mother and child may, in time, be veiled with every kind of ambivalence, but the baby's first smile is as yet uncontaminated by the difference between subject and object, or between subject and signifier. This first mirroring of smiles is pure play, the gift mother and child give to each other, as one subject recognizing another. With his smile the baby makes his first discovery of himself as the creator, the I AM at the center of the world. The baby's smile, signifier mimicking signifier, is the first sign of awakening self-consciousness.

But, again, what has a baby's smile to do with apotheosis? Here we draw on a myth, articulated first in Plato, and surfacing again in Wordsworth's "Intimations of Immortality." At birth, when we descend from the field of the subject (Wordsworth's "fields of light") into what Wordsworth calls "the light of common day," we exchange the unmediated archetypes for the complex mediation of our signifiers. The parent, as the infant's first mediating image, the surrogate that recalls the original archetypes, is the child's consolation for the loss of Eden. The god and goddess in the last line of Vergil's Eclogue are both the archetypes themselves, the Lord and Lady if we like, and the child's biological parents, whose function is to activate in the child's imagination the memory of the archetypes. By bonding with his parents, and recognizing himself as first the object, and then the subject, of their gaze, the child agrees to accept the substitution of icons and signifiers for the unmediated presence of the subject.

The child who will not smile for his parents, Vergil admonishes the baby in the cradle, cannot expect to join the gods. Once we have entered the world, the only road to the subject is through the signifiers in the field of the Other. But transcending the signifiers, the god and goddess wait to welcome consciousness back into the home of the subject. We are born into alienation, as myth and the great religions tell us. Mothers know this as well as anyone. Why else would they coach the infant in the ceremony of the smile, if not to secure the presence of the subject in the newborn consciousness before alienation works its damage?

The *puer* receives his first intimation of his godhood in his mother's smile. Seeing her smile, he finds reassurance that the world is a living, welcoming presence. Smiling in return, he discovers himself as that living, creating presence in the world. The smile is the infant's first linguistic sign, with which he bonds the subject that is himself with the subject that is the Other. The sacramental exchange of smiles between mother and child are the outward sign expressing the joy of the subject creating itself anew in the hazardous eclipse of meaning in the world of the Other.[53] Whitehead shows a sensitive recognition of these archetypes, whose hospitality Vergil invokes in the communion of the smile: "The image—and it is but an image—the image under which this operative growth of God's nature is best conceived, is that of a tender care that nothing be lost."[54]

2

Job's Noble Euphemism

It is the glory of God to conceal things,
but the glory of kings is to search things out.
—Proverbs 25:2

Job was a righteous and God-fearing man, so scrupulous in his religious observances that he would sanctify his sons and daughters, offering sacrifices to God for each of them in turn. "It may be," he said, "that my sons have sinned, and cursed God in their hearts."[1] Job took every precaution against even the inadvertent sin, the sin in the intimate recesses of the heart, and in this he was as concerned for the spiritual well-being of his children as for himself. Job's piety was rewarded. He was a prosperous man; the greatest, our scribes tell us, of all the people of the East.

One day the sons of God came to present themselves before the Lord and, strange to say, the Adversary was among them. Who were these sons of God, and how did the Adversary come to be of their number? The Ground of Being does not split into parts; it is neither male nor female; it has neither sons nor daughters. And God, from a monotheistic perspective, can have no adversary. Even if such beings as these sons of God could exist, who would know of them?

This is a vision of a seer, privileged to penetrate the veil between the conscious mind and the numinous Ground. As is the way with dreams, we are suddenly in the middle of things. No explanation is given, no history; simply, numinous beings present themselves, in defiance of logic and theological orthodoxy. Returning from the numinous field of the Subject, the seer translates his vision into the forms of everyday experience: fathers and sons, judges and advocates, trials and defendants. He sees a vision of the one and indivisible God conversing with His own thought forms, His aspects as they are manifested in the manifold phenomena of the world; among them is the Adversary, the archetype of all resistance, contradiction, and negation; the opposition by which that which is comes into being.[2]

God said to the Adversary, "Have you considered my servant Job, that there is none like him on the earth, a blameless and upright man, who fears God and turns away from evil?"[3] How could the Adversary not have noticed such a man? Job was an adversarial opportunity too splendid to overlook. Satan answered God, "Does Job fear God for nought? Hast thou not put a hedge about him and his house and all that he has, on every side? Thou hast blessed the work of his hands, and his possessions have increased in the land."[4] Who would not be godly, given such godly protection. "But put forth your hand now," Satan continues, "and touch all that he has, and he will curse thee to thy face."[5]

To curse God is the ultimate tabu. By comparison, violations of the social tabus are mere misdemeanors. To curse God is to sever our relatedness with the Ground of Being. The curse produces no ill effects on God, since the Ground cannot be damaged by any of the creatures that it supports; rather, it negates the person who utters the curse, cleaving the I-Thou covenant asunder, and leaving only the ego standing with no ground to stand on. The ego, thus bereft of relationship, is rendered a mere It, though strictly speaking an It with no relatedness is not even an It; it is less than nothing. To curse God, in the days when the word was the creator, was to repudiate both the unconscious, wherever it conflicted with rational consciousness, and the universe itself, wherever it presented any opposition to consciousness.

Job was a true hero; that is, a human in a direct relation with the numinous. Like all heroes, he was put to an ordeal, and his was the greatest ordeal of all, since the contest was for his soul. Job was elected to demonstrate that no change in his external circumstances, no catastrophe whatsoever, could destroy his covenant with his Ground of Being.

God accepted the challenge. The Lord said to Satan, "Behold, all that he has is in your power; only upon himself do not put forth your hand."⁶ And Satan went forth from the presence of the Lord.

Who are these beings who make wagers over human souls as lightly as if they were gamblers at the card table? Is God so hungry for power that he will wager a human soul for His own greater glory? The story violates all canons of justice. The conscious mind sees in Job's suffering a story of a conspiracy between the forces of good and evil, with the human soul a plaything for their sport. The human mind, endowed with a perception of order, responds in its innermost depths to a call for justice, equality, and a reverence toward the universal law based on a relationship of trust and fair dealings. But what does the universe know of justice and fair dealings? The conscious mind creates archetypal images of gods, as signifiers of its own values; yet these gods are apparently unencumbered by the restraints of justice, oblivious to moral values for themselves, even while demanding from their human creatures submission and adoration. It is a cruel double bind, to be called to worship a Creator who consorts with the adversary to rain the severest afflictions upon his most devout worshippers.

The vision of good and evil treating the world as their playing field makes no sense to the mind. Yet the conscious mind seems to be a structure created to apprehend, and so to reflect, the universal order. If anything is created in the image of God, surely it is the faculty of consciousness. "Why is light given to him that is in misery?" Job cries. "Why is light given to a man whose way is hid?"⁷ The vision of God and Satan bartering for human souls defies the very basis of conscious thought. The conscious mind, structured to apprehend coherence, finds instead a universe subject to apparent randomness, governed only by the law of universal entropy.

God and Satan place their bets, with the soul of Job as the prize. Satan goes forth from the presence of the Lord, and suddenly, on the human plane, an inexplicable series of catastrophes erupts in Job's life. The Sabaeans and the Chaldeans fell upon his lands, robbing him of all his oxen and camels, and killing all his servants but one survivor who escapes to report the calamity. A fire falls from heaven and wipes out the sheep flock. A great wind sweeps across the wilderness; the house in which Job's sons and daughters are feasting falls in on them, killing them all. All the disasters are natural disasters. Everything here is in the natural order, except that the old mythographers condensed the body's petty losses into one catastrophe, so that the mind might plumb catastrophe to its depths.⁸

Job arose, rent his robe, shaved his head, fell upon the ground, and worshipped God. Job said, "Naked I came from my mother's womb, and naked I shall return; the Lord gave and the Lord has taken away; blessed be the name of the Lord."⁹ The natural order makes no promises with a man; it offers no guarantee of happiness or prosperity. If a man's possessions are taken from him, that too is the natural order. Job accepts. He does not violate the tabu.

Again God and the Adversary meet. And the Lord said to Satan, "Have you considered my servant Job, that there is none like him on the earth, a blameless and upright man, who fears God and turns away from evil? He still holds fast his integrity, although you moved me against him, to destroy him without cause." [10] To destroy him without cause? The conscious mind is all cause and effect, and yet it perceives a universe indifferent to causality. Ego-consciousness, studying to assimilate its own being to the structure of the universe, discovers a universe hostile, it would seem, to consciousness itself. It interprets this hostility in the image of a superego who actively opposes the attempt of the consciousness to discover true cause and effect, and places a barricade between the ego's consciousness and the workings of the superego. At the same time, this superego demands from ego-consciousness the love of heart and soul. The double bind is intolerable. The logical mind every day proves it is connected with the universal laws. Structured for survival, it discovers the links intervening between the libido and the food supply; it cultivates the soil, builds houses, domesticates animals, invents tools, cures diseases. Yet this same logic, which builds a world by observing the circling stars and the rhythm of the seasons, finds itself adrift in a universe contemptuous of human logic. The temptation to curse the Creator is very great.

"Skin for skin!" the great Adversary replies to the Lord; "all that a man has he will give for his life. But put forth your hand now, and touch his bone and his flesh, and he will curse thee to thy face." [11] And the Lord said to Satan, "Behold, he is in your power; only spare his life." [12] *Behold, he is in your power.* So lightly God hands over to the Adversary a man whom God himself recognizes for his piety and courage. We are in a world much like Homer's, where the Olympians casually negotiate the fates of their favorites on the earthly battlefields, where humans are puppets and easily expendable.

Satan goes forth and destroys Job's physical health. To remove man's physical capacities is truly to cut close to his Ground of Being, but this too is natural. The natural order makes no promises to sustain a man's health. Job's wife said to him, "Do you still hold fast your integrity? Curse God, and die." [13] Job said to her, "You speak as one of the foolish women would speak. Shall we receive good at the hand of God, and shall we not receive evil?" [14] Job's wife is a realist, for whom the universe is either unconscious or, if conscious, immoral. From the realist's perspective Job's integrity is but infantile fantasy, and his God merits not adoration but contempt. Job's wife is the ancient version of a modern existentialist like Meursault in Camus's *The Stranger,* who chooses scorn and hate as the only honorable attitudes to maintain toward the universe.

To prove that God does not exist is easy, but to prove the existence of God is impossible, since God is, as Soleri writes, a pursued hypothesis. [15] A finite

particle cannot prove that the universe has an order, much less that it has
intention and will, and that its intention is good. However many signs of
order or design that logic reads in the book of nature, the order and design it
discovers are local events, and no logic can prove, from local events, the
design of the whole. Hence the ancient tabu against cursing God. "The idea
of a whole," Dewey writes, "is an imaginative, not a literal idea. The limited
world of our observation and reflection becomes the Universe only through
imaginative extension." [16] To curse God is for the ego to cut off that "imaginative extension," but in doing so the ego would be cutting itself off from its
own imagination, which is the source of its power.

God must not be cursed; the tabu is absolute; it admits no exceptions, or
extenuating circumstances. Yet God sets Job in circumstances just short of
death, to force Job to capitulate—or so it seems. Job sits among the ashes,
wordless in his grief. Three friends come to comfort him. They sit with him
for seven days and seven nights, unable to speak a word themselves, for they
see that his suffering is very great. On the eighth day Job opens his mouth
and curses the day of his birth.

Job said: "Let the day perish wherein I was born, and the night which said,
'A man-child is conceived.' Let that day be darkness! May God above not
seek it, nor light shine upon it. Let gloom and deep darkness claim it; let the
blackness of the day terrify it. That night—let thick darkness seize it! let it
not rejoice among the days of the year, let it not come into the number of the
months. Yea, let that night be barren; let no joyful cry be heard in it. Let
those curse it who curse the day, who are skilled to rouse up Leviathan. Let
the stars of its dawn be dark; let it hope for light, but have none, nor see the
eyelids of the morning; because it did not shut the doors of my mother's
womb." [17] Job honors the tabu. He does not curse God, but what he cannot
do to God he turns on himself. Singled out to endure the full weight of the
numinous, Job sees himself as the tabu person, a man accursed. Job is angry,
and his anger, once released, can be stopped by nothing. Forbidden to curse
his Ground of Being, he searches in all directions for another target. The
curse, which cannot be uttered, cannot be suppressed either; and the only
target, outside the Almighty, is Job himself.

Everything Job's friends offer by way of consolation or explanation only
fuels his anger. They talk of the justice of God and human sin. If only Job
will acknowledge his fault, they say, the connection will be reestablished.
Theirs is the world of cause and effect. For every disaster in human life there
is a reason, and since the reason cannot be an arbitrary whim in the mind of
God, the reason for Job's suffering must lie with Job. But Job too knows the
world of cause and effect. His mind has contemplated as well as theirs the
world of morals and logic. He does not deny his human fallibility, or claim
for himself divine perfection. Job's logic, like theirs, tells him that the Al-

mighty cannot be measured by human logic, and piety is to accept Being as it is.

Logic is cognitive and discursive, a fine tool for the theorist, working on matter externally. But Job is living in the experiential world beyond the reach of logic. With his being caught in the maze of his signifiers, Job flails the air with the rage of a mind immobilized, all too conscious that afflictions are the very reason for the existence of the tabu against turning signifiers into engines of destruction against the Ground of Being. Who, in the midst of prosperity, is tempted to curse God? The temptation arises in the disjunction between reality and logic, between Being and our signifiers of Being. Was Job singled out to be God's victim? No. Was his torment the decision of a malicious being on high? No. Job was singled out for his piety and his courage, to manifest the function of the tabu, and its terrible necessity.

Job may curse his own day of birth, but his anger is directed at God. "Why hast thou made me thy mark?" Job cries out to God. Job's anger blots out any consolation his friends may offer. Who are they to defend God? Do they know something Job does not already know? Has God appointed them Job's teachers? Bildad, holding firmly to cause and effect, says, "Does God pervert justice? If your children have sinned against him, he has delivered them into the power of their transgression. If you will seek God and make supplication to the Almighty, if you are pure and upright, surely then he will rouse himself for you and reward you with a rightful habitation."[18] Easily said, from the secure position of the objective theorist. We, with our privileged perspective on the hidden workings of the numinous, know something that, if told to Bildad, would destroy his belief system utterly: Job's children died not for their transgressions but because Job was blameless in God's eyes. "The arrows of the Almighty are in me," Job cries; "my spirit drinks their poison."[19] The Adversary is the arrow of the Almighty.

Job knows what Bildad knows, and his knowledge goes one step farther. "How can a man be just before God? If one wished to contend with him, one could not answer him once in a thousand times."[20] The terms of the relationship are unjust. "If it is a contest of strength, behold him! If it is a matter of justice, who can summon him?"[21] How can the particle argue with the universe? Even worse when the particle has a consciousness of universal justice, but the justice is apportioned from unequal scales. Job's comforters hear in Job's words his claim to righteousness, and therefore a denial of God's justice. Zophar answers Job, "You say, 'I am clean in God's eyes.' . . . Know that God exacts of you less than your guilt deserves."[22] Small comfort, to be told that the justice of the universe is the relationship of the master to the slave.

Then Job answered, "No doubt you are the people, and wisdom will die with you. But I have understanding as well as you; I am not inferior to you.

Who does not know such things as these?"[23] Job's comforters have become his adversaries, too, but it is a strange kind of adversarial relationship, based more on agreement than disagreement. Whatever Job's friends offer as universal principles, Job acknowledges, and even reiterates. When one friend speaks of God's majesty, sovereignty, and justice, Job will respond with sarcasm, yet his very rejection of his friends' arguments becomes a hymn as eloquent as theirs to the glory of God. Even in anger Job cannot stop his praises. The argument seems never to advance, but to circle around the same issue. In fact, it is not an argument at all. Whatever arguments and theses can be made, Job's friends make in their opening exchange with him. Job concedes the truth of their arguments and proves himself equally capable of reasoning about cause and effect, justice, and the universal law. He is willing to concede too that no human can be blameless if the contest is between human purity and the Absolute.

The debate, which Job carries on with his friends, is really a struggle in the human soul, as consciousness wrestles to map uncharted Being with its own signifiers. But Being ignores, contradicts, and transcends human signifiers. It is a trial, but with no charge, no judge, no proceedings, no acceptable defense, since consciousness is in argument with itself, both plaintiff and defendant, advocate and judge. However far consciousness extends its understanding of secondary causes, it faces, in the end, the same unanswerable question: Why suffering? Why death? This is the great dialectic, which Hegel outlines in his *Phenomenology of the Spirit*. The dialectic begins when consciousness discovers absolute negation, called in this ancient myth the Satan.

As in a dream, Job's mind splits into components. The argument between Job and his friends never advances to a resolution because each of the speakers, Job included, is a moment of experience, presenting its perceptions, its values, its claims, in the tribunal of the ego. The mind traces and retraces its steps, talking through its hypotheses to itself, offering to itself the wisdom of the ages, only to reject that wisdom as inadequate, ranging near and far for the ideas and images adequate to the experience of suffering and death, and finding only itself. The mind is trapped in the circle of its own signifiers, which can detect the inconsistencies between their constructions and the world, but cannot reconcile them. All the accusations that Job's friends bring against him, Job brings against himself, and he can direct them with equal validity back on to his friends. Their righteousness is not more impeccable than his, when weighed on the scales of the Absolute, but they are not suffering as he is. The vindications which they make of God's inscrutable justice are Job's thoughts too. That Being is inscrutable is no consolation, if we are endowed with intellects that search for, and require, significance. The mind accuses itself of error and arrogance, and then denies its own charges. The mind accuses the Creator, and the universal law, but that accusation too it

must immediately retract. The several human voices in this drama are a soliloquy of the conscious mind speaking into the chasm of Being, and hearing
only its own echoes.

Job is bitter, and with good reason, since he sees himself judged, but by a
judge who will not reveal himself or declare the charge. While Job's comforters can offer only pious theories, Job cries out for a personal revelation
from God—not that he really expects to win the case by personal pleading.
The issue is both larger than a question of lawsuits with their procedures of
prosecution and defense, and more intimate. Job holds fast to his certainty
that he has not, on his side, severed the I-Thou relationship with his Ground
of Being. It seems to him that the relationship has been severed from the
other side. If the first commandment is to honor the I-Thou covenant, surely
the Thou will do no less than reciprocate. "Oh, that I knew where I might
find him," Job cries. "Behold, I go forward, but he is not there; and backward,
but I cannot perceive him; on the left hand I seek him, but I cannot behold
him; I turn to the right hand, but I cannot see him." [24]

Pain itself Job could endure, but when the numinous Subject vacates its
place in the I-Thou relationship, this is a pain of the soul. This is the outrage
consciousness experiences in its dealings with the unconscious. The unconscious intimates that it is the real, that it is wholeness, totality, presence, and
yet it reveals itself as the Ground only by its absence. Job will not trespass
on the tabu, but when the subject of the tabu disappears, what form can the
relationship take other than adversarial? Job's anger against the Almighty is
very great, but even in his anger, while acknowledging that his perfection is
imperfection in the light of the Absolute, he holds fast to his integrity: "I
know that my Vindicator lives." [25]

Job is a warrior, and his tenacity is rewarded. When his friends are done
with all their talking, the numinous bursts through to Job as the voice of the
Almighty speaking out of the whirlwind: "Gird up your loins like a man; I
will question you, and you shall declare to me. Where were you when I laid
the foundation of the earth?" [26] The tone is one of accusation, the approach
adversarial. Does Job presume to summon God to the witness stand? Very
well. God appears on the witness stand—such is the force of Job's will to
conjure the Almighty. Now, the voice thunders, cross-examine me if you
dare. If the ego presumes to approach the numinous as an adversary, the
numinous responds in kind.

The numinous responds to Job's will by entering directly into a relation
with Job's consciousness, but the form the numinous takes is confrontation.
Even in God's magnificent litany of his creative powers, adversarial relations
predominate. The fierceness of the elements; the relations of predator and
prey; the horse snorting at the smell of war; the flashing spear and javelin;
the Behemoth, with bones of bronze and limbs of iron; the Leviathan, whose

sneezings flash forth lightning, and terror dances before him, king over all
the sons of pride—all are manifestations of the numinous. God's hymn to
power hardly addresses Job's questions, except to obliterate them. Furthermore, God's hymn seems to reiterate both the theme of Elihu's speech, and
even much of Job's own statements acknowledging the vast complexity of
Providence.

What has the voice from the whirlwind added to the words already spoken
by Job and his counselors? It brings forth no new arguments; it passes in
silence over the question of Job's righteousness or unrighteousness; it gives
no explanation for Job's catastrophe; it does not share with him the insight
given to us into the relations between God and the Adversary. It asserts Being
in its manifold contradictions, and the reality of the Adversary within the
universal order. More important, it proclaims, even in the seemingly adversarial structure of the world, the primacy of the I-Thou covenant, between
the ego and the numinous Subject, and between God and the Leviathan.

Job humbles himself before this voice proclaiming the awesome incompre-
hensibility of the numinous: "I had heard of thee by the hearing of the ear,
but now my eye sees thee; therefore I despise myself, and repent in dust and
ashes."[27] After such heroic defiance, this sounds like abject capitulation, and
it would be, if the voice were the response of a merely superhuman poten-
tate.[28] But this is the voice of Being itself, and what argument is there against
Being?

The tabu against cursing the Almighty was so charged with power in ancient times that the pious scribes who recorded this parable could not permit
themselves even to write the prohibited phrase. In contrast to our modern
ideology, which idolizes objective facts, archaic consciousness honors the
word over all material or objective manifestations. The Book of Job testifies
throughout to this ancient belief, as indeed do all sacred Scriptures, which
assert the primacy of the metaphysical over the physical. If Job were the kind
of man to place his faith in objective fact, he would certainly have good
reason to deny the existence of God. But Job was chosen to be God's hero
because he had the courage to maintain his belief in the primacy of the spirit
over matter. God's contractual agreement with the Adversary is a mythical
way of talking about a man who, even in circumstances that made a mockery
of his faith, would not surrender the power of his word. Job kept his lips from
speaking the prohibited phrase, knowing that to speak the word is to create
the fact: to curse the world is to make the world accursed. In the days of his
prosperity Job performed sacrifices—apotropaic rituals—to redeem the
world from even the wordless curse that might lie deep in the heart of his
children, so great was his belief in the power of the mind to work good or ill.

The scribes well understood the significance of this no doubt traditional
tale. In their reverence for the creative power of the word, whenever the tale

required them to write the prohibited blasphemy, they veiled it under a euphemism. Where our English translations read "curse," the pious scribes substituted its antonym, "bless," being unwilling even in writing to bring the blasphemy into conjunction with the sacred Name. "Put forth thy hand, and touch all that he has," the Adversary says, as the Hebrew scribes put it, "and he will *bless* thee to thy face." "*Cursed*. Literally 'blessed'. A standard scribal euphemism," is the full extent of the commentary that Pope has to offer on this passage in *The Anchor Bible*.[29] So far have we come from archaic consciousness, in which word and act were synonymous, that we can dismiss the thought at the heart of the Book of Job as a mere scribal discretion. "To bless, to curse—it is a kind of contrapuntal minor theme," is Terrien's exegesis of this theme, in *The Interpreter's Bible*.[30] A minor theme? The holy Name itself was so tabu that it could be expressed only as a cipher, in the sacred tetragrammaton. How much more terrible to blaspheme the Name. Whether Job will bless or curse the Name is no minor theme; it is the only theme of the wager between God and the Adversary.

Job does exactly as Satan prophecies. "Then Job arose, and rent his robe, and shaved his head, and fell upon the ground, and worshipped. And he said, 'blessed be the name of the Lord.'"[31] Again the Adversary wagers with God. The text, bearing the scribal euphemism, continues: "Put forth thy hand now, and touch his bone and his flesh, and he will *bless* thee to thy face." Again Satan afflicts Job, and Job's wife says to Job: "Do you still hold fast your integrity. *Bless* God, and die." And Job answered: "'Shall we receive good at the hand of God, and shall we not receive evil?' In all this Job did not sin with his lips."

We call this substitution of a benign for a negative or pejorative term *euphemism*. But our translators, believing themselves under obligation to strip the text of the scribal discretion, present us with the prohibited word in all its nakedness, thus both violating the tabu and casually occluding the most significant point of the parable. The Greek translators, more circumspect than we, never allowed themselves to lapse into blasphemy in translating this text. Where our texts, so casual with regard to the ill effects of blasphemy, use the word "curse," the Septuagint reads *eulogia*: "to speak well of God."

Euphemism we think of as a trait of the superstitious mind, of which only relics survive in our own language, when we substitute a polite term where the cruder synonym would be considered vulgar. The euphemisms in ancient languages and cults we interpret as signs of a magical thinking, as if all thinking were not magical. If biology insinuated itself into matter by mimetically adapting itself to "the habits of inert matter," as Bergson puts it, magical thinking is the same biological process translated into consciousness.[32] The world, in which myth is a living force, is not a collection of inert objects but, as Eliade writes, "a living cosmos, articulated and meaningful. In the last analysis, *the World reveals itself as language*."[33] Removed from that ancient reverence for the living correspondence between the linguistic structure of the world and human language, we classify euphemism as an obsolete magical practice faded, as here, into scribal decorum. Thus we give ourselves permission to name what must not be named, and mark it with the blasphemy that the scribes took care to circumvent.

The sympathetic magic, from which euphemism arose in antiquity, expressed an attitude both intellectual and religious. The word *euphemé* (from which we derive "euphemism") was an utterance of good omen. A soothsayer, sighting a bird flying past on the right, might make the event significant by publicly proclaiming it an omen of success; he would *euphemize* the bird's flight, to read it as a signifier of nature's concordance with some intended human enterprise. Even if we dismiss the soothsayers' claims to a superior knowledge of nature's laws, their euphemizing expressed a positive psychological attitude. By reading in nature a continuous play of signs guiding human endeavor, soothsayers asserted the power of the intellect (which was identifying and validating those signifiers) to find meaning in nature, and a corresponding meaning in human nature. By euphemizing the world, the intellect learned to overcome its doubts as it moved forward into the future, finding by slow degrees evidence of its ability to fashion tools to bring nature into greater conformity with the mind, if not vice versa.

Euphemé had a specific use in cult, in relation to a god's epiphany. A prayer or a hymn to a god, in ancient cult, was both a pious remembrance of the god's majesty and benevolence and an invocation; that is, a magic conjuration of the god into existence. Prayer was the magical practice by which consciousness took hold of the formless and ineffable, made it take on form, and lend its form for human service. In formal cult hymns, of which we have literary examples in the poems of the Alexandrian poet Callimachus, the hymnist would invoke (that is, conjure into being) the desired god, by naming the god, by specifying the god by his titles, attributes, and customary haunts. If this act were done in such a way that, as Parmenides would put it, thought and the object of thought were one and the same, the god would materialize out of the void, ready to do his worshippers' bidding. The hymn, moving in a crescendo, would culminate in the epiphany of the god. At the moment of the epiphany the priest, or hymnist, would utter the warning: *euphemeite*— "let only words of good omen be spoken." By custom, this was an injunction to observe complete silence, silence being the best way to minimize the hazards of an ill omen. What would be the consequence of an ill omen at this time? Who knows, since this is the moment when the full power of the numinous transects the mundane. The god might not appear or, worse, might materialize not in the form invoked by the worshippers but as a malevolent demon. So great, in mythical thought, is the effect of the word upon the world.[34]

Euphemism is an essential law in mythical thought. It is the belief that as the world was created by the word, so now it is still created by the word; that human thought creates even the gods, and gods can take form according to human will.[35] The law of the euphemism is the theme of the Book of Job. Job, like every human being, has the power either to euphemize the world or to withhold his word of good omen.

Job's piety, before Satan's intervention in his life, was a piety still only half-conscious of the negative. Prosperity and piety were equally yoked in his life. Job maintained a correct attitude toward the Almighty, and the Almighty rewarded him with an I-Thou relationship, in which was no shadow of doubt. The shadow entered when Satan crossed that I-Thou relationship, thus demonstrating that the relation of piety and prosperity is not always one of clear cause and effect. Job discovered the negative; that is, the Other. His choice now was to negate the Other, by cursing God; or to negate himself, by directing the curse onto himself. Job's friends see these as the only possible terms in Job's predicament. If God is good, the evil must be situated in Job's will; if Job is good, God must be the evil principle. Good and evil must exactly balance out, in the cosmology of Job's friends.

For Job this equation will not compute. The world, so much more powerful in its being than Job's limited and mortal state, threatens to negate Job entirely. From the perspective of the universal Subject, Job is a mere nothing, and Job's well-being a seeming irrelevance in the universal order. Job, seeing this truth, negates himself, cursing the day of his birth. But this solution is inadequate for either heart or mind. How can Job negate his own consciousness, which is the very shrine of the God-image? How can the Almighty demand I-Thou relations, in which only the I exists, and the Thou is a zero, or in which the I exists only in order to negate the Thou? Can Job choose the opposite alternative—to assert his own identity, while negating the world? No, the world will not so easily suffer itself to be negated. What kind of integrity would it be for the individual ego to reverse the I-Thou equation, and make the ego the truly existent, and the world the nonexistent? "The unification of the self," Dewey writes, "cannot be attained in terms of itself."[36] The individual ego can find its wholeness only in its relations with something transcending its own finite identity. The ego requires the Other for the sake of the ego's identity, yet this Other must also be the ego's Thou; that is, the Subject.

If the ego refuses to be annihilated by its own God-image, and God in turn refuses to be annihilated by the ego, the two must coexist, but as enemies, mutually irreconcilable opposites. This is the Adversary's temptation, and the solution Job's wife adopts. If God is the Adversary, why not respond in kind? Dare to be God's enemy. This is the skeptic's position, but Job will not accept it as his solution. The ego cannot survive without an I-Thou relation to the world, but survival is a terrible condition if the partnership takes the form only of enemy set against enemy. "Blaspheme the Almighty, and die," says Job's wife. To choose to be God's enemy is to choose a living death.

Figure dissolves into ground, ground resolves into figure. Which is the ground? Which is the figure? Is God the ground and the ego the figure? Or is the ego the ground and God a figure that the ego creates in its own image? What is Job to do? It would be foolish to negate God—"you speak as one of the foolish women," Job replies to his wife. But Job will not surrender his own integrity and negate himself. Yet negation, here personified in the form of the Adversary, is real; sentimental optimism will not make it disappear. Job's heroic labor is to keep both terms of the equation—God and Job's own independent ego—intact. Job must affirm his own integrity, yet he must also affirm God's integrity, since his own integrity, indeed his very existence, depends on the integrity of the whole; he must affirm the Adversary, who works to dissolve all integrity; and he must maintain at all moments in this heroic labor his I-Thou relations with the indivisible One, in which can be no Other, or even the shadow of an Other.

Job's struggle is Hegel's noble dialectic, in which consciousness first appears as consciousness of the Other. As the ego wrestles with the Other, acknowledging negation, unable to negate, yet refusing to be negated, consciousness discovers itself. The law of the euphemism, here expressed as the tabu against negating the Almighty, was instituted to prevent consciousness from short-circuiting its progress to self-consciousness through fear, anger, or guilt. Consciousness begins when the Adversary first introduces distinction into the indivisible One. When ego-consciousness comes upon the Adversary, the obvious and simple solution, by which the ego can maintain its own integrity, is to deny God. But this solution arrests the ego's development and fixates it at the I-It level of consciousness, where the ego is the despot, and all the world its object.

The law of the euphemism rules that the Adversary must be negated; and, in negation, affirmed. The negative must be acknowledged, validated, and transcended. Consciousness wrestles with the Adversary as Herakles wrestled with the river Acheloos, as Menelaos wrestled with Proteus, the ancient, polymorphous creature of the deep, whose wisdom transcends the signifiers of the intellect. The hero is ego-consciousness, which wrestles with Proteus while Proteus goes through his manifold transformations, until, at last, polymorphous appearances focus into a unified whole. At this point Proteus reveals his deeper function, not enemy but oracle, a direct conduit between the ego and universal wisdom.

"Behold, Behemoth," the voice in the whirlwind speaks to Job, "which I made as I made you. . . . He is the first of the works of God."[37] Behemoth is the Adversary, in one of his many mythical forms, and he is the first of the words of God. "Canst thou draw out Leviathan with a fishhook?" the voice asks. "Will he make a covenant with you to take him for your servant for ever? Will you play with him as with a bird, or will you put him on a leash for your maidens? Will traders bargain over him? . . . Lay hands on him; think of the battle; you will not do it again! He makes the deep boil like a pot. . . . Upon earth there is not his like, a creature without fear. He beholds everything that is high; he is king over all the sons of pride."[38] Who is this Leviathan, whose majesty the voice of the Almighty extols in his hymn to Creation? Leviathan is "the twisting one."[39] He is Proteus; he is the hydra with which Herakles wrestled; the Python, Apollo's antagonist; and the serpent, with whom Adam and Eve sported in the Garden of Eden. Satan, Behemoth, Leviathan—they are all forms of the same archetype: the primal chaos demon.[40] But this chaos demon is first among the works of God; he beholds everything that is high; when the sons of God present themselves, he is numbered among them.[41] God and the Leviathan have a covenant with each other, and converse with each other as I and Thou.

The Lord and his Adversary make a covenant to show forth the law of the euphemism in all its glory. "Put forth your hand now, and touch all that Job has," the Adversary wagers, "and he will bless thee to thy face." Only a hero can bless God when the indivisible One splits, and takes the form of the Adversary. Truly to bless God is to bless the Adversary.

Are we surprised when the voice of the Almighty turns in anger against Job's counselors? They had thought to vindicate the ways of Providence, but their pious truths are an offense to the Lord. "My wrath is kindled against you," the voice says to Job's friends, "for you have not spoken of me what is right, as my servant Job has." The Lord commands them to ask for Job's intercession: "and my servant Job shall pray for you, for I will accept his prayer not to deal with you according to your folly."[42] Had Job, who dared to stand fast and defend his integrity before the Almighty, spoken rightly? Had his comforters who, in justifying God's integrity, had accused Job of solipsism, if not narcissism, misrepresented God? Paradox upon paradox. Job, angry and defiant, is blessed by the Almighty, because he kept the covenant, while his counselors, though they speak so piously of God's perfect will, are rejected.

Modern commentators speak often like Job's counselors, who judge that if God is to be vindicated, Job must be condemned. "The poet," Terrien writes in *The Interpreter's Bible,* "daringly portrays a blasphemer, a doubter, a frenzied rebel, a proud giant, a challenger of God, who in the end must cast himself down and repent in dust and ashes."[43] A proud giant, yes; a challenger of God, certainly; but hardly a frenzied rebel. And a blasphemer? Never. What evidence could we use to justify such an accusation? Terrien's evidence seems to come from passages where Job scornfully dismisses his friends, and no longer content with being the plaintiff in this case, decides, as the Jerusalem Bible puts it, "to cross-examine God."[44] Terrien seems to read Job's words at 13.13–15 as blasphemy, where Job says, in the Jerusalem Bible translation, "Let him kill me if he will; I have no other hope than to justify my conduct in his eyes."[45] Granted, Job grazes the edge of blasphemy; even so, he dares the Almighty to vindicate him, and He does.

Self-assertion is not blasphemy in this parable, and neither is doubt; both, in fact, seem to be respected by the Almighty, who turns on Job's friends, as if their servile obedience were the blasphemy and Job's doubts and defiance were the mark of true understanding. Only the Name is tabu. Nowhere in our text does Job say anything that God construes as blasphemy, and where the Almighty finds no blame, why should we? So sacred is the Logos in Job's consciousness that he cannot even bless the Almighty, without risking the violation of the tabu. "Blessed be the *Name* of the Lord," Job says; or rather, even then he does not name the Name, but says (or his scribes say) only "Blessed be the *Name* of the *Tetragrammaton.*"

How could God lose his wager? And if he could, and did, what scribe would record the defeat? Job's God, whether he be named YHWH, Elohim, or Eloah of the Edomites (and all three signifiers are used in our text, to intimate, and protect, the Subject), expects to be cross-examined. People who fear to cross-examine God will certainly find God all the same, since there is God enough for everyone. But they will not find Job's God. We may agree with Whitehead that throughout the Book of Job runs an "undercurrent of fear lest an old-fashioned tribal god might take offense at this rational criticism."[46] But that, surely, is the intention of the Book of Job, to remove the ethical debate from the purview of the old tribal god, who proscribes rational criticism. This God expects a good wrestling match. Why else would he lay such fantastic odds on the match, and send his wrestling master into the ring? Job was chosen to advance consciousness, ours or God's, by wrestling with the Satan at the edge where euphemy and blasphemy exactly touch.

Job's friends do not blaspheme the Almighty, but they are fixated at an earlier moment in the development of consciousness, a majestic moment, to be sure, when the old tribal patriarch god stands guard over his children, obliging the faithful with rewards, and punishing the evil with evil. Their god is the superego fixated on its monarchical prerogatives: a superior ego, waiting to punish any trespass on its domain. Their god enjoins complete compliance upon them, claiming metaphysical questionings as his province alone. If the work of the Adversary is proof of God's anger, they need look no further into nature, or into their own minds. Let their god assume all thought and consciousness into himself; on their side, they will oblige by delivering themselves as his obedient, but unthinking, flagellants. At the first appearance of the Adversary they counsel immediate capitulation, as a child would capitulate to an angry father, who brooks no questioning of his authority.

The God who, in the end, vindicates Job, is not the patriarch Job's friends take Him for, though his demands, in fact, are more strenuous than the simple prescripts of the old tribal patriarch. The patriarch promises security for his believers in return for unexamined obedience. Job's God promises no security, and demands that Job risk everything—his meanings and his being; in short, consciousness. Since the relations of Job's friends with their god are fixed in the mode of the slave bowing to his lord, they cannot enter into dialogue with Job's God. Do they need the punitive patriarch for their God? So be it. Let them prostrate themselves, and confess themselves the blasphemers, who must approach God through Job's mediation. If this is unjust compensation for their piety, they will keep their silence, given the proof of God's persuasive power. On the other hand, the voice in the whirlwind gives Job no satisfaction, if by satisfaction we mean a logical accounting of the cosmos, and of Job's place in the purposes of Providence. By its silence, the voice relegates Job's case to something less than a footnote in the dynamic movement of Being. But we know, despite the bluster on Job's side, and on God's, that Job has been cleared of the slightest taint of blasphemy, and is esteemed in the courts of heaven for reconciling in himself God and Leviathan, the signifier and its negative.[47]

Edinger has discussed the Book of Job as the encounter of the ego with the transpersonal Self, the term Jung adopted to connote the Atman of Vedantic thought, the universal Spirit.[48] So it is, but the ego in this parable is not simply dissolved into nonidentity by the revelation of the universal Self. Job blesses God by holding fast to both his own integrity and God's integrity at the same time. What is this universal Self? The Self is the world translated into consciousness, and consciousness is the vision granted to Job as the goal of his dialectical questioning, when he sees Jehovah and Leviathan meet each other as I and Thou, neither canceling the other, but each maintaining the other's integrity for the sake of his own. "Self-consciousness," Hegel writes, "attains its satisfaction only in another self-consciousness."[49] Only when a self-consciousness has another self-consciousness before it, Hegel writes, does it come to have "the unity of itself in its otherness."

Otto writes of Behemoth and Leviathan, to which the voice in the whirlwind alludes, as examples of "the wellnigh daemonic and wholly incomprehensible character of the eternal creative power."[50] True; but if we see these primordial beasts as only exemplars of the awesome mystery of the universe, we may miss the full significance of the parable. Jahweh does not simply turn Job's attention to Jahweh's grandeur, but calls upon him to wrestle with the numinous powers. At the first level of consciousness the Adversary is the enemy separating the ego from the universal Self, the chasm between subject and object, the doubt that shadows every certainty. But a hero with Job's stamina discovers that the Adversary is also the river of Being, which sustains even the individuating ego with undivided attention. Behold, Behemoth, luxurious in the river of life: "Under the lotus plants he lies, in the covert of the reeds and in the marsh. For his shade the lotus trees cover him; the willows of the brook surround him." [51]

Behold, Leviathan, the servant of the Most High, luxuriating in the marshes of matter, ready to seize the smolt and hurl it from its alpine streams down to the open sea. But behold, Leviathan (again!), waiting now at the river mouth to receive the wandering hero and enfold him back to his home, with his mind made more supple in its wrestle with time. For this was the tabu against blasphemy and the law of the euphemism ordained, to give the neonate time and space enough to distinguish between automatism and choice, impulse and intention, and reconcile the differences.

3

Hesiod's
Archaic Cosmology

I. The Prime Elements

As the forms and laws from the universal matrix impinge on our biological being, the imagination responds by ordering them and translating them into the images that become the ground of our language, indeed of all our thinking. The archetypes, as Jung tirelessly repeated, are beyond form; they might as well be formless, and so they have been called by many philosophers and in religious thought. The Tao that can be named is not the Tao. The old Jewish commentaries on the Old Testament repeatedly insist that the Almighty cannot be qualified by any attributes. Jung, in introducing the ancient term *archetype* into modern psychology, quotes the *Corpus Hermeticum,* where God is called "the archetypal light."[1] Light manifests itself to our vision in a variety of forms—as sunlight, moonlight, incandescent light, the sociable light of the campfire. How inadequate our vocabulary is for express-ing even the commonest forms of visible light. The light that physicists study is theoretic, so theoretic that it has neither color nor visibility, the qualities that ordinary experience takes for the very essence of light. The physicists' light is dark. How can light be dark? Physicists too search for something like an archetype transcending the light our senses perceive.

If the archetypes are beyond any particular form manifested in time and space, we cannot immediately lodge them in some completely transcendental realm. Hegel has taught us to understand that we perceive the universals only as they engage in the dialectic of our daily experience, in what he calls par-ticular, determinate existence. Buber makes the same point in his own way when he says that each moment of the I-Thou consciousness points to the eternal I-Thou.

We can liken the archetypes to the structure of a crystal. The patterning structure that determines the specific form of a crystal has no existence sepa-rate from the existence of the crystal. It must coexist with the crystal, yet the formal patterning is not the crystal. Though the form is realized only in the specific, in real crystals in our material world, its being is, as we say, of a different ontological order. A crystal is geometry made visible, and geometry, Kepler said, "is the archetype of the beauty of the world."[2]

The DNA coding in our biological cells offers another analogy for the relationship between archetype and particular. As the structuring principle determining our biological form from the moment of conception until our organic being is dissolved in death, DNA is our whole genetic history, a memory bank of records going back millions of years. It is also everything we will become; in it are already contained our laughter, our griefs, our thoughts, ideals, accomplishments. It is even prepared for our mistakes. In fact, biology *introduces* error into the material world—how can inorganic matter be in error?—and in doing so *sanctifies* error. How could there be trial without error, accomplishments without failures? In biology every error is an opportunity. Inorganic matter knows nothing of opportunities. DNA, which codes not only our specific physical features or mannerisms but even our hesitations, choices, and miscalculations, is truly the homunculus of medie-val thought, a miniaturized self placed at the center of every one of our cells to guide the unfolding of our unified, organic form through the bewildering maze of natural objects and laws. For each of us the DNA in our cells is the archetype of our individual form; it is our destiny.

DNA is a microscopic piece of matter, a chain of protein molecules, con-taining bits of information. But what do we mean by information? Biologists tell us that the genome that contains all the genetic material in our cells is composed of several billion bits, each bit coding, presumably, a certain quan-tum of information. But already we can construct computers with microchips containing as many bits of information, and computers have given no evidence as yet of anything resembling human behavior. Quantity of information alone is not what distinguishes our thinking from the operations of a computer. The information inscribed on a microchip is inert data, but the information in a genome *informs*: it draws matter to itself and not only regenerates itself but generates new forms. Most amazing of mysteries, DNA is the source of ideas that have not yet been thought, of inventions not yet invented.

Though our genes are composed of matter and function in accordance with the laws that govern all material substances, they operate in a different manner than the materials that form an inorganic machine. The arrangement in a machine, Köhler points out, "consists of given materials, just as a rock, or any piece of iron, contains the same solid material day after day, more probably year after year."[3] Hardly any part of an organism, Köhler says, is a solid object in this sense. Instead, organic structures "prove to be processes, so-called steady states, the materials of which are gradually and slowly being eliminated and, at the same time, replaced by metabolic structures."[4] To talk, then, of DNA as if it were a substance is to talk crudely, since the material of which DNA is composed is in a continuous state of decay and replacement.

DNA is not so much a storehouse of data but a process, a dynamic set of relations so complex it must encompass not only the immediate materials on which the cell depends for its nourishment but also all the elements and hazards that the whole organism may expect to encounter in its life cycle. DNA is not only embedded in an individual cell; it is embedded in the universe. One species of tree requires for its survival certain species of birds that will be lured to eat the fruit of the tree and deposit the indigestible matter, the seeds, elsewhere. A flowering bush seduces the busy bee to suck on its sugars and so carry on the bush's work of pollination. A wise bush will time its blooms to coincide with the arrival of the bee population. The genetic codes of sugar-saturated bush and honey-making bee engage in a truly Hegelian dialectic of the I-Thou relationship. Each, to maintain its own separate and independent identity, must seduce the other and be, in turn, seduced.

The deeper our meditation takes us into DNA, the less it appears to be a material compound, and the more it approaches what theologically minded people call the soul, the individual soul intimately related to all other individual souls, and emanating from the World Soul, whose reflection it is. Heisenberg, discussing the modern scientific concept of matter, writes: "I think on this point modern physics has definitely decided for Plato. For the smallest units of matter are in fact not physical objects in the ordinary sense of the word, they are forms, structures, or—in Plato's sense—Ideas, which can be unambiguously spoken of only in the language of mathematics."[5] What Heisenberg says of material particles must certainly be as true of DNA. If subatomic particles are archetypal Ideas, then so too must be the genetic code.

Is DNA conscious? We do not ordinarily think so since we are object-minded and cannot as yet find consciousness in any of the materials or particles of DNA. If it is not conscious, where, then, does consciousness enter into the process? DNA is not conscious, we say, yet it determines the form of consciousness. How can a nonconscious material substance code consciousness into being? We are back at the distinction between archetype and particular, or to the Kabbalistic distinction between the Sefiroth and the En-Sof, which, though beyond form and consciousness, emanates as both form and consciousness in the material world, or to the distinction in Plotinus between particular forms and Form itself, from which, though it is prior to all forms, all particular forms emanate.

Wherever we turn, we reach the same mystery. Unconscious nature (for so we like to think it) translates physical matter into organic life; organic life translates into consciousness; then consciousness, in examining itself, finds itself to be made in the image of nature. Consciousness responds with the sense of rapture that Plato wrote of when it discovers that its apparently subjective laws coincide with the objective laws, the archetypal forms of nature.

Since Jung's use of the term "archetypes" has been taken by some as evidence of his lapse into mysticism, let us invoke a physicist, Pauli, whose reputation for objective thought stands secure beyond criticism. What is the bridge, Pauli asks, between our sense perceptions, which are our registers of physical data, and our concepts?

> All logical thinkers [Pauli writes] have arrived at the conclusion that pure logic is fundamentally incapable of constructing such a link. It seems most satisfactory to introduce at this point the postulate of a cosmic order independent of our choice and distinct from the world of phenomena. . . .
> The process of understanding nature as well as the happiness that man feels in understanding, that is, in the conscious realization of new knowledge, seems thus to be based on a correspondence, a "matching" of inner images preexistent in the human psyche with external objects and their behavior. This interpretation of scientific knowledge, of course, goes back to Plato.[6]

Pauli concludes that something like the Jungian archetypes must provide the necessary link between the world and our concepts:

> When modern psychology brings proof to show that all understanding is a long-drawn-out process initiated by processes in the unconscious long before the content of consciousness can be rationally for-

mulated, it has directed attention again to the preconscious, archaic level of cognition. On this level the place of clear concepts is taken by images with strong emotional content, not thought out but beheld, as it were, while being painted. Inasmuch as these images are an "expression of a dimly suspected but still unknown state of affairs" they can also be termed symbolical, in according with the definition of the symbol proposed by C. G. Jung. As *ordering* operators and image-formers in this world of symbolical images, the archetypes thus function as the sought-for bridge between the sense perceptions and the ideas and are, accordingly, a necessary presupposition even for evolving a scientific theory of nature.[7]

It is a mistake of our modern times to suppose that primitive peoples do not think in abstractions. Dialectic did not begin with Socrates, though Socrates, or rather Parmenides before him, was the first in Western philosophy to articulate consciously the formal principles governing the process. Dialectic is the process by which the intellect works. The human mind processes data by moving from specific to specific, by grouping specifics into categories, by weighing category against category, by moving from the particular to the universal and from the universal back to the particular again, and at each stage of the process altering its definitions of both the particular and the universal. A child, speaking its first word, has already mastered the fundamental principle of abstract thought; its mind is already moving in the world of the universal.

The One and the Many, Being and non-Being, Self and Other, the phenomenal and the metaphenomenal—whatever the questions philosophy poses for itself, we find the same questions posed in the images and the dynamic structures of mythology. Historical circumstances affect the form in which the questions are posed, of course, and the answers obtained. But human consciousness has always been committed to the same quest—to discover the nature and source of consciousness itself. The God-image of even the most primitive culture is an advanced thought, for in it is already encoded the whole dialectical process of the philosophers. In the God-image, consciousness discovers itself in dialogue with itself.

Hesiod's *Theogony* is one of the oldest systematic accounts of the creation and ordering of the cosmos that has survived from our past. Scholars date the poem in its present written form to about the seventh century B.C., when the Greeks adopted the alphabet of the Phoenicians and initiated their own literacy. But the poem's formulaic language and its kinship with other cosmogonies of much greater antiquity in the Near East suggest that it is, in its written form, the culmination of a long oral tradition extending back centuries prior to the flowering of archaic Greek culture in the seventh century B.C. It is thus a priceless document revealing the workings of the human mind at the dawn of literacy. To us, who have become accustomed to the rigorous mathematical cosmology of modern science, the *Theogony* reads like the thought of a naive, even childish, mind, yet it is an abstract document through and through, a statement of the nature of the world and of the human psyche, which reveals a sophisticated understanding of symbol formation and symbol manipulation.

The *Theogony* imaginatively transposes its historical moment onto the cosmos. It traces the rise of the patriarchy from a presumed matriarchal origin, and for the psychologist (and the philosopher) the significance of the *Theogony* lies in its articulation of the process by which it validates the new patriarchal order and reveals the strategies by which the new order gained ascendancy. The poem is, thus, a veritable treatise in mythical language on the structure and dynamics of the human psyche. The rise of the ego; the conflict between ego and superego; the ego's fear of the libido; the dialectic of conscious and unconscious thought processes with its strategies of distortion and evasion for rerouting and disguising prohibited desires; conquest by castration; male fears of vaginal engulfment; the passive aggression of the trickster ego—such themes, issuing from profound depths in the human psyche, inform the *Theogony,* giving it its dreamlike structure, in which clarity and obfuscation lie side by side.

Every cosmogony is a psychological theory. Purporting to explain the origin and structure of the cosmos, overtly describing the gods and their functions, cosmogonies really validate cultural values, gods being values defined and embodied. All cosmologies arise as the attempt to explain the place of the individual in society and of the anomaly of human existence in the universe, but hypotheses regarding the origin of the world and society are, at the primary level, hypotheses regarding the origin and nature of human consciousness. The myth, which Hesiod tells in the *Theogony* of Prometheus and Pandora, is the story of awakening consciousness. The ego discovers its own power both over the natural environment and over the inner inhibitions imposed by the superego. But this discovery contains within it the discovery of the cruel fallacy of the image, the necessity for labor, the disjunction between labor and the product, and between desire and enjoyment, the dilemma of authentic existence, the split of the original unity into contradictions at war with each other. The myth of Prometheus and Pandora tells of the birth of desire, and Self-consciousness, Hegel said, is *Desire*.[8]

Once we see the myth of Prometheus and Pandora as one version of the mind's coming into its self-awareness, we can recognize that the *Theogony,* as a whole and in its parts, tells the same story. Differentiation of parts within an original unity, and then the reconciliation of opposing parts into a new unity, forms the basis of the scientific method. Hegel has taught us to recognize in this process the dialectic of consciousness itself, since any alteration in our concept of the object demands an alteration in the subject. This process of differentiation and unification gives the *Theogony* its overall structure.

The major difference between Hesiod's archaic cosmology and our modern scientific cosmology is not that the one is mythical and the other not. Certainly scientific thought has pushed the objective mode to the extreme, and the result has been a more precise knowledge of the laws of nature. But when, in subatomic particles, the object disappears into a realm of pure mathematics, when statistical probabilities come to replace older concepts of fixed objects and precisely definable events, when physicists talk of the importance of intuition in scientific discovery, we are in the world of myth. At its extremities, logical thought, even in the very process of following its own rules, passes into a world of archetypes, which are the ground of myth.

The distinction between our modern cosmology and Hesiod's is that Hesiod's is subjective. The subject is both the center and the circumference of his cosmology. Where we talk of force, Hesiod sees the will; where we talk of impulse, he sees intention; what we call magnetism and chemical affinities, he calls desire; and matter for him is still synonymous with the Mother. Our modern cosmology describes a world of things being acted upon by other things, all objects with no agent. Hesiod's cosmos, by contrast, knows only living beings acting on each other reciprocally. Even primeval Chaos in Hesiod's *Theogony* is not merely empty or inert; like everything else in his cosmos, it too is a living being, which generates its own offspring.

Hesiod posits a beginning that is, as it were, self-evident. His prime elements—Earth, Chaos, and Eros—come into being as if from nothing. They are self-generated, autonomous agents in his cosmology, primary entities, beyond which it is not possible to penetrate. Together they form the Ground of Being in Hesiod's cosmology; as such they are in some sense beyond the bounds of conscious knowledge, yet they are assumed to be agents, to whom Hesiod ascribes consciousness (in what has generally been called naive anthropomorphism). In short, they are pure subject. Everything that proceeds from them is a subject too because pure subject emanates only subjects.

"The idea of a whole," Dewey writes, "whether of the whole personal being or of the world, is an imaginative, not a literal idea."[9] Logical thinking alone does not lead to unification, since its work is separation and leads us in an infinite regress from unity. Unity is a subjective idea, but subjective here is not a pejorative. The truly subjective is that which possesses its own authentic experience, which is experience truly lived in the world of nature. Despite the continuous flux in our circumstances and our inner emotions, despite the disparity between our intentions and acts, our experience of ourselves as a unified field remains constant. As we examine the external world with the tools of logic, we separate matter into ever finer particles, yet our scientific probes and experiments continue to confirm our intuition of unity, however elusive that unity remains.

Mythology translates this intuition of unity into the image of a state of aboriginal unity existing in a primordial moment. As mythology gave way to philosophy, the intuition of unity opened into the scientific search for the fundamental elements underlying all phenomena and for the element in the human organism that corresponds with those fundamental objective elements. Philosophy and science took us far from the images of mythical cosmogonies, in which living beings create or emanate the world. Yet modern psychology, which reveals that each of us creates a personal, subjective cosmology, has brought us closer again to myth. The ancient cosmogonies, which science discarded, have been reinstated in modern psychological theory.

As we floated in the universal matrix—for so we may assume as a hypothesis at least—the rich amniotic sea flowed around us and through us, carrying the chemicals necessary for our survival and growth. Consciousness existed then in us only in potential. We had as yet no language in which to articulate it, and the synapses had not yet formed that would later translate potential into kinetic consciousness. That state of bliss, when we were truly children of nature, traditional mythologies call Paradise, the Garden of Eden. Some modern psychologists have called it the Ouroboric state, after the ancient figure of the Ouroboros, the great serpent that circles around to swallow its own tail, a symbol of that state where beginnings and endings join in one undifferentiated field.[10]

If the embryo's needs are satisfied by osmosis, simple osmosis will not suffice for the neonate. In the symbiosis of the womb the flow of nutrients was automatic, but after birth the flow requires choice and intention. In response to the external environment neural connectors begin sprouting at a prodigious rate, dividing the original undifferentiated field into separate channels. Our needs become differentiated, and the means for their satisfaction diversified and complex. Once out of the womb we need certain nutrients, but nutrition is more than a supply of physical substance; we need to be smiled at and talked to; we need to be fondled; in short, we need relationships. The symbiosis of the embryo translates at birth into relationships.

Once we are thrust from the womb we encounter obstacles and resistance. What Brown calls the first law of Form is also the first law of consciousness: *Let there be a distinction*.[11] Cleaving space in two is the beginning of creation, since, with the first distinction, the mind must discover, or invent, the crossing. Boundaries now come into existence not only in the external environment but in the baby's physiology. Nutrition, once elicited, must be tested by various receptors, by texture, shape, and size. To the autonomic processes of the body is added a new process of discrimination. How is the infant to correlate its own internal sensors and receptors with the chaotic swarm of external phenomena? The imagination creates an inner world that, for survival, must correspond closely with the topography of the outer world. The laws of chemistry and physics, which once impinged upon the embryo willy-nilly, must now be differentiated by the imagination; that is, they must be represented.

At birth a space intervenes between our needs and their satisfactions, and in that space is born the first archetype, the Mother, the source of the nutrition (in traditional cultures). Since our first experience of life is of being parented, it is not surprising that the first signifier of the subject, projected into consciousness by the imagination, is the Mother. The infant becomes a scholar who studies to decode the signifiers of this subject with a devotion born of desire and necessity. This archetype is a magician with protean powers of transformation. Before the infant learns to translate change in size of a moving object into change of location, this archetypal figure must appear a very wizard at shape-changing. A giant when she looms over the cradle to mesmerize baby with her gaze, she diminishes into a dwarf as she moves away, until finally she vanishes into nothingness. A giant in size and strength, she has also the will of a giant, as relentless as it is capricious. She is omniscient and omnipotent. She wears a thousand faces. Sometimes her voice is sharp, her touch impatient; at other times she is a garden of smiles, and the perfumes of the Orient float in the air as she moves.

This archetype in Hesiod's cosmology is Gaia (or Ge), the Earth. Gaia has no parent. Self-generated and self-perpetuating, she is the matrix, the ground of the baby's emerging consciousness. In Hesiod's cosmology Gaia is the ground for all figures, for all the subsequent gods no less than for all plants, animals, and humans. Gaia, in Hesiod's account, generates Ouranos (Uranus), Sky, as her partner, both complement and contradiction in one. Every action, in mythology as in nature, produces its reaction. Ouranos is equal in size to Gaia, yet in other respects her antithesis. He is the male that defines her as female, the father that defines her as the mother; he is above as she is below; he is the light that defines her as darkness. The first archetype no sooner appears than it generates its opposite. Each thought contains its own contradiction, and contradiction must be built into any serious cosmology.

Gaia, the self-generated mother, spontaneously configuring her own body into mountains and sea, is the child's representation of its biological mother, behind whom it cannot imagine any prior existence. But it would be impertinent to read Hesiod's cosmogony as merely the fantasy of a child. Hesiod's poetry contains much more in perceptive range, and a greater wisdom, than we are likely to see in any infant's vision of the world. To the infant's representation Hesiod's cosmology adds a multitude of images that a maturer vision creates of the world. It is not only a naive or primitive mode of thought that leads people to reverence nature as the Great Mother. In contrast to the simpler biological forms, humans are not neurologically complete at birth. The slate, as our mind used to be thought of, grows even as it is being inscribed. The contrast even between us and our nearest cousins among the apes is striking. The human brain does not reach the proportion found in the chimpanzee at birth until about the sixth month after birth. "Human babies are born as embryos," Gould writes, "and embryos they remain for about the first nine months of life." [12] Even at nine months or a year after birth, however, our neurology is far from complete. Some say that we are not neurologically complete until adolescence.

To speak of a second birth is no mere figure of speech; like all archetypal experiences, this image corresponds with reality. We are born once of our biology, as physical beings, and born again of the spirit; that is, into consciousness. We have two mothers, our biological mother and the world. The long period of immaturity in our species, which we call infancy and childhood, allows for the slow gestation of the imagination.

Archetypes formed in infancy do not die when we leave infancy, nor are they irrevocably fixed in infancy, unless we suppose neurological growth also to be completed during infancy. By a normal process, archetypes enlarge to include more features in an ever-expanding field of consciousness. As the necessity for the biological mother wanes, her function is replaced by a more general mothering principle. Since the symbiosis of mother and embryo translates, after birth, into relationships with the world, it should not surprise us that the communal relationships, which developed into the institutions of church and school, should be called the Alma Mater. As the biological womb is the safe enclosure in which our physiology can develop, so the communal structures reproduce that security in our childhood, our second gestation period, to provide the matrix in which the metaphysical body, i.e., consciousness, can develop. The mother becomes the community; the community becomes, as we mature, the Earth; the Earth becomes the Ground of Being. Hesiod's Gaia is a thoroughly abstract concept, both physical and metaphysical. She is the universal substance, the *prima materia* of the alchemists, the element Earth of the philosophers, the nurturing aspect of the world.

The first archetype is the product of the cleavage of the original undifferentiated field into two. But this cleavage is not as simple as it seems. At some primordial moment the Mother is the whole field, the ground. But the infant deduces this ground as a true existent not from her presence but from her absence. The baby experiences a need as a hunger, but the hunger is not immediately satisfied. She who was present drops into the void, and just as mysteriously emerges from the void again in her own sweet time. No sooner does the ground come into being than it disappears. In its appearances and disappearances it becomes a figure, and the ground recedes into the farther distance. The first archetype cannot exist without a second.

Hesiod's Gaia requires the coexistence of Chaos, which is not our modern concept of chaos, a confused mixture of elements, but the gap, the yawning abyss. From the Mother's disappearances the infant deduces a space. The ground comes into being now as a kind of negative, a vacancy, simply that in which matter exists and moves. Thus Hesiod's Chaos is self-generated like Gaia, and her coeval.[13]

Both matter and space claim priority among the archetypes. In the rivalry of their claims we see the oscillation between figure and ground that is a continuous process in the psychology of perception. Every cosmology codes this oscillation in its own way. Did the world exist before the God of Genesis created it? No, it was "without form, and void." How, then, could God breathe on the face of the deep? Because the world, once formed, becomes a figure, and every figure must have its ground. The "deep" in the Genesis account of creation is Hesiod's Chaos, the context that brings Gaia forward into being, as Gaia is the context that then manifests every subsequent being. Consciousness creates its topography by naming one object after another, separating one thing from everything else. Then it retraces its steps, moving from figure to ground, from ground to another figure, from figure to ground again, back to the ultimate ground, and behold, the ultimate ground is not one but two. The One cannot come into being, or at least it cannot be manifest, except it become two.

We have generated the two primal archetypes. The original cleavage of the undifferentiated field distinguishes this Here from the There on the other side of the boundary. We have created Matter and Space. But space is that which separates one thing from another, creating separateness and difference out of the One, which is indivisible. Zeno amused and perplexed his contemporaries by drawing their attention to this riddle. If space distinguishes one thing from another, how can we add up all the separate units and arrive at the original One? How can we cancel space?

Just as the One cannot exist without the two, the two cannot exist except it become three. Once we have cloven space into a Here and a There, we now require what Brown, in his Laws of Form, calls a crossing.[14] O Dialectic, why are no hymns sung in your praise? Why are temples erected to the Forms but none to you, who are the chorus master of all the Forms?

Matter is the world viewed as fixed, dense, stable. Shifting our consciousness to view the world as process, we discover energy; that is, change, instability, and direction. Gaia, in Hesiod's cosmology, is the world as Being; Eros is the world as Act. The primal energy, which bonds elements into compounds, and dissolves compounds back into their elements, and becomes, in biology, instinct and intention, is Eros in Hesiod's cosmology; that is, Desire. Eros is the force that overpowers both humans and gods. It loosens the sinews of all living creatures; it weakens determination, melts the rigid, and dissolves the solid. Eros is the universal solvent. No wonder that the gods too walk in fear of this force that threatens all boundaries and distinctions. Even the Forms must preserve their distinctions and their self-sufficiency.

The raw energies of nature become, in biology, the libido, at first a conglomeration of scarcely differentiated drives. Now energy is a motive, the motive of the life force to perpetuate itself. In a state of absolute symbiosis with its environment a biological organism would be a perpetual-motion machine. Biology has achieved remarkable success in this direction, but it has achieved this success only at the expense of its individual members. Each individual organism is only a partially successful accommodation of the life force to the environment. Thus the Eros of biology is twofold: it works to create individuated organisms, but it is also the force that dissolves the independent organisms back into the general reservoir. Eros both creates distinctions and dissolves them. Every erotic impulse in individual organisms is simultaneously the work of Eros and Thanatos; hence, even the gods fear the power of Eros.

Desire is born when the baby leaves the fluid world of the womb for the world of more rigid structures, which require a more complex matching of the baby's needs with the environment. Consciousness now discovers a hiatus between one sense and another, between the needs on this side and their satisfactions lying out of reach on the other side. Desire then begins its work to create strategies for dissolving the distinctions. Desire invents dialectic as the mind's best simulation, in the world of rigid forms and categories, of the fluid mobility it once enjoyed in its prehistoric period in the amniotic sea.

The primal elements are now in place. We call them Matter, Space, and Energy. We must have a substance that, through all its transformations, is never diminished in its total mass. We must have a space in which this matter can undergo its transformations. We must have a force of movement and change. We must have stasis and kinesis. With space, matter, and energy as our first principles we can create a world. We have abstracted from these principles all merely local or accidental properties and have arrived at Matter, Space, and Energy as mathematical concepts. In Hesiod's cosmology these first principles are abstractions too, though they are still clothed in what we consider accidental qualities—they are not separated out from historical and psychological traits. Matter for Hesiod is still this Earth, this ground, the Mother. Energy in Hesiod is not a simple mathematical equation but the pervasive experience of desire.

In Hesiod's vision the most abstract forms and principles are seen as relations of and with the Subject. Even here, however, in this archaic cosmogony, we see the trauma that Lacan finds in the conflict between meaning and Being. The fourth prime element in Hesiod's cosmos is the ego, which is not so much visible in itself as in its attempts to realize itself at each new level as the subject in the forbidden field of the Other. In the growth of the psyche the ego first realizes itself negatively, as that on which the world acts. The infant ego takes its own impulses, and the powers it wishes to possess for itself, and projects them onto the giants on whom its survival depends. The giants have, it seems, no needs, but only pleasures. Not constrained by space or time, they are autonomous beings, pure subjects. The gods are truly superegos—the ego magnified, able to realize their own desires, while inhibiting the desires of the fledgling ego. The ego discovers itself first as the victim of the superego, not realizing that it has created its own signifiers, but then displaced them into the field of the Other.

The succession myth in the *Theogony,* recounting the generational conflicts leading to the supremacy of Zeus, reveals some of the strategies by which the ego struggles to repair the schism between the ego and the Self.[15] The first stratagem is castration. Ouranos, when he mates with Gaia, refuses to separate from her, and suppresses their offspring in her womb. Gaia, groaning with the burden of her teeming womb, conspires with Kronos, her trickster son. Kronos, emerging from his place of ambush within Gaia's body, takes the sickle Gaia prepares for him, and castrates his father when his parents are engaged in sexual union, thus effecting an irrevocable split both in the fabric of the world and in the relations of the sexes.

Castration is certainly a graphic symbol to represent the traumatic origin of consciousness, in what Brown calls (more abstractly) "the law of distinction."[16] We are reminded of Lacan's thesis that "the *one* that is introduced by the experience of the unconscious is the one of the split, of the stroke, of rupture."[17] Many themes are woven together into this formidable myth—the secret conspiracy of mother and son against the all-powerful father; the relationship of the male ego to phallic potency; the role of the oedipal rivalry between father and son in the construction of ego and superego; the suppressive power of the superego, and the ego's subversive revenge. Significant also is the result of the castration: from the severed genitals of Ouranos Aphrodite is born, and from his blood the Erinyes, the avenging furies, who hound those guilty of bloodshed. Just as earth and sky, mother and father, male and female, are polarized at this point in Hesiod's cosmogony, so the once-unified Eros is now polarized into desire and guilt. The castration of Ouranos is a mythical image of the ego's desperation to realize its own Being, which has been eclipsed in the field of signifiers.

But castration does not solve the problem; the conflict between the ego and its signifiers moves to the next generation. The conspiracy between mother and son against the father is repeated in the new triad—Rhea, Zeus, and Kronos. Kronos, more circumspect than his father, swallows his children as they are born instead of suppressing them in the body of the mother, as his father had done. His strategy achieves several aims, or such is the intention at least: the father's potential rivals are suppressed as in the previous generation, but in the body of the father, not the mother; the mother and her children are separated; the father substitutes himself for the mother, and thus proclaims his body, rather than the mother's, as the Ground of Being.[18]

When Zeus is born, Gaia has him conveyed to a secret place in Crete, where he is raised, while she tricks Kronos into swallowing a stone, which he mistakes for his latest-born child. Suffering a great indigestion, Kronos vomits forth the stone, behind which emerge all the other suppressed children. Zeus returns from Crete, and with the help of his siblings overthrows his father, despatches him with the other Titans to Tartaros, and comes to power in his father's place as ruler of the world.

Zeus is yet more clever than his father. He consolidates his position by a series of diplomatic maneuvers: a judicious alliance with the Cyclopes; concessions to his siblings; appointments of his own progeny to positions of power in his government; and, finally, imprisonment of the previous generation in the depths of Tartaros. The young ego struggles once again to survive the oedipal conflict. Zeus, the last of the sons to usurp the power of the father in Hesiod's succession myth, proves himself more successful than his predecessors in establishing himself as the subject, master of all signifiers.

Alas, the problem of the signifier does not disappear with Zeus's accession to power. At this very point, if the problem appears to reach a certain resolution on Mt. Olympos, through various compromises among the gods, polarity now intervenes to rupture the unity not only between the humans and their gods but also between men and women. The signifiers now being well fortified on the heights of Mt. Olympos, which is forever inaccessible to human reach, the ego must contrive another stratagem to bridge the chasm and repair its alienation. The appearance of humans on the scene in the *Theogony* marks the beginning of that torment that Lacan has called "the Gaze as *Objet petit a*," when the gaze of the subject, which reassures us of our own existence, is located in the field of the Other.[19]

Prometheus now enters the drama, archetype both of the forever devious human ego and of the libidinal drive to self-articulation against all efforts at suppression. Prometheus, intending to give humans an advantage over the gods, tricks Zeus into accepting the worse parts of the sacrificial animal as his portion. But the lord of signifiers will not so easily surrender his prerogatives. Zeus retaliates by removing fire from earth. Prometheus retaliates in turn by stealing the fire and returning it to humans. Zeus retaliates once again by creating the cruelest of all deceits—Pandora, a mere simulacrum of the gods, seductive but totally meretricious. Hesiod can take us no further in his tale than to assert that humans are condemned to perpetual alienation, trans-

fixed by the all-seeing gaze of the subject, and tangled in the subject's signifiers. He could not see that the tangle, which he names Pandora, is but the
image of the gods seen through the eyes of frustrated desire. The contradictions in Pandora (who was, as "The All-Giving One," the Ground of Being,
before the image was warped by desire) grow out of the contradictions in the
ego, haunted by its own finitude and desperate for the fullness of Being.
Occupying that space between meaning and Being, Pandora is frustration,
distortion, and alienation personified.

The succession myth in the *Theogony,* though it takes us far from Hesiod's
prime elements, is central to Hesiod's vision of the cosmic structure. If the
manifest theme of the poem is the rise of Zeus and the Olympians to power,
the subtext is the origin and growth of consciousness in the cosmos. Though
humans are scarcely mentioned in the poem, the bitter rivalries of the gods,
which culminate in the creation of Pandora, the icon of deceptive appearances, reveal Hesiod's underlying intention to explain the alienated consciousness of the human mind.

"Consciousness of an other, of an object in general," Hegel writes, "is
indeed itself necessarily self-consciousness . . . consciousness of a thing (is)
only possible for a self-consciousness."[20] Consciousness in the *Theogony* begins with the prime elements and spreads out through the world, with each
new element creating its own contradictions, from which another level of
beings arise whose existence, in turn, generates another set of contradictions.
If human consciousness proceeds in an oscillating rhythm of differentiation,
followed by resolution of the difference, this is the same process that the
Theogony articulates for the cosmos as a whole.

We are tempted to smile at the naive anthropomorphism of a poet imagining a universe realizing itself in consciousness, particularly when the stages
in the process are marked by such primitive conceits as the son's castration
of the father, the father's ingestion of his children, or the birth of a daughter
from her father's head. But if inanimate matter has transmuted itself into
biological organisms with a life force that sustains itself in defiance of entropy; if the life force has transmuted itself into human consciousness; if the
energy of the atom has been transmuted into desire; and if every desire is the
desire for self-realization, is it naive for Hesiod to portray Nature desiring to
realize herself in consciousness?

If Hesiod could not reach farther in his vision of consciousness than the
tangle of signifiers in the space between the ego and the subject, who can
fault him for that? The modern solution has been to dispose of the subject
altogether. "I don't know whether this world has a meaning that transcends
it," Camus writes.[21] "But I know that I do not know that meaning and that it
is impossible for me just now to know it. What can a meaning outside my

condition mean to me? I can understand only in human terms. . . . If I were a tree among trees," he continues, "a cat among animals, this life would have a meaning, or rather this problem would not arise, for I should belong to this world. I should *be* this world to which I am now opposed by my whole consciousness and my whole insistence on familiarity. This ridiculous reason is what sets me in opposition to all creation." Camus is a modern-day Hesiod, poignantly alive to the absurdity of consciousness, as Hesiod was, but Hesiod at least glimpsed through the tangle of signifiers a vision of the subject. In place of that subject we have what Soleri calls "the god of the statistical universe, split into every granule of matter, fully segregated and moving in logical but blind fury on the space-time path of physical transformism." [22]

If consciousness was deeply problematic to Hesiod, and meaning always liable to distortion, our alternative has been to create a cosmology from which consciousness has been expelled and meaning declared nonexistent. Camus talks of "this fragmented universe." [23] On what grounds do we say that it is fragmented? Science can no more prove a fragmented universe than it can prove ultimate order and design. Hesiod's cosmogony proceeds by differentiation, but his cosmos is not fragmented. The fragmented universe is the construct of the modern fragmented self, when the subject has been removed from the center, leaving only fragments—"fully segregated," as Soleri describes them—circling in blind determinism on the periphery.

Even archaic cosmogonies know of a paradise state as only a distant memory. The trauma of consciousness is inscribed in Hesiod's cosmogony from beginning to end. We cannot retreat from our modern consciousness, nor can we revive the archaic gods. But if the ancient gods are dead, they were only, as Soleri calls them, "a pursued hypothesis." [24] Developing Teilhard de Chardin's concept of the Omega point as the goal of evolution, Soleri sees the myths of the old gods as eschatological. The human mind projected those old gods—what Soleri calls the Alpha God—back to the beginning in order to simulate the process of consciousness as it moves into the future. Human cosmologies are, in fact, future-oriented; they project into the past a blueprint to validate the movement of consciousness into the future. God is, Soleri writes, "*an idea form that we try desperately to fill with an adequate, functioning performance.*" [25] In projecting gods as the locus of consciousness, the human mind gave itself a matrix from which embryonic consciousness could grow into self-consciousness. If the human mind is to survive the weight of consciousness, we cannot be satisfied with mere skepticism, but must create a new cosmology with a center, and at the center must be reinstated the subject.

II: Pandora and the Revenge of the Mind

A woman is a symptom.
—Jacques Lacan[1]

Hesiod, our major source for the myth of Prometheus and Pandora, tells the myth twice; once in his *Theogony,* and again in his *Works and Days.* Though the two versions differ from each other in details and emphasis, they are clearly variants of the same archetypal myth. This myth, like most if not all myths, is etiological. Hesiod uses the myth in the *Theogony* to explain the creation of women and the reason for their duplicitous nature. In the *Works and Days* the myth is Hesiod's vision into the origin of evil, the explanation for the austerity of human life plagued by labor and disease. The two etiologies collapse into a single etiology. As in the myth of Eve, the archaic mind, or at least the archaic male mind, searching for the origin of evil, fixated on the duplicity of women as both symptom and cause.

Scholars have paid little attention to the figure of Pandora, preferring instead to celebrate Prometheus as the symbol of the heroic human spirit daring to assert the power of consciousness even in defiance of the tabu established by the gods. The Pandora component in the myth, if regarded at all, has been seen simply as the platform from which Hesiod could vent his personal misogyny. But this myth, in this context, is not simply a personal vision. The myth, we must assume, had a long tradition before it emerged in his poems. Hesiod, in using the myth in his two poems, which are not private but communal cosmologies, provides an archetypal charter for certain social structures and values of his time. If Hesiod tells the myth to explain the duplicity of women, we read his version of the myth now to understand why misogyny was encoded as an essential characteristic of archaic cosmologies.

To uncover the etiology of evil is the primary task of the philosopher. The good is self-evident, self-referential, self-sufficient. If all the goods of the world flowed freely and continuously into our possession, we would need neither myths nor theologies, but goods come to us erratically and unpredictably. Some fall spontaneously into our laps; some come only in response to our labor; yet others obdurately resist our most strenuous efforts to acquire them or to manipulate them into usable forms. Their good, when it comes, turns out to be marred. A worm lies coiled at the apple's core. Once we become conscious that between the good and our enjoyment of it lies the abyss, we idealize the good. We create images and ideologies for discriminating the good from the bad; we develop strategies for securing the good, or for mitigating the effects of the not-good on our pleasures in the good.

Hesiod's myth of Prometheus and Pandora opens up a view into this process as it operated in the archaic mind. Hesiod's myth, like all myths, has much in common with our dreams. It has the contradictions that are commonplace in dreams. Prometheus lays out the sacrificial meat in such a way as to deceive Zeus into choosing the less attractive portion for the gods, thus leaving the more attractive parts of the sacrificial animal for human consumption. Zeus is deceived. But how can the gods be deceived? Is Zeus not omniscient? Of course Zeus is omniscient; of course the gods cannot be deceived. Zeus is tricked and he sees through the trick. He is deceived and he is not deceived. How can this be? Because we are in the dream world, where A can also be not-A; where, as Freud discovered, the syntax of either/or is translated as both/and.[2] Counterforces are at work. One psychic force in the dream needs the gods to be deceived. Another psychic force needs the gods, once deceived, to know that they have been deceived. The underlying motive of the dream is not to explain how the gods were deceived but why the human mind is caught in deception. The gods must be deceived first so that the humans can be punished, with deception as their penalty. Two contrary forces do not cancel each other out; they produce a dialectic.

Hope is another ambiguous element in the myth.[3] Hope was one of the items that the gods put into Pandora's urn, but it was differentiated from the other items, given a privileged status. It was kept confined in the urn after all the other contents had escaped. The other contents were the plagues and evils that the gods have visited on humankind. Since the urn functions in the dream as the matrix of all evils, are we to consider hope too as an evil? If it is an evil, why is it differentiated from the other evils, as something to be kept within the urn? Is it the one good that Zeus allows humans to mitigate the curse of Pandora? If it is the mitigating factor, why is hope confined to the urn? Is this to say that not even hope is allowed us, that the human condition is hopeless? Or is Pandora offering us hope as the last and greatest of all evils? Is Pandora holding out hope, or withholding hope?

Logical analysis will not resolve the ambiguity in Hesiod's text. We are not in the Aristotelian world but in the world of dreams. Trying to determine whether Hesiod meant one thing or the other leads us, in fact, farther from the solution. Hesiod did not mean one thing or another; he meant both. The duplicity of the world is the subject of this dream. In the Aristotelian world we can discuss the problem of duplicity in a series of propositions, each of which we aim to make as free of internal contradictions as possible. When duplicity is the subject of our dream, however, we *experience* duplicity. The dream arises from the experience of duplicity, and, in its attempt to resolve the problem, re-creates the experience. A man is troubled by the deceptiveness of the world, by the discordance between the ideal and reality. Unable to resolve the problem on the conscious level, he goes into the dream state.

The dream state opens up to him the vision of the discordance among the archetypes. The dreamer awakes, convinced that he has traced the problem to its archetypal origin. But he is deceived. Deception is the experience that motivates the dream; deception is the mode in which the dream functions; and deception is the final result.

Hope, far from being a minor and confused detail, is one of the primary constituents of the myth, the emotional state out of which this dream arises. What is a dream but a hope? Freud defined dreams as wishful thinking, or more accurately as wish fulfillment, even when the dream on the surface seems to present us with a sense of hopelessness. Speaking of one of his own dreams, Freud writes, "The dream represented a particular state of affairs as I should have wished it to be. Thus its content was the fulfillment of a wish and its motive was a wish."[4]

Hope is by nature ambiguous, the admission of a negative state. Hope is a positive, we might argue, in that it acknowledges the disparity between reality and our expectations, but it is also a denial of reality, a refusal to accept reality on its terms, possibly a maneuver to restructure reality into closer concord with our desires, but possibly also an evasion. Hope may be a means to transform the negative situation, or it may compound and reinforce the negative. The ambiguity of hope is the ambiguity of dreams in general. The contradictory values that hope embodies determine the contradictory structure of Hesiod's narrative of this myth. Is hope an evil? No, it is the mind's compensation for its disillusionment. It is what keeps humans from despair. But how would we be disillusioned if we did not have illusions first? What is hope but an illusion? Hope, therefore, is the cause of our disillusionment since it always by nature promises what it cannot deliver. Hope is the worst of our delusions and therefore the greatest of our evils. Why, then, is Hope confined to Pandora's urn? Because the situation is hopeless; we are given no hope. The hopelessness of hope is the answer to the riddle.

In addition to its internal contradictions, Hesiod's myth of Pandora has another quality characteristic of dreams: sharp clarity in some parts and a vagueness elsewhere. The narrative is graphic in many details—in the description of Prometheus and his sacrifice, of the creation of Pandora by the gods, of her appearance, of the punishment Zeus inflicts upon Prometheus for his trickery. The myth is tight and coherent. But then we wake up and clarity becomes obscure. Why was hope placed in Pandora's urn? Why did Zeus keep hope in the urn when the other contents were released? Why was Prometheus so determined to advance the human cause? Why did the omniscient Zeus allow himself to be deceived? If Prometheus was as intelligent as his name suggests, how did it escape his notice that by allying himself with humans he was introducing suffering into the human world? And, being intelligent, why did he choose his own suffering, which followed as an inevi-

table consequence of his cleverness? These are the real questions that arise
when we read Hesiod's myth, yet on these very points Hesiod as the interpreter can give us no advice.

Perhaps the most significant similarity between the myth and our personal
dreams is the emotional force that gives the myth its strength and coherence.
The interpretations, which Hesiod offers of the myth in both poems, though
affecting a logical and reasonable stance toward the mythic material, are in
fact highly charged with emotion. Hesiod concludes his telling of the myth
in the *Theogony* with the interpretation that thus, through Pandora, women
came into being. He follows this direct proposition with a long passage,
twenty-two lines in all, which contains one of the most vituperative expressions of misogyny in our literary tradition (verses 589–612):

> For from her is the breed of women,
> A great bane, they dwell with mortal men,
> not sharing in hateful poverty, but in luxury.
> As when in their overhanging nests the bees
> Feed the drones, conspirators in evil works.
> The live-long day the bees, until the setting sun,
> Toil to lay down their white combs,
> While the drones, remaining within the hollow nests
> Scrape the labor of another into their own bellies.
> In just this way Zeus, who thunders on high, made
> Women to be an evil for mortal men, conspirators in
> Vile works. Yet a second evil has he given in place of
> The good. He who, escaping marriage and the bitter works
> Of women, chooses not to marry, comes to a mournful old age,
> Bereft of a companion. He lives with but a scant
> Livelihood, and the heirs of a vacant inheritance divide
> His estate. But if marriage befalls a man,
> And he gets himself an honorable wife, suited to his ways,
> Even so, the evil remains with him, balancing the good.
> But he who gains a cantankerous sort of wife lives
> With a bitter pain for his heart and spirit, for which
> There is no escape. So it is not possible to outwit
> The mind of Zeus.[5]

This emotional discharge is at variance with the manifest content of the
myth. True, a female figure is created in the myth and sent down by the gods
to deceive humans. But this figure is a fiction, even in the terms that the myth
itself uses. The myth does not suggest that women came into existence only
with the appearance of Pandora, though that is Hesiod's interpretation of the

myth. Throughout his narrative of the myth Hesiod refers to humans not as men specifically but as humans, using the Greek word *anthropos* to refer to the species—a usage our translations, and most of the modern studies of the myth, blur when they translate the species term into our gender-specific term "men."

The myth tells not of woman's deception of men but of a power struggle between two male figures, Prometheus and Zeus, who deceive each other. Objective analysis would suggest that the myth tells how woman has been made over into an artifice by the power struggle between males in the patriarchy. The passion that Hesiod vents on womankind should more properly be directed to the male principals in the myth. By the terms of the myth itself woman is the product of the male conflict, not its cause. The anger that the myth releases in Hesiod is clear evidence that the myth takes us to that psychic space where dreams originate, to the deepest ground of our fears and desires. The myth, under the guise of representing a moment in cosmic history, provides Hesiod with a charter for misogyny.

If an individual were to recount this myth as his personal dream to a therapist, using it as his explanation for both the presence of evil in the world and the universal treachery of women, the therapist would take the dream for evidence of a deep-seated psychic obsession in the dreamer. The myth, indeed, is obsessive. Hesiod tells it twice over, each time with emotional vehemence, and invokes the myth as sufficient explanation for everything negative in the human condition. The dreamer of this myth has the emotional intensity of a young man, an idealist, who is deeply disillusioned to discover that reality perverts his every ideal. He is angry, and fixated on his anger. He dreams a solution to the problem. He dreams the dream over and over again, but the wound will not heal. The wound reopens and discharges more negative emotions every time the young man contemplates the dream. Since this myth is Hesiod's explanation for every failure of reality to coincide with his ideals, he finds confirmation of the dream everywhere he looks. The dreamer is trapped in his own cosmology, in which the gods have doomed him to failure, and to the helpless anger born of failure.

The myth of Pandora, together with Hesiod's interpretations, reveals the mind of a child who has been traumatized by loss. Hesiod reacts to the trauma exactly as Freud found his patients reacting to psychic traumas of their childhood. Endeavoring, on one hand, to relive the trauma, "to make it real," as Freud said, he becomes fixated on the trauma in a repetitive, compulsive way; on the other hand, he develops defensive reactions that have their own compulsive logic, though this logic defies the logic of impartial, objective observation.[6] The mind behind this myth is fixated on its own hurt, on what Freud calls "injuries to narcissism."[7] The obsessive quality of the myth and the overdetermination in its content (what Freud called the dream material) reveal that Hesiod is not only remembering an original, personal trauma; he is re-creating it in order to reexperience it.

Here is the first version of the myth (*Theogony* 507–616):

One day the gods and humans are gathered sociably together at Mekone, the "Poppy Fields." This is the first mention of human beings in the *Theogony*. How did humans enter the cosmos? This is a dream; we cannot ask from dreams what they do not choose to reveal. All we know is that the humans and gods are gathered together, drowsing no doubt in the poppy fields of the unconscious. Apparently the humans and gods have been enjoying an easy relationship with each other, but the time has come for a breach to open up in that relationship. Hesiod says that the gods and humans were gathered at "the time when gods and mortals *were being separated*." West, in his edition of the poem, notes that the word used here for separation (*ekrinonto*) connotes a legal settlement.[8] The law enters into consciousness, and the law is the law of separation.

How is the separation accomplished? A mediator comes between gods and humans. As in a dream, we must accept the myth's paradoxes on their own terms. A mediator arises where no mediator, it seems, was needed. Through the mediation of Prometheus, The Thinker, two parties in harmonious concord with each other are brought into violent conflict. Prometheus plays the part of the maître d'hôtel at the banquet, to which the two parties have been invited. He seems also to be an arbitrator, though we have no evidence that anything needs to be arbitrated until Prometheus intervenes.

Prometheus slices up a great ox in pieces. He serves it up to Zeus, with a friendly spirit we are told, and at the same time with the intention of deceiving Zeus. Prometheus divides the feast in two portions. He wraps the tastiest portions of the meat in the paunch of the animal. With "devious skill" he prepares the second portion by wrapping the bones in succulent fat. Zeus will no doubt find the paunch and hide repulsive, and will be seduced by the savory fragrance of the roasting fat to select the worthless portion. A theme first occurs here that will recur throughout the dream: the good and the not-good are to be found almost always in exact reversal of our expectations; furthermore, this reversal is the result of a deliberate intention at work in the world. The world is composed of deceptive appearances, and this deception is by deliberate intent—these are the two fundamental thoughts coded into the dream.

Zeus, "the father of humans and gods," is displeased. He sees through the deception and reproaches Prometheus for his unfair division of the meal. Prometheus, "with his bent mind," smiles, and "does not forget his cunning." He invites Zeus, "greatest and most honored of all gods," to select whichever portion pleases his heart. Zeus, "who knows thoughts that are imperishable," is not deceived. He sees what Prometheus has in mind, but he chooses to be deceived, because he has sinister plans in mind for death-bound humans. Despite his all-seeing mind, or rather, in the myth's own terms (again, as in a dream), because of his all-seeing mind, Zeus falls into the trap. He chooses exactly the portion that the script calls for him to choose. Why does the omnipotent and omniscient god choose the worse portion? Because the dream requires an angry god. The god makes his selection and, true to the determinism of the dreamer, becomes very angry. Anger takes hold of his spirit, Hesiod says, when Zeus picks up the bones and sees the worthless content so cunningly decked out.

This is Hesiod's explanation for both the institution of sacrifice and the schism between humans and gods. Sacrifice itself is a complex of human motivations, and Hesiod's myth reveals much of its complexity.[9] The rituals of sacrifice have both a manifest and a latent ideology. The manifest function of sacrifice is to propitiate the great powers of the universe and to engage their cooperation in human ventures. Overtly, sacrifice is a means for reconciling the human and the divine orders. But the myth reveals also a covert etiology for sacrificial rituals. Sacrifice, as Hesiod understands it, is the means by which humans outwit their gods, masquerading human advantage as pious reverence to the gods. The hallowed human practice of inviting the gods to the communion table is revealed in this account as a specious arrangement whereby humans can keep the best goods for themselves, while sanctifying the discards by offering them to the gods. The first communion was, in reality, the cause of the irreparable breach between humans and gods.

Hesiod's myth of the first sacrificial meal expresses the ambivalence humans continue to feel regarding their carnivorous tastes. As things turn out in the myth, the sacrificial meal becomes the means whereby the gods maintain their superior rank and separation from the human species. The double bind in this myth is that each sacrificial meal, by which humans hope to placate their gods, only serves to drive the human and divine orders farther apart. The sacrificial meal, overtly the middle term that reconciles two opposites, is in fact the term that cleaves them asunder and makes them antagonists forever. Sacrifice does not reconcile opposites, but confirms the superior in his superiority, and the inferior in his inferiority.

Burkert argues, with a convincing body of ancient evidence, that our ancestors created the rituals associated with animal sacrifice to appease the guilt they experienced when they became hunters and predators.[10] No wonder Hesiod is so bemused when he attempts to account for the catastrophe that occurred when blood sacrifice was first instituted. The ritualized killing of animals is shot through and through with paradox and contradiction. Of course humans, in Hesiod's account, are not responsible for the charade. They are victims dragged into a dispute between two gods. Human cunning disguises itself as innocence. The human ego is a trickster beyond compare.

The myth continues. Zeus, in his anger, resolves to keep fire from humans. Retaliation now enters as the response to deception. Retaliation provokes counter-retaliation. Prometheus retaliates against Zeus with a new deception. The dream is certainly obsessive. The plot moves, yet it stays in the same place, fixated on the same problem. Prometheus steals the forbidden fire from the gods and delivers it to the human species. Once again Zeus is deceived and knows that he has been deceived. And deception, as we have already seen, provokes the deceived to anger. Zeus is now angered the more, seeing that the humans are now enjoying the profits from the forbidden fire. Zeus devises yet another counter-retaliation. He will create an object that will be the ultimate delusion and retaliation in one. At his instructions Hephaistos fashions from earth the figure of a chaste maiden. Athena dresses the figure in silver, and places a wondrous veil on her head. Over the veil she places a crown, also wondrous to look upon; on the crown Hephaistos fashions the figures of animals of land and sea, marvelous, graceful, like living forms. This "beautiful evil" Zeus then parades before the assembled gods. Amazement grips the gods when they see this "precipitous trick, from which there was no means of escape for humans." Here ends this version of the dream.

Hesiod now offers his own interpretation. This myth explains, he says, how women came into being. He begins to unravel a tirade of misogyny. Women, he claims, are a heavy woe to men. Women will not share in a man's poverty, but only in luxury. Women are like drones that idle away their time in the beehive, waiting to feast on the produce harvested by the worker bees. This is the curse that Zeus has devised for men, that they should be given women as their partners.

Now here, says Hesiod, is something even more terrible. If a man chooses celibacy, to avoid the snare of women, he comes to old age without a family to support him, and when he dies his property passes into the hands of strangers. And here, Hesiod adds, is yet another evil. A man may, by some quirk of fate, find a wife who is good and intelligent. Even so the good will be balanced by evil. The woman may be a "baneful breeder." Then the man will suffer pains in his heart from which there is no escape. The text is problematic at this point, but whatever reading we choose, the thesis is that any and all relations men may have with women are doomed. Even the man with a good wife will not be free of the curse. Hesiod ends his interpretation with the observation that it is impossible to deceive the mind of Zeus. Even Prometheus, for all his intelligence, could not deceive Zeus, and is suffering punishment for his attempt. This indictment of women Hesiod professes to find validated in the myth of the conflict between Zeus and Prometheus.

Here is Hesiod's second version of the myth (*Works and Days* 42–105):

In the *Works and Days* Hesiod sets forth the agricultural calendar that humans should follow to be in harmony with the rhythm of the seasons, if they wish to minimize the hazards of failure. These hazards are inevitable, including that great hazard, death. The gods have decreed that humans must labor to extract their livelihood from a resistant world. Why have the gods ordered the cosmos in this way? It could have been different, Hesiod imagines. He fantasizes a time when humans needed no ships to ply their trade, no beasts of burden to work the land. But such a condition, if it ever existed, is now only a remote fantasy. Hesiod invokes the myth of Pandora now to explain necessity in the largest sense, the necessity for human labor, the necessity for human suffering and death.[11]

In this version of the myth Zeus, angry because Prometheus has cheated him in the sacrifice, takes fire away from humans, and thus hides the substance of life from them. Prometheus steals fire, hiding it in a fennel stalk, and returns it back to the earth for human use. Angered again, Zeus responds that he will give humans an evil to balance the gift of fire, an evil that humans will embrace to their hearts. Zeus laughs to think how humans will delight in this terrible gift. He instructs Hephaistos to mold a figure from earth and water, to endow it with human voice, and to give it the form of a maiden, like the immortal goddesses to look upon. Zeus instructs Athena to teach this artificial creature women's crafts. He instructs Aphrodite to shed golden grace on the figure, together with "the cruelty of desire, and longings that wear out the body," as Lattimore translates the phrase.[12] Hermes' assignment is to give the figure the mind of a bitch and a treacherous disposition.

The gods do as Zeus instructs them. Hephaistos creates the figure. Athena dresses it. The Graces and Persuasion place necklaces of gold on it. The Seasons put a crown of flowers on its head. Hermes puts in its heart lies, wheedling words, and a treacherous disposition. Hermes also endows it with a voice, and names it Pandora, signifying that this seeming woman is the gift of all the gods, receiving from each his or her particular power or attribute. When Zeus has created this deception, he sends her down as a gift to Epimetheus (Afterthought), the brother of Prometheus. Prometheus had warned his brother not to accept any gift from Olympian Zeus, but to return it to its source. Epimetheus forgets these instructions; he accepts the gift, and only then understands Prometheus' warning. But now Pandora opens her urn and scatters evils among humans. Only Hope remains in the urn because, by the will of Zeus, Pandora stoppers the urn before Hope can escape. But all other woes now pursue humans, thousands of woes, on land and sea. Diseases come upon humans by day; they wander about at night, working their evil spontaneously and in silence. So it is not possible, Hesiod concludes, to escape the mind of Zeus.

This myth is worse than a dream; it is a recurrent nightmare. It might seem that women have been created to be men's companions and partners; in fact, their appearance in the world creates suffering, disillusionment, and death.

The indictment is total since, in this cosmology, woman introduces death into the world. With such a cosmology Hesiod has nowhere to escape.

A kernel of truth lies at the base of this indictment. Death appeared in the world together with sexual reproduction. Cellular mitosis knows nothing of death; the organism replicates itself exactly. Sexual reproduction seems, by comparison, a cruel sport of Nature, since replication of the self now requires sexual attraction for the Other, and therefore loss of the self in the Other. When simple cellular replication is sexualized, the life instinct is translated into desire. Since desire is, as Lacan insists, the desire for the Other, it is by necessity the desire for death.[13] Sexual organisms achieve immortality only through death to the self. This myth that finds in sexual desire the origin of evil is to be found wherever we look in ancient cosmologies.[14] The archaic mind shows a deep understanding when it reads in sexual reproduction both the birth of consciousness and the origin of death. The one element Hesiod ignores in this equation is that, in a sexualized world, both male and female suffer the same fate.

Anger, arising out of hope forever deferred and disappointed, dominates this myth of the origin of sex and sexual desire. Unwilling to own his anger openly and consciously, Hesiod displaces it elsewhere. Zeus, in both versions of the myth, is a tornado of anger. Zeus is angry first when he sees the unequal division of the sacrificial meat, then again when he chooses the portion containing what humans discard as refuse, and angered a third time when Prometheus steals fire from him and gives it to humans. The myth not only describes the anger of Zeus; it embodies his anger in action. Zeus's decision to hide fire from humans and his scheme to invent the desirable but deceptive Pandora are both acts of anger. The punishment Zeus inflicts on Prometheus is another act of anger. For punishment Prometheus must be chained to a rock, where an eagle, as Zeus's personal *agent provocateur,* descends every day to devour his liver. What more graphic image of anger than the liver gnawed at day after day, consumed as often as it is renewed, in an eternal cycle from which there is no exit?

What kind of theology is this? Angry people legitimize their anger by projecting it onto their gods. In projecting his anger onto his supreme god, Hesiod disguises from himself his own responsibility, while validating his anger at the same time, by claiming the great Zeus himself as its source. The dialectic is subtle, as always when the ego is engaged in its work of self-justification.

Pandora is the embodiment of anger, the vehicle through which anger carries on its deadly work. Zeus manifests his anger in the duplicitous figure of Pandora, who passes it on in turn to Hesiod. Hesiod wakes from this dream in a state of anger, and searching through the dream for the cause finds Pandora as the only fit target, though she is the product of his anger, not its cause. Even awake, Hesiod is still dreaming.

If Zeus is the kind of god who can play a terrible hoax on humans, why does Hesiod not direct his anger back at Zeus? Because the gods are tabu. Even an earthly king is tabu, but gods, being more numinous than kings, are even more protected by the tabu. Hesiod, prevented by the tabu from directing his anger at Zeus, the archetypal father, displaces his anger onto women, as a more available target.

Hesiod's thinking is confused yet marvelously consistent. To his mind women were created to generate his anger. Zeus, in this myth, is good enough both to validate Hesiod's anger and, at the same time, to provide it with a target. The reasoning is a self-perpetuating cycle. As Hesiod increases his animus against women, their reactions will no doubt confirm his expectations and justify the escalation of his animus against them. Women, at the effect of men's anger, become duplicitous; then, being duplicitous, they instigate Hesiod's anger. Woman, in Hesiod's myth, is both the fit object of anger and the source of all anger. Hesiod finds in the myth of Pandora his god-given authority, indeed his obligation, to nurture and enjoy his misogyny.

In the *Works and Days* Hesiod tells us that Zeus, our patriarch, laughed when he told Prometheus of his scheme to entrap humans with an alluring deception. Anger is a clean emotion compared with the emotion behind this jovial laugh. This laugh, of a superior who knows that he has the weaker person in his power, is the laugh of malice. Malice is anger first frustrated and then twisted. Malice looks for devious and perverted satisfactions. Anger is violent; malice, sadistic. Pandora, with her alluring beauty masking a cruel intention, is sadism embodied.

Hesiod is no more willing to acknowledge his malice than his anger. He must displace this malice elsewhere, and where else but onto womankind? Since women are Pandora's incarnation on the human plane, they are, *ab utero*, malicious. Anger strikes out, it reaches its target, and is dissipated. Malice is never dissipated; it looks always for new victims and new methods of torture, its objective being to prolong suffering. Such is the cosmology Hesiod has invented or inherited, in which he is doubly the victim: the victim first of his gods and then of his partner, Woman, who conspire together to cheat and torment him.

A person who ascribes all evil to one segment of the human species is not a rational thinker, but a person possessed by an emotion so violent that it exceeds an objective correlative. Hesiod parades his misogyny as the rational response of a man who sees things as they really are. Both Hesiod's interpretations of the Pandora myth have the mysteriously logical quality of the completely irrational. They are the arguments of a man who prides himself that he can see through the veil of illusion to the fundamental law of the universe, which is, as he deciphers it, that women are malicious and men their helpless victims. Hesiod's sadism becomes acceptable as long as he can disguise it as masochism. Hesiod dissociates himself from his own malice by projecting it onto the patriarchal authority, who is beyond criticism, and then onto women, whom he may openly hate, convinced that his reading of their nature is free of any personal bias.

Freud theorized that the function of dreams is to provide a mechanism to allow us to continue sleeping.[15] Hesiod's dream of malice in heavenly places, translated into the malice of women, allows Hesiod to continue his privileged sleep. Even when awake he can remain in the dream, secure in his own integrity, even if that integrity requires him to be the victim of a relentless hostility coming at him both from his gods and from his human partner, Woman.

The misogyny in Hesiod's myth of Pandora is the overt expression of an even more terrible emotion. Pandora, the sum of all the divine powers and attributes, has only one function: to thwart all human aspirations, and to torment the human heart with desires, which cannot be fulfilled, or whose fulfillments are so perverted that the heart is weighed down with even heavier sorrows. This is a terrible theology. We dream our gods to be our ideals. In projecting our thoughts of beauty, integrity, and justice as ideal forms, we validate our own aspirations. We strive toward these images of the absolute, as if we were made in their image, as if we too were transcendent beings like our gods. Hesiod's myth of Pandora gives the lie to this fond fantasy. In the theology of this myth all our ideals are false illusions.

The situation is worse. Insofar as truth and beauty apparently exist, they exist as the gods' instruments of torture. The gods emanate, in Pandora, an appearance of goodness and beauty, but only to lure us to our damnation. Whatever our senses interpret to us as beauty is only a screen that the ruthless powers of the world have placed between us and them in perpetuity. In short, we are endowed with senses that are deceived, feelings that are manipulated by higher powers for their own inscrutable ends, and hearts that must be broken.

For consciousness, all relations with the world are double binds. Theologies arise both to explain these double binds and to encode, and so to validate, them. The double bind in this myth of Pandora is obvious. The gods, being our ideals, are worthy of our reverence. In fact, they demand reverence from us, such is the compelling authority of our ideals. But then the gods reveal that they do not share our values. The values we attribute to them are mistakes in our own confused sensorium. The gods turn out to be false ideals, yet they still demand to be reverenced. The person who values them is a fool, since the gods themselves live by no values but the ruthless exercise of power. To refuse allegiance to the gods is to invalidate ourselves, yet to give them our allegiance is to invalidate our highest ideals. Prometheus's liver grows night after night, only to be devoured day after day by the predatory eagle of the father; such is the pain of consciousness.

Hesiod's angry gods surely have a provocation. Gods are, by definition, motivations. The dream calls for a motivator. Enter Prometheus, *agent provocateur*. Prometheus is a Titan, of the generation of gods who came into being prior to the emergence of the Olympian gods. In Hesiod's myth the conflict between Zeus and Prometheus is a power struggle between the two orders of gods. It represents the resistance of the old regime to the attempts of the new to usurp the powers of the old regime. The new sky gods, though they are the victors in this struggle, must learn that they cannot rule as absolute monarchs in this world, but must reach an accommodation with the earlier, primordial powers. The cosmic conflict of the *Theogony* is the conflict within consciousness itself. Each newly emerging order of consciousness cannot eradicate the previous order, but emerges in a dialectical process with its forebears. The cortex cannot do away with the libido of the serpent brain.

Why are humans brought into this power struggle among the gods? What kind of benefactor is Prometheus, who drives a wedge between gods and humans, and cleaves a chasm between our ideals and reality? Before the intervention of Prometheus in the cosmic plan, human work was easy (Hesiod imagines); humans had not experienced the deception of appearances or the pain of disease. Prometheus is depicted in ancient literature as a culture hero, who brings to humans inventions that change the course of history, indeed the very nature of human civilization. In Hesiod's myth Prometheus introduces fire into human life, and thus makes possible the beginnings of human technology. In other accounts he is a master craftsman, who teaches humans various skills, for example, writing and astronomy. He is the agent who teaches humans to study the signs; that is, to apply the rules of symbolic thought to the study of nature. In some accounts Prometheus and his brother Epimetheus were the creators of the human species, fashioning the first human beings from the soil. Taken together, these various myths suggest that in the archaic Greek tradition Prometheus was the proto-anthropos, the primal human, who either fathered the human species, or gave humans the skills and thought processes that were to form the basis for human civilization. Yet this same benefactor creates the great schism between gods and humans. In this Greek version of Paradise Prometheus is the old serpent, the adversary who, by opposing, brings consciousness to light and banishes us from paradise.

As a god Prometheus is an archetypal signifier, whose being and function transcend any conscious human decisions. Prometheus is Forethought, or thought itself, a mysterious process prior even to conscious, rational thinking. Who can say where ideas originate, or how connections link one idea with another to produce the webs of causality that we recognize as thinking? The thinking process itself the myth projects as a divine personification, a force that is indestructible, with its origins in the Titanic depths, far below the surface that we call conscious thought.

Prometheus is the trickster. The trickster's morality, at least on the surface, is minimal. The traditional trickster figure appears to be both amoral and autonomous.[16] His function seems to be to upset the existing order, whatever that order may be. On the most primitive level, he is entropy personified, the impish principle that, disregarding our wisest plans and our best theories of causality, works to erase all ordering structures and reduce the phenomena back to primordial chaos. The trickster is, as Kerényi notes, one of myth's representations of the evil principle.[17] The gods should receive the better portion of the feast; therefore the trickster will engineer it that the gods choose the inferior portion for themselves. The cosmic order establishes a hierarchy, in which the gods are superior and the humans inferior. Therefore the trickster will steal power from the gods and distribute it to the humans. The trickster does not look to the long-range consequences; his work is of the moment. Wherever he finds stability, he must destabilize. Humans are as much victims of his tricks as the gods. Humans work to stabilize their condition in the world; the trickster introduces, therefore, confusion and deception. Where he finds clarity, the trickster sows ambiguity. The trickster embodies the universal principle of instability. The trickster is the libido.[18]

This cosmic trickster embodies both the victories and defeats of human consciousness. Hesiod's myth of the conflict between Prometheus, the rebellious trickster, and Zeus, the primal father, is one version of the myth of the relations between the ego and the superego. Like the ego first discovering its own powers, Prometheus is audacious and cunning, undaunted by threat or punishment. But the willful Prometheus and the patriarchal Zeus have much in common. They are both credited, in Hesiod's text, with *metis,* the kind of intelligence that carries the connotation of cunning and deviousness.[19] They both have the same crooked smile. They are both tricksters. Zeus had tricked his own father, Kronos, into surrendering his power to his son. Now Prometheus continues the tradition, by playing a trick on father Zeus, and Zeus in turn plays a trick on humans.

Zeus and Prometheus, playing father and son, are made in the same image. Zeus maintains the patriarchal authority; Prometheus undermines it. Then Zeus, as the superego, undermines the victories of the growing ego. Prometheus gives humans the spermatic fire, the seed of intelligence. Zeus erases the advantage by sending Pandora, an eloquent image of the human mind too clever for its own good, caught in the web of its own signifiers.

Since humans are the focus for this conflict, the primary agents in the myth, the gods, are clearly archetypal forms, and their conflict takes place within the human mind. The superego is jealous of its prerogatives; its law is absolute. It maintains its numinous authority by powerful tabus. The ego, unable to compete with the superego on equal terms, resorts sometimes to outright defiance, sometimes to guile. But each advance of the ego provokes a new retaliation from the superego. The product is the phenomenon Freud observed in our dreams, where we may enjoy simultaneously the satisfaction of our illicit desires and the satisfaction of being caught violating the tabus of the superego. The dialectic between Zeus and Prometheus is so desirable that humans cannot resist embracing Pandora to their hearts.

The myth of Prometheus and Pandora is the same myth that the book of Genesis tells of our first parents' discovery of desire and its deceptions. The emergence of consciousness destabilizes the cosmos. The cordial relations between gods and humans are disrupted. Eating of the tree of consciousness, humans become gods themselves, as the subtle serpent promised Eve, but at the same time they lose the paradise that the gods enjoy. Humans become gods only by becoming alienated from their own gods, from nature, and from themselves. As the ancient myths tell the story, humans were once in harmony with their gods, but then the gods, fearing this newly emerging species called *Homo sapiens,* created a perpetual schism between themselves and their feeble human imitators. Writing the myth in reverse, we would say that when consciousness first appeared it *idealized* itself by creating gods. But in creating these images of itself, it discovered that it had created a conflict between the image and the reality. Unable to understand its own part in this drama, consciousness then ascribed the conflict to those primordial beings that it had created, in order to justify both its separation from its ideals and its own progress toward those ideals.

When humans discovered in themselves the power to see into nature, what humans found was not nature pure and simple but nature as represented in symbolic forms. Pandora, though she embodies all the powers of all the gods, is not the gods, but only their image, as it is received and translated by the human imagination. She is the troublesome signifier of the subject. Hesiod is so bemused by this two-faced signifier that he ascribes to it the necessity for labor, the alienation of human culture from nature, the pain of disease and death—in fact, all human suffering.

Using symbolic forms humans create technologies to overcome the resistance of nature, but these same technologies make human culture into something other than nature. Symbolic thought leads humans to idealize a world transcending physical constraints, and beings free of disease and death. The ego, thwarted in its desires, compensates by idealizing itself as the superego, a being of absolute autonomy, which is also in absolute concord with nature. Yet through this idealizing power the ego creates its own estrangement, a trespasser in the world of ideals and absolutes.

The dilemma of the ego is that it cannot be united with its own images without surrendering its own identity.[20] At the same time, given the power to behold the ideal forms, even if only in their distorted images, the ego believes itself the rightful heir to those forms, yet both excluded from its inheritance and compelled by the inscrutable will of the archetypes to pursue those ideal forms regardless of the cost. Consciousness, once begun, cannot be stopped, even though, in Hesiod's myth, it is hopeless.

Consciousness discovers—or should we say invents?—the principle of polarity. In Hesiod's myth the gods become polarized as Prometheus and Zeus, two opposing aspects of the same intelligence, and Pandora is the synthesis produced of their antagonism. Humans and gods become polarized into two opposing orders of consciousness, and again Pandora is the synthesis born of their opposition, the form through which each order relates to the other. Even the human species is now polarized. Nothing in Hesiod's account suggests that humans were differentiated as men and women before the intervention of Prometheus; humans, in Hesiod's text, were *anthropoi,* the human species collectively, as Adam and Eve were not sexually polarized before the incident in the Garden of Eden.

The archaic mind imagines a state prior to our human consciousness that could include opposites without opposition. But once consciousness intervenes in the world of nature, this state of concord becomes, on one hand, the lost paradise, and on the other hand, the final goal of consciousness. Consciousness, cast out from its primordial unity, must now progress through the world of difference to arrive at sameness.

In Hesiod's cosmology Pandora's appearance, which is simultaneously both true and false, marks the schism between the self and the Other. Everything is now polarized. The woman-nature is polarized into image and whatever unknowable reality may be concealed behind the image. Man-nature too is polarized into father and son, forever hostile to each other. Men's thinking is polarized between hopeful illusion and hopeless reality. Men and women are polarized into two separate orders, two genera that do not communicate with each other, since they are at odds in their desires, and the one—Woman—is only a mimesis, a copy of reality. The human mind itself is polarized in this myth, not only as Prometheus and Zeus, ego and superego, but as Prometheus and Epimetheus, forethought and second thoughts, dazzling thought and thought that misses its mark, as Hesiod describes them.[21]

Pandora, the mirage produced by all these polar oppositions, is an oxymoron: an evil gift, as Hesiod calls her, a beautiful curse, hope and hopelessness, love and hate, inextricably blended. Pandora is both the tabu and the force that compels men to violate the tabu, since the function of the tabu in psychic topography is to mark the erogenous zone.[22] Consciousness is first consciousness of the Other, and the Other is what is desirable because it is the Other. The desirable, however, is also terrifying because to attain it is to erase the self. Hesiod's myth of Pandora, taken with the *Theogony* as a whole, places the origin of polar consciousness within the historical context of the rise of the patriarchy. Pandora is created, as MacCary notes, out of the oedipal conflict between father and son.[23] In the conflict that Hesiod represents as the opposition of two male egos, woman is transformed from whatever she is by nature into an image, an object, the object of men's desire. Pandora, the phantom, recalls the son's lost mother, but in doing so she signifies the extent of the loss, since the recall is hopeless. Pandora is the projection of a double bind since she is, as MacCary points out, the conflation of two conflicting desires: the son's "nostalgic feelings for reunion with the mother and equally strong feelings for the establishment of the self independent of the mother."[24] We may add a further complexity: with every advance of the son toward the father's prerogatives, the son increases not only the hostility of the father but also his estrangement from his mother. In such a paradigm misogyny is inevitable.

The *Theogony* is the patriarchy's revision of biology. The Mother is the primal being in Hesiod's cosmology. But once Gaia produces her first son, Ouranos, as her counterpart, the battle of the sexes begins. Conspiring with her trickster son Kronos, she pushes the ambitious Ouranos into the background. The drama is replayed in the second generation, when Rhea conspires with another trickster son, Zeus, to seize the power from his father, Kronos. Zeus is more cunning than his forefathers in defending himself against the conspiracies of the mother. Ouranos aspired to prevent the reproductive process in utero; Kronos attempted to take over the mothering function by ingesting his offspring. His offspring now have two gestations and two births; the first gestation in the maternal womb, and the second in the paternal abdomen; one birth from the mother, and a second from the father. Zeus carries this process one step farther. He takes control of the reproductive process. He removes the spermatic fire from Gaia's domain, thus placing the seed of consciousness in the celestial realm, leaving Gaia to be only the womb, the passive material. Now humans must steal the seed of consciousness from the superegos on high. Zeus now makes woman over into his own image. Woman, once the mother, the principle of fertility, becomes her father's daughter.

If the maternal womb is our common experience, then biological experience must be rewritten, as it is rewritten in the Genesis account of Creation, so that the female issues from the male. Fatherhood must precede motherhood, and the mother must issue from the mind of the father. Her appearance is now the result not of mere blind biology but of conscious male will and technology. Pandora is not begotten but made, conceived first in the mind of Zeus, then brought into being by the artisan gods, Athena and Hephaistos, whose province is not biology but technology. Pandora is the triumph of the father's technology over the blind instinctual nature of the mother.

Pandora represents an antibiological revision of a cosmology that was once biologically oriented. Jane Harrison was the first scholar in modern times to see that behind Hesiod's artificial Pandora is the more ancient figure of the first goddess, the Earth, the all-giving.[25] Gardner refers to one vase in the British Museum that shows Pandora rising from the ground, with Epimetheus standing at her side, mallet in hand, and to other vases depicting male figures beating with hammers on a woman's head rising from the ground.[26] Linking these vases with Harrison's identification of Pandora with Gaia, Gardner interprets them as representing the sky deity subduing the earth. Put more philosophically, they are images of the divine principle manipulating formless matter into form. Even in Hesiod's disguised version we can trace the character of the ancient goddess. Pandora, who wears on her head a crown depicting the animal life of land and sea, is *potnia theron*, mistress of the animals, as the Great Mother is often represented in classical iconography. The Graces and the Seasons adorn Pandora with the flowers of spring, another image representing her as the face of nature. Pandora is the source of all life, as even Hesiod must acknowledge when he treats her as the archetype of Woman, and therefore the mother of us all.

Pandora is the Greek version of what in Sanskrit was known as Māha-Māyā, the illusory aspects of the phenomenal world. In Hindu mythology Māyā is the power specific to each deity. Gonda defines Māyā as "the wisdom, judgement and power enabling its possessor to create something or do something, ascribed to mighty beings."[27] Māyā is the power of the gods to create forms in the void, and to assume forms in which to manifest themselves. As the *Ṛg Veda* expresses it, the Godhead becomes every form through its Māyā.[28] This original concept of Maya as the power of the formless to assume form develops into the concept of Māyā as illusion. Like their Greek counterparts, the Hindu gods have the power to assume manifold forms. Māyā is the magic they possess to project illusions.[29] Zimmer calls the Māha-Māyā of the Vedas the World Mother. He interprets her as "the dream-force of his [sc. Vishnu's] universal sleep, by which, as a yogi manifests his inner visions, he moves all the fulness of the world within himself."[30] Māyā is the play of the mind, which can both generate images and materialize its images in the world of phenomena.

Māyā is thus both the intrinsic power of the gods and this world as the manifestation of the play of their inscrutable intentions. Māyā is nature, the veil that both reveals and screens the workings of the gods. Pandora performs the same function, being both the collective power of the gods and the play of their manifold forms on our senses. Like Māyā, Pandora is the interface between the mind of the universe and our limited human minds, which can reach the vision of the absolute Unconditioned only through the dialectic of opposites in this world of phenomena.

Pandora is also the signifier; the mythical image of the system of symbolic forms through which we interpret the data of our senses. Pandora is the world's duplicity, as we perceive it, the duplicity of the universals in their participation in the flux of phenomena, the duplicity of the good and the not-good yoked in partnership, the terrible affinity between the image and the archetype.

But why should women bear the blame for this cosmic baffle? In a world ordered by the universal Forms, why should women be the mere image, the false copy of the Forms, *the-not-truly-existent?* Woman becomes, in this cosmology, as Zeitlin puts it, "the mimetic creature par excellence."[31] Hesiod mistakes the object of desire for desire itself. Caught in the play of his own images, he cannot see that the object of desire is created by desire, precisely to protract desire, and desire being the desire for the Other, the subject aggressively frustrates himself with his own phantoms. Hesiod is betrayed by his own desire. "The subject," Lacan writes, "sustains himself as desiring in relation to an ever more complex signifying ensemble."[32]

Mother's womb was our first cradle, the fountain that flowed spontaneously to satisfy our needs. But one day mother was not present. In that catastrophe we discovered desire, the time lag between need and satisfaction. We were betrayed. In this new world of emerging ego-consciousness desire became our teacher. In place of the absent mother desire created a phantom mother. Not understanding the dynamics, we did not know that this phantom mother was the creation of our own memory and desire. Desire taught us to supplicate this phantom mother by prayers, tears, and charms. With the proper rituals we discovered that we could manipulate this phantom into materializing. But our magic was never completely successful. Out of our failures desire created new phantoms and taught us new inventions.

But always, in the manifold phantoms, a recalcitrant element remained, a degree of failure. Even mother, when she materialized, did not always match the perfection of some of our idealized phantoms. Then, for sons at least, came the oedipal trauma, when the father entered the world, whose word was the law. The law of the father delivered us up to the confusion of the signifier, in punishment for the ego's illicit desires. The young ego cannot eliminate its desires, since desire creates the web of relationships with the world, nor can it escape the punishment of the law. Frustrated, it displaces its anger onto the mother image.

We grow up and elaborate our childhood experiences into a cosmological vision. Deceived once, we will never forget. Each new experience of absence, each recurrence of the disparity between our images and the hard reality of matter, confirms the child's cosmology. Experiencing the betrayal of the image again and again, we inscribe the betrayal on the face of Nature. Mother Nature is meretricious. Mother Nature brings us into the world through no choice of our own—the ego discovers choice only when it is too late, when the only choice possible is to choose what fate has already decreed. Nature endows us with desires, and clothes herself in beauty to attract our desires, but as we move toward the beautiful, Nature reveals her true face: the ego discovers that its desire is the desire for death. "The glamor of Pandora," Pucci writes, "hides the grin of death."[33] Nature, charming our senses with the harmony of colors and sounds, seduces us into an agreement with life. Nature seduces us into relationships with the world, only to reveal the absence at the heart of every relationship. Hope is the ultimate betrayal, for to hope is to create another phantom, to compound illusion with illusion.

Meditation on this truth brought the Buddha to his enlightenment. Nature seduces us into a round of existence that leads only to disease, old age, and death. Even hope is but another form of desire. The Buddha reached enlightenment when he realized that desire itself must be transcended. Hesiod believes that he has found enlightenment because he has discovered the polarity of image and archetype deep in the structure of the universe. He, or rather the archaic mind thinking through him, has indeed seen deeply into the contradiction in our biology. But his personal animosity, and the malice that he must project onto women, show that he is arrested at an early stage in the process of consciousness, when the mind cannot yet disentangle desire from the object of desire.

In Hesiod's myth Aphrodite endows Pandora with desire—a classic instance of displacement. Pandora's fault, to accept the terms of the myth itself, is not that she desires but that she is desirable. As long as desire and the desirable are mixed in confusion, the mind remains trapped in its own syllogisms.

Hesiod's myth of Pandora articulates into a cosmological theory the experience of an infant traumatized by the loss of the mother and by the law of the father. At the core of the myth is the obsessive anger of the child, which, harbored in the heart, grows into malice, and sweeps every experience into its vortex, finding everywhere confirmation of its theory. The anger is validated by being projected first onto the gods, and then onto Pandora, who is their image in nature. But displacement only inverts and intensifies the anger. The child is trapped, angry at the mother who brings him into the world of disease and death, and at the father who substitutes the signifier, a mere phantom, in place of the mother. It does not take much insight to see in the spiteful image of Pandora a young boy's revenge on his mother; he has not forgiven her for bringing him into the world, nor the world for seeming so desirable. But the perverted image of Pandora is also the boy's revenge on his father, whose inviolate law places him beyond the reach of revenge.

Hesiod's myth of the struggle of Zeus and Prometheus to outwit each other, and of Pandora, inflicted upon men as a punishment for thought, strikes us as quaint today, yet it is our myth too. Self-consciousness is our common human heritage, and the common riddle of all humankind. Like Prometheus, we all carry the psychosomatic symptoms with which the mind punishes us for its own thoughts. Like Hesiod, we too have grown up in the myth that Mother Nature has played us false, and we are her miscarriage.

Hesiod's myth tells of a reconciliation between Prometheus and Zeus. Much later in the history of the world, after the fall, Herakles killed the eagle feeding on Prometheus's liver and freed Prometheus, as Hesiod says, "from his evil disease and from the bitterness in his heart"[34] Herakles did not perform this healing service, Hesiod tells us, except by the will of Zeus, who wished to magnify the glory of his great son. How could Zeus glorify his son Herakles by allowing Herakles to kill the eagle of Zeus and release Prometheus from the punishment of Zeus? We are in dreamtime again, where the author of the punishment and the liberator are one and the same. By Herakles' act of compassion Prometheus and Zeus are reconciled, father and son, ego and superego. Ego-consciousness need no longer bear the guilt for thinking itself an infraction of cosmic law.

Who more appropriate to heal the trauma of self-consciousness than Herakles, the hero who endured a life of agony until he achieved a successful integration of the mother archetype? True son of the Animus, Herakles came also to be named; that is, recognized, as the glory of the Anima. As Hesiod tells the story, at one time Hera hated Herakles more than she hated any god or mortal, but now she loves him and honors him above all other gods except only the mighty son of Kronos.[35] The myth of Pandora comes to a closure only when Herakles reaches his own godhood on Mt. Olympos, and discovers that the monsters that tormented him were all phantoms of the estranged mother. Self-consciousness liberates itself by slow degrees from the fear of the father. Then it learns too that it must forgive the mother. When the mother and father archetypes are integrated, no longer at war with each other, the ego begins to understand that consciousness is not the revenge of the gods visited on humans for daring to imagine a possible godhood. The radiant signatures of the world, which enchant our hearts and minds, are not delusion but allusions to the universal Subject.

III: The Serpent in the Garden

The Olympians, emerging into the light, must defend their existence against the threats from the previous generation, the Titans. The conflict between the two generations is a world cataclysm, encoding no doubt the collective memories of great natural catastrophes and the memories of the individual ego's internal struggle to defend, as its birthright, the principle of individuation. The outcome hangs in the balance. Will the new ego succeed or will it be swallowed up again in the matrix? But Zeus draws on all his powers and allies, and the old order is consumed in flames. The Titans are despatched to Tartaros.

With the defeat of the Titans and the creation of their underground prison, space, originally bifurcated into earth and sky, is now marked with a vertical axis, with Olympos at one pole and Tartaros at the other. Olympos rises up from the surface of earth, and its apex, shielded from human sight by a cloud cover, merges into sky.[1] Tartaros mirrors Olympos, but in inverse relationship, being as deep beneath the earth as the sky is high above it. Tartaros too is invisible but for the contrary reason, that it is hidden in the darkness beneath the earth. Olympos is airy, and spacious the lives that the gods live there. The Olympians, each with his or her own palace, visit back and forth; they gather for feasts or councils, for music and dance; they travel airily through the sky, from sky to mountain peak, from mountain peak to the earth. Tartaros, by contrast, surrounded by a bronze moat wrapped in triple folds of darkness, descends to a point of absolute constriction.[2] On the inner side of the moat is a wall with a gate of bronze over which the Hundred-Armed monsters keep perpetual guard, by the orders of Zeus. The climate on Olympos is always temperate, but anyone who falls into the chasm of Tartaros "would be cruelly tossed this way and that by storm after storm."[3]

As Olympos is freedom, pleasure, and beauty, Tartaros is confinement and deprivation. The chasm of Tartaros, located amid "the springs and at the farthest edges of earth, sea, and sky," as Hesiod puts it, is darkness absolute, matter in its absolute density, and space without definition.[4] To use the language of philosophy, Olympos is Being in all its fullness; Tartaros, hidden in darkness, racked by storms, and confined by walls of bronze, is non-Being in all its vacancy. To this prison the new sky gods condemned the old gods.

No sooner are the Titans vanquished, however, than a new monster arises to threaten the newly victorious sky gods, exactly as the unconscious continually rises up to threaten the orderly structure of the conscious mind. Gaia, as if reaching into her depths, unites with Tartaros to produce Typhoeus, also called Typhon, a creature compacted of earth-matter in double density. Hesiod's Typhon is a great beast with a hundred dragon heads, all of them flickering their black tongues and flashing fire from all their eyes (lines 820ff.). These heads resound with terrible noises—hissings, the bellowing of bulls, the bark of dogs, the roar of lions. More uncanny still, the hundred heads of this polymorphous monster could speak the language of the gods (lines 829–35). So great an emanation of Gaia's creative energy would have become the new world ruler, Hesiod says, had not Zeus seen the danger and acted promptly to muster the sky gods. The battle is pitched, and once again the world is racked by catastrophe. But the sky gods are again victorious. Zeus hurls the great dragon down into Tartaros, though we still continue to feel his effects in the destructive windstorms that are his offspring. With Typhon vanquished, Gaia at last acknowledges Zeus as the supreme god, and the rule of Olympos is now legitimized.

The battle between Zeus and Typhon has many parallels in the mythologies of the ancient Near Eastern peoples. Fontenrose, in his encyclopedic study of this myth (which he calls the combat myth), has traced the parallels extensively in Hittite, Canaanite, and Sumerian references and documents.[5] *Enuma elish,* the Babylonian creation poem, tells of the combat between the god Marduk and his monstrous opponent, Tiamat. Tiamat and Apsu were the original deities from whom all subsequent deities were generated. Female and male, they were the world-matter before it had materialized, the waters of chaos before the forms of creation arose out of them. As one generation of gods emerged from another, conflicts arose parallel to those in Hesiod's *Theogony.* Apsu was killed, leaving Tiamat as the sole image of the primordial powers.

A new god was born, Marduk, whose superior qualities so aroused the envy of the older gods that they entered into an alliance with Tiamat to wage war against Marduk and his fellow gods. Tiamat called up her reinforcements—snakes, vipers, dragons, lions, scorpion men, and other awesome beasts. An agreement was reached that the victor in the combat would win the kingship of the gods. Marduk, riding forth to battle at the head of the host of the sky gods, challenged Tiamat to single combat. In the combat he caught Tiamat in his net, and with an arrow from his bow pierced her entrails and split her heart. From Tiamat's body Marduk created earth and sky, and her foul hordes he consigned to the underworld along with the other rebellious gods.

The parallels between the Greek and Babylonian combat myths are obvious. Both are cosmogonic myths, which tell of a new generation of gods arising and of a rebellion, or a resistance to their power, among the older gods. In both cases the new gods are the sky gods, while the enemy rises up from the earth or is the primordial element itself. The enemy is either reptilian or brings reptilian forces to the battle. In the Egyptian version of this myth Seth, with whom Typhon was identified by the Greeks, changes into various wild animals (lions, snakes, crocodiles). In the Greek version the enemy, with his hundred heads, is a conglomerate of deadly creatures, whose cacophonous voices parallel the plurality of forms characteristic of the monster in other versions of the myth. In such versions of the combat myth the victor in the combat becomes the world ruler under whom a new order is established.

From India comes a similar myth. Vṛtra was a snake who encircled the primal waters and kept them from flowing. His name means "The Suppressor." He is described in the Vedic tradition as tricky, insulting, and godless. The gods go forth against this monster, with Indra as their champion. As his reward for his success in this exploit, Indra is promised the kingship of the world. Indra, wielding thunderbolts as Zeus does in his battle with Typhon, slays the dragon and thus frees the waters that were in confinement. Indra's feat is commemorated in his epithet: Vṛtrahan—Vṛtra Slayer.

Vṛtra consorts with a whole host of demons, many of them snakes, and others are endowed with the forms of savage beasts or monsters. Vṛtra himself, called in one place "firstborn of the snakes," is the great Dragon.[6] In Hesiod, Typhon simply opposes the power of Zeus, whereas Vṛtra shows more clearly the primordial nature of this beast. Vṛtra confines the waters of the world, which are also imaged as cows, the source of all nutrition. Vṛtra is either said to encircle the waters, or to block their approaches, or to drain them because of his insatiable appetite. As the principle of resistance at work in creation, the suppressor, Vṛtra opposes the emerging sky gods in their work of establishing order.

The combat myth appears in other forms where the cosmogonic significance is not so immediately apparent. Greece gives us another great version of the myth, in the conflict between Apollo and Python.[7] Apollo, looking for a favorable site for his shrine, came to a place charged with oracular power, sacred variously to Gaia or Themis; a site, that is, where the numen of the old pre-Olympian gods was most concentrated. At the site was a spring, the famed Castalia, guarded by the dragon whose name was Python. The young god of the new sky consciousness did battle with the guardian of the old earth consciousness, killed the dragon, established his shrine on the site, and thus appropriated for the new gods the ancient oracular powers of the site. The place then was named Pytho, so named, according to the ancient interpretation, for the rotting carcass of the defeated monster. Apollo became known as the Pythian god, in commemoration of his defeat of the great Python. Modern linguistics reveal an even more ancient etymology for Pytho: the dragon's name derives from the root *pyth-*, which appears in the Greek verb *pythano:* "to inquire, ascertain, understand." Strange to say, the dragon in this myth is "He who has achieved understanding."[8]

Apollo's battle with Python for the rights to the oracular power at Delphi recalls the battle between Zeus and Typhon. In addition to the several obvious parallels, the two myths are linked by various connections beneath the surface. In the Homeric *Hymn to Apollo* Typhon was the offspring of Hera, conceived by her as an act of retaliation against Zeus for the birth of Athena from his head, and was reared by the serpent at Pytho.[9] It was not always clear, in fact, whether Python and Typhon were two entirely distinct characters, so closely were they aligned in their mythical functions. The cosmogonic significance has been slightly disguised in the Apollo myth because the myth is centered on one particular locale and, on the surface at least, Apollo is not represented as defending all the sky gods against insubordinate opponents. Yet both myths express the same theme—the emergence of the new gods, the resistance that the new gods encounter from the primordial powers, the conquest of the primordial powers by the new gods, and the establishment of a new order.

The primordial character of the site in the Python myth is expressed in its oracular powers, its connection with Earth or the Titans, and by the presence of the spring. In Greek mythology all fresh water streams flow from Okeanos, the stream that encircles the world. Hesiod makes Okeanos one of the Titans, but ancient Greek sources—Homer, for example—suggest other cosmogonies in which Okeanos with his wife, Tethys, were the original parents of the gods.[10] Fontenrose points to the evidence that links Okeanos with Ogygos, and Ogygos with Ophion (literally "the snake").[11] Ophion, as Fontenrose points out, is another cosmogonic serpent, a primal god who was overthrown by Kronos.[12] "Ophion and Typhon," Fontenrose suggests, "were two forms of the same dragon, the antagonist of the combat myth."[13]

Python was no mere serpent. In some accounts Python himself delivered oracles at Delphi before being slain by Apollo.[14] Our sources are late, but, as Fontenrose argues, they are corroborated by evidence that Python held a revered place in the cult at Delphi.[15] Python was, in fact, the ancient god of the site, whose original rulership was overshadowed by the prominence of Delphi's new ruler, Apollo. But even in the historical period, it seems, Python continued to receive worship at Delphi. The Pythian games were first instituted as funeral games to honor the dead god. An oval-shaped stone was set up at Delphi, which people said was the rock that Kronos was tricked into swallowing in place of his son Zeus and then forced to disgorge. This monument the Greeks called the Omphalos, the navel, to signify Delphi as the center of the world. Other evidence suggests, however, that the omphalos was originally the tomb of Python. The omphalos marked Delphi as both the burial ground of the old gods and the birthplace of the new Olympians.[16]

The same myth, though more distant from obvious cosmogonic significance, appears in association with the heroes. Herakles spent his life in one great combat after another, and his antagonist took diverse forms: the hydra, a many-headed serpent; the serpentine river god Acheloos; giants and brigands; the three-headed hound of Hades; he even descended into the underworld and did battle with Hades among the corpses. The cosmogonic combat myth is serialized in Herakles' case into a whole lifetime of separate combats.

Among his exploits Herakles does battle specifically with the serpent, in the garden of the Hesperides. The Hesperides, daughters of Night, have their garden in the far west, in the darkness beyond the boundaries of the world, where stands a tree gleaming with golden fruit. The guardian of the tree is a dragon or serpent, Ladon by name, said to be the son of Typhon, and represented sometimes as many-headed, as monsters so often are in myth. Herakles either enters the garden and kills this serpent or, in one version, tricks Atlas into fetching the apples for him while Herakles sustains the world on his shoulders for a spell. Ancient interpreters played with the homonyms— *melon* ("apple") and *melon* ("sheep")—and supposed that the golden apples were originally sheep with golden fleece. This interpretation takes us back again to the myth of Vṛtra. Herakles, like Indra, must liberate the flocks held captive by the great serpent in the darkness of chaos, which is the realm of death.

In another of his exploits Herakles wrestles with the river god Acheloos. Acheloos was closely associated with Okeanos, sometimes even identified with Okeanos, and sometimes said to be the offspring of Okeanos and Tethys, the primal waters. The horn, which Herakles tore from the brow of Archeloos and carried off as his trophy, is identified, in some accounts, with the horn of Amaltheia, a daughter of Okeanos, who was also the goat who nursed the infant Zeus in the Dictaean cave on Crete. From her horns, so tradition said, poured forth ambrosia and nectar. The horn of Amaltheia, fused in mythical imagination with the horn of the great river Acheloos, is the archetypal cornucopia, the horn of plenty. Once again we discern the outlines of the Vṛtra myth. Herakles, in wrestling with Acheloos, is another Indra doing battle once again with the great beast who withholds the waters of creation. Herakles, in defeating Acheloos and capturing Amaltheia's cornucopia, unlooses the creative fluids of the world, as Indra rescues soma, the magical drink, from Vṛtra's possession.

Every hero, it seems, has at least one encounter with a serpent or a serpentlike enemy. Hera, angered at the philandering of Zeus, sends two serpents to do away with Herakles as soon as he is born. But the infant, a hero even in the cradle, grabbed the serpents and strangled them both. Perseus did battle with Cetus, the sea monster to whom Andromeda had been offered in sacrifice. In some of the representations on vase paintings, Cetus is another Acheloos, fluid and serpentine in form and movement. Perseus meets the serpent again in the Gorgons. The Gorgons, like so many of their kind, live at the far extremity of the world. The triple Gorgons, each with her snaky locks, are the serpent multiplied many times over. Ovid tells us that as Perseus flew over Libya carrying the head of Medusa, the blood that dripped from the head generated snakes in the Libyan sands, and that is why the desert swarms with snakes.[17] In this myth Medusa is the great mother of all serpents.

Kadmos, in founding the city of Thebes, has a set of adventures reminiscent of Apollo's adventure in establishing his shrine at Delphi.[18] Weary from his futile search for his sister Europa, Kadmos is instructed by Apollo's oracle to follow a cow until she should lie down. She by this act would signify the site for his future city. At the site, as Ovid tells the story, was a trackless forest, and deep within the forest water flowed from an abundant spring into a sequestered cave. The spring was guarded by a serpent as enormous as the serpent constellation visible in the night sky, both beautiful to look on and horrifying. He had a body swollen with deadly venom; his eyes flashed fire; a triple-pronged tongue flickered in his triple rows of teeth; his skin was protected by scales of iron. The Phoenician men, who had accompanied Kadmos on his journeys, dipping their vessels into the spring, aroused this serpent, who emerged from the nearby cave and killed them all.

Kadmos, being of heroic mettle, takes on the dragon, and in Ovid's narrative the combat is truly cosmic. Kadmos hurls a stone with force enough to collapse a city wall, but the beast scarcely feels the blow, protected as he is by his scales of iron. Kadmos then hurls his javelin, which strikes home, but the serpent rears and struggles, writhing in coils as high as trees, rolling like rivers in flood. When the beast succumbs in the end to Kadmos's javelin, Kadmos takes the dragon's teeth and plows them into the ground. Instantly the Spartoi, a breed of armed men, rise out of the earth, who fall upon each other until all are killed except for five, who make peace with each other. The five survivors, together with Kadmos, become the founders of the new city of Thebes. One of the survivors was named Echion—Viperman, as Fontenrose translates his name.[19] Kadmos himself and his wife, Harmonia, were later transmuted into serpents that slithered into the woods and disappeared forever from human company. But that is another story.

Once again a serpent, at first sight simply the guardian of a spring, is revealed as the great cosmogonic god of river and flood. In some accounts this serpent was once the king of Thebes, whom Kadmos deposed and killed when he arrived with his Phoenician band. Here, then, localized at the Greek city of Thebes, we find yet another exemplar of the primordial beast, representative of the old gods, which obstructs the progress of the new order.

As we would expect from a creature so widely prevalent in myths, dreams, and fantasies, the dragon has a multitude of forms. The dragon is sometimes male, sometimes female. The dragon can be a pair of dragons, sometimes sexually nondifferentiated, at other times differentiated as male and female, whether as husband and wife or as mother and son. The dragon can be winged or wingless. It can be specifically a snake, or it can look more like the dinosaurs of old, or the dragons of our popular culture. It inhabits watery places and breathes fire and venomous fumes. It can be a mixed breed, like the Chimaera; or have a hundred heads, like Typhon, all breathing fire and howling with the voices of savage beasts; or change from one monstrous form to another. Even the Sphinx who obstructed Oedipus and the Gorgons with their snaky grimaces are versions of the archetype. Sometimes this beast may be represented as a large and terrifying monster, like Behemoth or Leviathan, with whom Jahweh did battle, with little specifically to signify a reptilian form.

This serpent's lair may be in the pit or simply in the darkness of primeval Chaos. This serpent may be a sea monster like Cetus in the Perseus myth, or Leviathan; it may be a river creature like Acheloos; or, like Vṛtra or Okeanos, the primal sea itself. Even Proteus, the Old Man of the Sea, with his magical powers to change his shape and with his oracular knowledge, reveals that he too is an allomorph of the great cosmogonic beast of the primal sea. This ubiquitous beast may lurk at the edge of the world, whether in the darkness of the west, like Ladon in the garden of the Hesperides, or in the remote east, like the serpent guarding the golden fleece. The serpent is associated (at least in our Western tradition) with the earth—born of Earth herself, or born to one of Earth's many surrogates, or nursed by Earth or her surrogates, or raised up by Earth in opposition to the sky gods or heroes.

The serpent may be confined, like Typhon, in a dismal place, shunned by gods and humans. Just as often, however, the serpent is found occupying a highly desirable site, like the site at Delphi that Apollo found ideal for his oracular shrine, or the site where Kadmos planned to build his new city. In the darkness of the west we find a paradise guarded by a serpent. So too, in the far northeast, somewhere in the land of the Hyperboreans, a mythical place beyond the boundaries of terra cognita, we find paradise again, where the sheep are golden, but here too a serpent bars the way. The serpent hides in the Garden of Eden. No one knows how he got there, yet there he is, as if Eden were his own habitat.

The serpent of myth marks the locus of some treasure, highly prized but difficult of access. He may be the tutelary deity of a river or spring; or we may find him coiled around a tree whose fruit has a special potency and fascination. Sometimes too the serpent holds cattle or a fair princess as his hostage. The more desirable the treasure, the more terrifying and monstrous the forms in which the serpent appears.

Who, then, is this serpent, whose power threatens the gods, with whom gods and heroes must wrestle again and again, the antagonist in a thousand myths? Fontenrose calls this beast the chaos demon, the representation of "not only primeval disorder, but all dreadful forces that remain in the world and periodically threaten the god-won order: hurricane, flood, fire, volcanic eruption, earthquake, eclipse, disease, famine, war, crime, winter, darkness, death. They (sc. the ancients) imagined either that the demon himself came back to life and renewed the combat, or that his progeny continued the war against the cosmos, ever striving for disorder and a return to primeval inactivity. His death amounted to no more than banishment from the ordered world: he was cast into outer darkness beneath the earth or beyond it, that is, he was thrown back into the primeval chaos from which he came, where he and his minions lived on, ever ready to invade the god-established order and undo the whole work of creation. For the cosmos has been won from the chaos that still surrounds it, as a cultivated plot from the encompassing wilderness." [20]

The serpent is certainly the chaos demon in the great cosmogonic combats, as in the myths of Zeus and Typhon, Marduk and Tiamat, Indra and Vṛtra, Apollo and Python. The many labors of Herakles, the myth of Perseus and Medusa, of Perseus and Cetus, of Oedipus and the Sphinx, the myths of heroes wrestling with great river gods, or freeing the waters from water demons, the serpents that crush Laocoön and his sons, thus persuading the Trojans to introduce the Wooden Horse—in all these myths we see the archetypal theme of the warrior's battle against the demon of chaos and death. Likewise the serpent who insinuates himself into the Garden of Eden, and undoes Jahweh's work by introducing the signifier into the Lord's perfect creation.

The battle between Zeus and Typhon, or between Apollo and Python, is the mythical representation of creation itself, the act by which God or the gods bring a world into being out of the original chaos. Typhon, Tiamat, Seth, Vṛtra, Leviathan, call him what we will—the dragon is the mythical emblem for the formlessness of the original matter and its resistance to the informing, creative act of the gods. But if the dragon is the chaos demon, what are we to make of the snake cults in antiquity? If the snake was abhorred and feared in antiquity, it was also venerated. The so-called snake goddess of Crete, represented as wearing snakes or holding them aloft in both hands, indicates that the snake was a prominent icon in Minoan cult. [21] This icon had a long history behind it. "The snake and its abstracted derivative," Gimbutas claims, "are the dominant motifs of the art of Old Europe, and their imaginative use in spiraliform design throughout the Neolithic and Chalcolithic periods remained unsurpassed by any subsequent decorative style until the Minoan civilization, the sole inheritor of the old European lavishness." [22]

Archaic Greece too, though it seems to have elevated the serpent to the status of the archenemy, still retained the snake as a cult idol. Athena had her snake totem or emblem. Her temple on the Acropolis in Athens housed a snake, which we interpret as embodying the tutelary spirit of the shrine. Why should a snake guard the shrine of the goddess of city crafts; that is, of civilization? If Athena's shrine houses a snake, the snake is Athena, in one of her functions at least. The prominence of snakes in the cult of Dionysos is well known. Nonnus tells a myth in which Dionysos discovered wine by observing a snake sucking the juice from grapes ripening on the vine. [23] The maenads, who celebrate Dionysian ecstasy, are represented much like the Minoan snake goddess, holding snakes in their hands, or wearing snakes entwined in their hair or as decorations on their dress.[24]

Even Zeus had his snake cult. Athenagoras, the Christian apologist, preserves what is no doubt an ancient tradition, that Zeus and Demeter mated as serpents.[25] As Athenagoras tells the story, Zeus pursued Demeter; she, to escape his amorous attention, transformed herself into a serpent; Zeus did likewise. Then the two, sky god and earth mother, joined as serpent with serpent, in "the so-called Herakleotic knot." The caduceus of Hermes, with its two serpents entwined around a central staff, adds Athenagoras, is the symbol of this union.

From antiquity comes another tale, that Zeus took the form of a serpent to mate with their daughter Persephone, and from this union Dionysos was born. Ovid mentions this myth briefly, but Nonnus tells it at greater length.[26] In Nonnus's tale Demeter, fearing the prophecy that her daughter would be ravished by a cunning half-monster, carried Persephone in her car, drawn by dragons (*drakones,* in Greek), to a rocky grotto. She hid her daughter away in the grotto, posting her dragons as guards, one to the left of the entrance and the other to the right. But Zeus, taking the dragon form himself, lulled Persephone's dragons to sleep, entered the cave, and mated with Persephone. From this union was born Zagreus, the horned infant. Nonnus calls this mating Persephone's marriage with the "etherial dragon"—one of the few surviving references in our Western tradition to the celestial dragon who still reigns in the Orient. Kerényi argues that these tales preserve relics of the ancient myth of the Cretan snake god, whom the Greeks later assimilated to their sky god, Zeus.[27] But even in the historical period Zeus continued to have his snake form. In one of his manifestations he was worshiped as *Meilichios,* "The Kindly God." This gentle Zeus is portrayed on Athenian votive tablets in serpent form.[28]

What are we to make of the serpent to whom Psyche's parents were commanded by the oracle to sacrifice their daughter? The serpent they feared was indeed one of the great primeval gods—Eros himself—but instead of devouring Psyche, as she and her parents had feared, he transported her to a secret paradise and there made her his bride. Psyche's parents grieved for her as one dead, as indeed she was, but they were mistaken in supposing that she had been killed. She had been initiated by the serpent god into a life far transcending the mortal life her parents knew.

Remove or change the names of the myth of Eros and Psyche and we have a variant of the myth of the Cretan snake god's mating dance with Demeter or Persephone. We can even dimly recognize in Psyche's adventures a version of Eve's story, as it might have been told by someone sympathetic to the serpent. That the serpent who threatened Psyche with death should be Eros, that he should have his palace in paradise, and initiate Psyche into the mysteries of love—all this is strangely consistent with the habits of the polymorphous serpent archetype.

Athena wears the Medusa head on her breastplate, as the victory trophy that Perseus gave to her in return for her aid. Manifestly, Medusa's head on Athena's armor commemorates Athena's victory over the chaos demon. But just as manifestly, Athena, as she goes into battle with writhing snakes at her breast, proclaims herself Medusa. Athena the virgin, a goddess to her friends, becomes the chaos demon incarnate to any man who dares to look on her with sexual intent. Under her Olympian persona as the goddess of civilization, Athena is the ancient snake goddess herself.

Zeus is the dragon slayer and the dragon, both in one. Apollo too is dragon and dragon slayer. Apollo, coming upon the oracular site at Delphi, saw Python as the enemy to be eliminated from the garden. But Python's name tells a truer story. *Python* is "He who understands," or rather, "He who has achieved understanding." The cognate of this name is Sanskrit in *Buddha*. So well has our Western culture buried Python that we must go to the Orient, where the Buddha and the serpent remained on friendlier terms, to uncover his true identity. As the Buddha sat in contemplation beneath the tree of enlightenment, a great storm raged around him. But the serpent king Muchalinda came out of the earth, enveloped the Buddha seven times with his coils, and spread his hood above the Buddha's head, saying "Let neither cold nor heat, nor gnats, flies, wind, sunshine, nor creeping creatures come near the Blessed One!" After the storm was spent the serpent uncoiled himself, assumed human form, and did reverence to the Buddha.[29]

The Greeks themselves of the historical period mistakenly supposed that Pytho derived its name from *pythein* ("to rot"); that is, "the rotting carcass" of the slain serpent.[30] But the Buddha too reached enlightenment by meditating on disease and decay. Even a confused etymology tells its own mythical truth. If Python is "the Enlightened One," the treasure that the Delphic dragon guards is consciousness itself. With the old god dead, the new god can rest secure in the belief that all wisdom originates with him. But Python, whose death is celebrated in the great Panhellenic festival at Delphi, whose name is attached to the site, to the cult, to the priestess, and to Apollo himself, attests that every pilgrimage to Delphi, the site of understanding, is an encounter with the old serpent who lurks in the new god's shadow.

Though slain, Python does not die as mortals die. Apollo himself becomes the Python god, honoring the old serpent in his name and cult. In antiquity some argued that Apollo and Python were related as brothers. Róheim goes so far as to argue that Apollo himself was originally a dragon too, the son of Python, the young dragon who killed his father to gain the old dragon's prerogatives.[31] Whatever of the old dragon's nature Apollo did not appropriate was transferred to Dionysos, Apollo's unruly brother, to whom Apollo was obliged to surrender his lordship of the Delphic shrine during the winter months.[32] Dionysos is the old serpent born anew every year.

Who calls Python the chaos demon? Why, Apollo, of course. Who calls Typhon the chaos demon? Zeus, of course. Who are these Olympians, who dare to proclaim themselves alone the champions of order? Zeus freely hurls his thunderbolts at those who arouse his displeasure, and rapes nymphs that charm his amorous eye. Athena leads the troops into battle. Artemis rejoices in the victory of the predator over the prey. Poseidon rejoices in earthquake and tidal flood. The sky gods are as much agents of destruction as those they call their enemies.

Comparative mythology reveals that this dragon was, in fact, the ancient deity who was venerated throughout the Near East until he or she was deposed by the gods of the new consciousness, which was brought into the region by newer waves of settlers from the north. Whether among the Indo-European peoples like the Greeks or among the Semitic peoples, the serpent had once ruled as the supreme lord.[33] According to an ancient cosmogony preserved in the *Argonautica* of Apollonios of Rhodes, Ophion, "The Snake," was the first ruler of Olympos.[34]

The serpent, as he or she has survived in mythical imagination, has thus been subject to a political campaign of vilification. "In Eve's scene at the tree," Campbell writes, "nothing is said to indicate that the serpent who appeared and spoke to her was a deity in his own right, who had been revered in the Levant for at least seven thousand years before the composition of the Book of Genesis."[35] The serpent was the gardener in Eden, but mythology was rewritten to cast that primordial gardener into his new role as the arch-enemy of the true god or gods. Leviathan, the primal serpent in ancient Hebrew consciousness, disappears almost completely from the record. Without the benefit of hermeneutic scholarship, we might suppose Leviathan and Behemoth, to whom the voice in the whirlwind alludes in the Book of Job, to be simply large beasts such as might be found in nature, if exaggerated by a fanciful popular imagination; or the serpent in the Garden of Eden to be simply the reptile known to biology. But Leviathan, whose name means "The Twisting One," Behemoth, and the serpent in the Garden are all versions of the same figure—the ancient deity predating Jahweh, whom Jahweh deposed.[36]

Wherever they could, the new gods deposed the old serpent god and appropriated not only their rival's privileges and sanctuaries but many of the earlier god's characteristics. Harrison, speaking of Zeus Meilichios, writes: "the human-shaped Zeus has slipped himself into the place of the old snake-god."[37] Just so, Apollo slipping into Python's place, became Apollo *Pythios* and assumed the oracular functions that once were Python's. The symbiosis of god and serpent-*daimon* is revised into a ritual antagonism, and what was once essence is first negated and then transformed into an attribute.

Aelian describes a cult of Apollo at Epirus.[38] Within a grove sacred to Apollo, Aelian writes, was a circular enclosure in which snakes were kept. Only the priestess of the sanctuary was permitted within the enclosure, and she was required to enter the precinct naked; that is, in a state of nature, as Eve was naked when she encountered the serpent in Eden. If the snakes were gentle when she approached them during the great festival of Apollo, that was an omen of good health for the community for the coming year. If they frightened her, and did not take the honey cakes she offered them, that was an ill omen for the year. The people of Epirus, according to Aelian, claimed that the snakes in their sanctuary were descended from Python at Delphi. Epirus preserved into historical times what had been, surely, an ancient snake cult, which long antedated Apollo's arrival at Delphi.

The snakes were kept in the sacred precinct, Aelian adds, as "playthings, surely, for the god." Playthings? In Aelian's conjecture we glimpse the nature of the pre-Apollonian Python. The old serpent was, if we may be so bold, "the plaything" of his worshippers before the new gods transformed him into the chaos demon, as the snake is the plaything of his female votaries in Cretan paintings, and of the maenads, the votaries of Dionysos. The playfulness of the serpents at Epirus and their oracular powers are vestiges of the old god's original character. Apollo's playful relations with these descendants of Python, in contrast to the adversarial relations between Apollo and Python at Delphi, are testimony that the cult god at Epirus was indeed the old god (or goddess) of the serpents, who was in the course of time rehabilitated under the new name, Apollo. Is the story of Eve and the serpent a revision of an older story of the snake goddess or priestess sporting with the snakes in her garden?

The new gods projected a "negative moral judgment," as Campbell notes, onto their opponent.[39] Typhon became a subhuman monstrosity, a beast conceived in the deepest pit, brandishing a hundred snake heads, which uttered terrible subhuman noises. Indra's enemy became Vṛtra, the Suppressor. Acheloos, a great and gracious river flowing through a parched land, became a restless demon whom the hero Herakles must subdue. The lovely Medusa became the gorgon with the paralyzing stare. If we were to be guided by visual iconography alone, we would surely interpret Athena, displaying on her breast the head of Medusa encircled by snakes, as the old goddess of the serpents, playing with her snakes as Apollo plays with his snakes at Epirus. But the old goddess, no longer either the mother or the bride, has become the daughter, sprung from the head of the new sky god Zeus and subject now to the authority of the head. The snakes that once played on the bosom of the mother have become the weapons by which the daughter preserves her virginity, and thus her fidelity to the father. The Olympians, as they moved into "the upper air," as Harrison puts it, "were, it seems, ashamed of their earth-origin and resolved to repudiate their snake tails." [40]

The transformation of the serpent from venerated god to loathsome demon marks the shift from a matriarchal to a patriarchal consciousness. History and, indeed, biology itself were revised to conform to the newly emerging ideology. The ancient goddess, when not erased from the scriptures altogether, was transformed into the daughter obedient to the father and ruthless toward the father's enemies. The woman, the new biology decreed, was born from the man, whether from his rib, like Eve, or from his head, like Athena. In the new ideology Pandora, once the great, all-giving Mother, became a mere *eidolon,* an idol created by the will of the father to entangle his rivals in confusion.

Human consciousness fell victim to it own polarities. The polarities observed in nature, which might have been marked by merely neutral signs, became more rigidly differentiated, and marked as good or evil. "All that is good and noble," Campbell writes, "was attributed to the new, heroic master gods, leaving to the native nature powers the character only of darkness." [41] Pandora, transformed from the mother to the puppet of the father, becomes the sum of all contradictions. Adam and Eve, eating of the tree of enlightenment, introduce shame where none had existed before. In the new consciousness the human mind, even when pursuing its natural functions, is marked as irredeemably sinful. Sin, from the inner perspective, is the consciousness of the rupture between humans and nature, the mind's consciousness of its own guilt.

The polarity that the myths find in the orders and powers of nature is, in fact, the polarity arising in the human ego. At variance with itself, the ego projects its own inner dynamic onto nature as a whole, and then invents myths to substantiate its own projections. The complete and thoroughgoing externalizing property of myth further substantiates the ego's belief that its projections are not of its own making but are, indeed, the eternal truths. But all myths record the history of the human psyche in search of itself, and the myth of the combat between the sky god and the subterranean serpent is one of the remarkable documents of the ego's self-discovery.

Fontenrose calls the archetypal serpent antagonist the symbol of "all the dreadful forces that remain in the world and periodically threaten the god-won order." [42] True enough. But the dragon, conceived of Earth or nurtured in the dark recesses of Earth, is the consort or champion of Earth, symbol of Earth's prodigious vitality, which breeds new forms in utter disregard for the ego's fears of its own extinction. In marking the serpent with the sign of all that is irrational and evil, the new gods passed judgment on Nature herself. Hesiod's cosmogonic vision is colored throughout by the belief that Nature is devious, capricious, and lawless. Nature must be brought under the rational, hierarchical control of the new sky gods. The Titans, the Cyclopes with their lightning bolts, Typhon breathing fire and uttering subhuman noises, the hundred-armed monsters—all are exemplars, in Hesiod's *Theogony,* of Earth's natural proclivities. The ambiguous movement of life horrifies the rational mind, whose instruments are most precisely calibrated to work on matter, provided the matter be stable and inert.[43]

The serpent was vilified because he embodied whatever in the more archaic consciousness conflicted with the new ideology. But is a cultural shift from one set of gods to another sufficient to account for the extreme hatred that has pursued the serpent throughout our Western history? Other animals are as threatening to human life, but the serpent alone, of all God's creation, must forever live under God's curse, cast out from the circle of grace that redeems all the rest of God's creation. We wonder not only at the absolutism of Jahweh's curse, laid even upon the harmless and graceful garter snake, but equally at the ambiguity of the attitudes expressed in myth toward this creature. Why is this species marked with God's curse yet posted to guard the sacred tree or spring in the sacred garden? Why is the serpent of myth endowed with oracular powers? Why is the serpent, who might be thought the farthest removed of all biological orders from human consciousness, God's humble ally to bring Eve to her self-consciousness? If the snake is the chaos demon, why does Apollo maintain his snake cult, and even Zeus need his snake persona?

The modern mind may find it absurd that in antiquity one single creature was held responsible for all natural disasters, yet this fearsome dragon is the very creation of the rational mind. Such is the paradox of human consciousness. By the law of compensation, the higher Olympos reaches into the heavens, the more monstrous its serpent enemy grows. The serpent is, in Jung's iconography, the Shadow that the Olympian pantheon casts on earth. The greater the desire of the Olympians for rational control, the more irrational grows the adversary who dares to oppose Olympos.

The myth of the combat between the Olympians and the serpent is the ego's own, inner cosmology. The emergence of the Olympian gods from the universal matrix to a position of authority over the rest of creation is the myth that the ego projects to describe its own emergence from its matrix in the human soul. The Olympians' ambition is the ego's assertion of its own rationality; conversely, the serpent, the Olympians' chthonic antagonist, embodies the fears of the ego's own irrationality. The loathsome features of the serpent express the ego's fears of the impulses and desires lurking within the human soul, which threaten to bring down its towers in ruin.

The serpent is both the polymorphous libido and the tabu imposed by the superego against the libido's entrance into consciousness. To look upon Medusa is to be turned to stone. "God saw everything that he had made," the author of the book of Genesis writes, "and, behold, it was very good."[44] But, as if from nowhere, the serpent appears, and upon this creature alone God lays his curse: "Thou art cursed above all cattle," the Lord says to the serpent in Eden, "and above every beast of the field."[45] The loathsome form of the serpent and its terrifying disposition guarantee that the territory it guards will remain out of bounds.

Every tabu is Janus-faced, a prohibition, which also demarcates what is desirable, and thus excites the very desire that it prohibits. The dark and desolate habitat of the serpent is also a *locus amoenus,* grove or garden, and in the garden flows the river of life or stands the tree of forbidden delight. The serpent, who entices the hero to transgress the tabu and seize the golden fruit, is compounded of fear, desire, and guilt.

Róheim, following a conventional Freudian interpretation, reads the serpent as a phallic symbol.[46] But this is to translate one signifier into another. The phallus, as it functions in post-Freudian criticism at least, is an archetypal symbol, charged as are all archetypal symbols with emotional contents beyond any and all explicit meanings. The serpent who takes Psyche for his bride may express a woman's fear of male sexuality. Medusa, however, may with equal cogency express a man's fear of female sexuality. The serpent, who has his lair deep in the earth or in the boundless sea, is simply the polymorphous libido, the primal energy itself, which the ego fears even when it recognizes that it depends on that energy for its own survival.

The serpent is, at the first level, the raw energy of nature, which erupts in violent catastrophes and spawns creatures that prey upon each other. This energy appears intentional, yet perversely so, since its intentions seem flagrantly indifferent to the intentions of its own individual creatures. The icon of this overwhelming natural force is the many-headed hydra, the fire-breathing cosmic dragon, the grinning gorgon. The Mother who spawns this creature is Siva, Nature who destroys as freely as she generates new forms. To the hero of ego-consciousness this force is profoundly alien, since consciousness sees all too clearly that entropy is the universal fate that devours every form and motive.

The raw energy of nature, entering consciousness, becomes the libido—voracious, lecherous, polymorphous, a creature that regenerates itself as often as it is suppressed. The serpent who takes Psyche for his bride is Eros, both the libidinal drive in its biological force, so to speak, and the libidinal energy translated into desire. The splendid garden into which the serpent guides Psyche is, of course, the same garden where Eve discovered desire and its bitter fruit.

The serpent of the libido rises from the depths of the unconscious, from the bowels of nature, and it must be thrust back whence it came if it is not to undo the ego's systems and hierarchies. Where it cannot be extirpated, it must be transformed, though this transformation is more likely to be deformation and degradation. Vṛtṛa is named the Suppressor when, in fact, the sky gods are the suppressors. The sky gods cast the serpent into outer darkness; they decapitate it, or imprison it in a subterranean prison. The victory of the sky gods over the serpent testifies to the superego's success in defining the territory of the illicit.

Snakes, profoundly alien, put in question the whole human enterprise. Ego-consciousness, affronted to find itself related to a form that slithers on the ground, goes so far as to assert that the reptilian order stands outside of God's creation altogether. The serpent has been declared the absolute Other. So the human tribe goes forth to tread this subtle creature underfoot. Named the Suppressor, the serpent may legitimately be suppressed.

Yet the serpent is as profoundly familiar to us as it is alien. The serpent of myth inhabits the primal elements, but these are our primal elements. We are as much creatures of water and earth as they are. The serpent guards a prize that we desire or offers us an arcane wisdom that we need. Kadmos, a dragon slayer at the apogee of his career, at the end of his life surrenders his human form, becomes a serpent himself, slips into the forest, and disappears from human habitation. The kinship between us and the serpent is as compelling as it is repugnant.

In myth this kinship between the sky gods and their dragon adversary survives all their hostilities. Apollo and Python were brothers, some ancient sources attest. Asclepius, Apollo's son, not only carries the serpents on his caduceus but takes on himself the serpent form. Where the family connection is faint, the kinship is expressed in other ways. The voice that speaks to Job out of the whirlwind treats Leviathan and Behemoth as if they were on familiar terms with God, perhaps even God's allies. Behemoth is, according to the voice, "chief of the ways of God."[47] The voice grows eloquent in describing Leviathan's beauty and might: "I will not conceal his parts, nor his power, nor his comely proportion," the voice proclaims; "upon earth there is not his like, who is made without fear. He beholdeth all high things: he is a king over all the children of pride."[48] To call Leviathan king of the children of pride is hardly a pejorative, not when such an expression comes from the voice that speaks of the Leviathan's "comely proportions." The serpent who promises Adam and Eve that they will become "as gods, knowing good and evil," if they eat of the forbidden fruit, speaks the truth.[49] Adam and Eve, eating of the tree of knowledge, are initiated into godhood. The serpent who guards the tree of life, or the oracular spring, is the demiurge—God's first minister, or (dare we say it?) God himself in one of the most numinous of his personas.

The serpent is the ground of all biological energy. As we walk erect, proud of our bipedalism, we assume that all our movements are straightforward. We are the Olympians. Fond delusion! In fact, all our movements are reptilian rotations around the spinal column, though the final product in our bipedal species looks so different from the movement of the snake. Our locomotion begins as a tidal surge of energy from side to side. We are, in our first movements, amoebas, but as our free flow becomes progressively articulated by bones, muscles, and tendons, we evolve from amoeba to serpent, from serpent to alligator, from alligator to lumbering primate, until finally we stand on our own two feet, as nature's latest experiment in bipedalism.[50] We are articulated serpents. The staff of Asclepius is the symbol of all biological movement.

Just as our gross movements are serpentine, so are all our internal movements below the articulation of motion by bone and muscle. Each of us is a river, with numerous tributaries, each river a meander of eddies and undulations. The deeper we penetrate into our physiology, the more the dragon reveals his presence. Now consciousness, looking directly into the cell, finds the double helix of DNA coiled around a central axis. The microcosm reproduces the macrocosm; the macrocosm reproduces the microcosm.

Biologists talk of the human brain as a structure built up of three quasi-independent structures, much like a building to which stories have been added in the course of time. MacLean calls these three structures the reptilian brain, the old mammalian (or limbic) brain, and the neomammalian brain (the neocortex).[51] Each of these structures, MacLean writes, "has its own peculiar form of subjectivity and its own intelligence, its own sense of time and space and its own memory, motor and other functions."[52]

"Man's oldest brain," MacLean writes, "is basically reptilian."[53] This old brain "seems to be hidebound by precedent."[54] MacLean suggests that the reptilian brain in humans governs "such genetically constituted forms of behavior as selecting homesites, establishing territory, engaging in various types of display, hunting, homing, mating, breeding, imprinting, forming social hierarchies, and selecting leaders."[55]

Can the humble snake be held accountable for this catalogue, which sums up most of the behavior patterns characteristic of all living species, including the human? Are reptiles more prone to forming social hierarchies or electing presidents than other biological orders? Surely the limbic brain, with its influence on our emotions, and the complicated superstructure of the neocortex have as much to say in our choice of mates or nests, or on our social structures and traditions, as the old reptilian brain. We might do better to allow for a reptilian factor in all our actions, an instinctual element stereotypical yet spontaneous. Sagan is closer to the mark when he suggests that our reptilian brain corresponds (loosely) to the Freudian id.[56]

Modern biological theory converges strangely with Hesiod's topography. If the irrational and lascivious serpent is the mythical image of our old in-

stinctual brain, then Olympos is the neocortex. The neocortex has not eliminated the functions of the old brain but has modified them by introducing
analysis, conjecture, and hypothesis into a process once automatic and instinctual. With its symbols and signifiers the neocortex evaluates, and thus
brings into consciousness the processes that would otherwise lie below the
threshold of conscious perception. The neocortex creates gods.

The conflicts, which figure so prominently in our myths, are the shadow
play of the conflict within our own brains, which are nature's experiment to
adapt three separate structures, with their conflicting modes of perception and
behavior, into a single harmonious organ. The neocortex introduced conflict
into the human organism by imposing will upon impulse, cogitation upon
instinct, evaluation upon sensation.

The Freudian model of the id as a seething swamp of uncontrollable and
divisive impulses, over which the superego must maintain perpetual surveil-
lance, corresponds closely to the old mythical model, in which the Titans and
the great serpent, thrashing about in the pit of Tartaros, must be kept under
control by the Olympians with their superior intelligence. Again, we suspect
the propaganda of the dragon-slaying gods in the neocortex. Are the reptilian
orders more prone to uncontrollable impulses than our species? Why should
instinct be racked by internal conflicts, if left to its own devices, or more
ruinous than intellect to the organism? No, the neocortex is the subtle beast,
which by its fine discriminations dismembers the unity of instinctual life and
musters one idea to war on another. As the neocortex expanded its capacity
to modify the functions of the reptilian brain, so the gods on the peaks of
Olympos enlarged their territory, introduced divisions and complexities into
what was once undifferentiated, and placed their tabu on what they regarded
as the blind autonomy of the older, simpler, instinctual gods.

Each of the three brains has its own orientation on the world. The neocortex, as MacLean writes, is externally oriented, both physiologically and so-
cially. MacLean surmises that the limbic cortex may be constantly bombarded
by impulses from the internal world, whereas the neocortex "performs many
of its nice discriminations without interference from signals and noise generated in the internal world."[57] Another distinctive trait of mammals with a
developed neocortex is their sociability. The human neocortex, in MacLean's
view, is responsible for our emphasis on education and culture, and for our
empathetic and altruistic values.

Transpose this modern biological model into myth and we would have a
world of gods much as Homer and Hesiod portray them. The Uranian gods,
who have claimed Olympos, the vault of sky, and the thin ether, for their
watchpost, are far-seeing, far-shooting, far-traveling. These gods delight in
the pleasures of the neocortex. They are sociable beings who enhance basic
biological functions with ritual and ceremony; they do not merely eat; they

banquet, and the banquet is not complete without music and dance. They are social, yet individualistic. Like any human family, they are quarrelsome, yet at their best they are altruistic and compassionate. They respect integrity; they admire honor; in short, the Olympian gods are cultured.

The neocortex, MacLean suggests, is "futuristic." It teaches us the principle of delayed gratification, by drawing us away from earth's gravitational field into the thin atmosphere of outer space, where the Olympians have their home. The neocortex creates ideals. The Olympians, we admit, have the narcissism of children who must have instant gratification. Yet they are future-minded also. In the *Iliad* Zeus can hold an overall plan to honor Achilles even while several subplots, and even counterplots, run their course. The Olympians certainly have their ideals, however tarnished they may be by the gods' rivalries. The ancient combat myth tells of the suppression and inhibition of the instinctual life, but on the positive side it tells also the story of the neocortex wrestling to bring the contents of the unconscious up into the light and so to extend conscious understanding. Apollo incorporates Python as Athena incorporates the gorgon. Hermes and Asclepius carry serpents on their caduceus. What appears, at one stage, as a combat between the ego and the unconscious is, at another level, the integration of the serpent's wisdom into consciousness. Adam and Eve, listening to the serpent, became subtle themselves. They became the new gods.

The greatest difference between the neocortex and the lower brains is language. "Neural machinery does not exist," MacLean writes, "for the reptilian and the limbic brains to communicate in verbal terms."[58] The neocortex goes its own way, processing its own data, largely indifferent to the work of the other brain systems, which MacLean calls "those two ever-present animals which are conscious and wide awake, but hopelessly inarticulate."[59]

If the old brain structures cannot translate their functions into verbal language, how do they communicate? When the major functions of the neocortex are turned down in sleep, perhaps then the limbic and serpent brains can emerge and play in our dreams. The grid of the signifier, with which the neocortex restrains our swarming sensations and perceptions during the day, unravels, and the mind becomes again a river of free-floating images. The dream world is the last asylum of the old brain, and we dream, perhaps, to give the serpent time to share its thoughts with us.

Small wonder that the combat between the sky gods and the serpent has taken hold of the human imagination as the great cosmogonic myth, when the serpent at the base of our brain speaks in a foreign tongue. The rhythms of the lower brains the neocortex must take for mulish obstinacy, or worse; and their signals it reads as the gibber of animals. By the law of action and reaction, however, the more the signals from the lower brains are ignored or misinterpreted, the more serpentine their communications must become.

Little does the neocortex suspect that instinct becomes devious only when distorted by the signifiers of the intellect. "Electrophysiological studies," MacLean concludes in his discussion of the limbic brain, "have shown a functional dichotomy ('schizophysiology') of limbic and neocortical systems."[60] Instinct must translate its wisdom into the signifiers of the cogitating ego, but for the problems in translation the serpent is judged solely responsible.

The communications from the reptile are ineffable. Small wonder, if they must pass through the babble of the neocortex, that they come as though epiphanies from another order; whether from superior beings, who use fear to extract our submission; or from infernal beings, beguiling us to slip back into precortical unconsciousness.

Not every culture, however, has instated the serpent as the signifier of all that is evil and destructive. The celestial dragon, now only a faint constellation in our night sky, in the Orient still enjoys a vigorous popularity. Eastern thought understands the serpent as the primal energy coiled at the base of the spine. Approached arrogantly or naively, the serpent will surely be the demon of chaos. But it is also the source of all creative energy. If correctly understood, this force spirals up around the spinal column to enliven the higher energy centers in the body. In the West we communicate somewhat haphazardly with the serpent through dreams and fantasies. Meditation techniques, as they are practiced in the East, aim at a more systematic discipline for lifting the dam of the signifier, to allow the old serpent to meander more freely through the land.

The truth shines through, if enigmatically, in spite of the myth's degradation in our culture. The serpent coiled around the base of a tree in our iconography, or dangling from the tree over the heads of our first parents, is the kundalini, the dragon both chthonic and celestial. Adam and Eve must invoke the wisdom of the serpent to become fully conscious beings.[61] Apollo needs the waters that flow from Python's well. Herakles needs the golden fruit hidden in the garden of Night. The horn of Acheloos is the horn of plenty, flowing with nectar and ambrosia. Psyche, when she surrenders to the serpent Eros, discovers herself in paradise.

For all the vituperation that the sky gods have heaped upon the serpent, we have not been able to eradicate the image of the serpent as the source of health. The caduceus, with its entwined serpents, is the same totem that Jahweh commanded Moses to raise in the desert to heal the Israelites, which the Israelites continued to worship until King Hezekiah had it destroyed.[62]

Modern medicine, studiously Apollonian, reveres clinical accuracy and dispassionate observation. Nothing would seem farther removed from medicine's concept of its methods and functions than the serpent of ancient myth. Yet the whole profession—doctors, nurses, pharmacists, clinics and hospitals—stands even today under the sign of the coiling serpents, the aboriginal gods. Potent indeed is the icon that can flourish as the river of life even when cursed for bearing the signature of the devil.

Piety bids me conclude with Ovid's happier myth of the cult of Asclepius at Rome, surely the finest celebration in classical literature of the beauty and majesty of the serpent.[63] The Romans, suffering a plague against which all their own medical skills were powerless, sent an embassy to solicit a cure from Apollo's oracle at Delphi. The god instructed the Roman delegates to consult the god's son Asclepius. The Romans, following instructions, proceeded to Epidaurus, famous for its cult of Asclepius. At Epidaurus they requested the citizens to grant them the loan of their god (their cult image, no doubt). The people of Epidaurus were of two minds, some in favor of the request and others against.

That night Asclepius appeared to the Romans in a vision, stroking his ancient beard with his right hand and holding his staff in his left hand. The caduceus is, in Ovid's imagination, *baculum agreste* (line 655), the god's field staff, bearing the serpent as the insignia of the fields, magical talisman of Earth's instinct for regeneration. The god, calming their fears, agreed to accompany them to Rome. Pointing them to the serpent entwined around his staff, he promised to assume that very form the next day, enlarged, of course, to the size appropriate to celestial bodies.

The next day the people of Epidaurus joined with the Romans to gather at the temple of Asclepius, where they prayed to the god to reveal his will by celestial signs. No sooner had they spoken than "the golden god" (*aureus deus,* lines 669–70) appeared in his serpent form. The trembling of the temple on its marble foundations and the gentle hissing of the serpent bore witness to a god's epiphany. The gigantic snake filled the whole temple with his arching neck, and his rolling eyes flashed fire. A priest, recognizing the presence of the *numina* (line 765), calmed the terrified crowds. "Behold, the god," he cried, and commanded the people to observe a reverent silence. "Whoever you are, O most beautiful one," he addressed the serpent, "may your appearance bring good to those who honor you." The serpent nodded his crest and hissed to ratify his covenant with the Romans, who had been foremost in their veneration.

The serpent, gliding down the steps of the temple, turned to make his farewell bow to his ancient altar and home. Then he slid sinuously through the city, along streets strewn with flowers, and came to the curved harbor. There he stopped to give his blessing to the people of Epidaurus, then raised himself up and slid into the Roman ship. The ship, sensing the presence of the numen, sank lower into the water with the weight of the god.

This is the good dragon of our childhood. If Ovid has dipped his pen in Walt Disney's colors, so be it. Ovid's smile reaches the child in us, who laughs to see the dragon festival come around. Being mere minnows, children can more easily follow the magician's wand through the nets of the signifier, less terrified than we, with our more articulate frames, to chance a meeting with the subject face to face.

All gloom and fear were exorcised by the god's happy presence, to accept Ovid's account. The Roman sailors first feasted the god on the shore at Epidaurus; then they unloosed the cables and put out to sea, their ship garlanded in flowers. The snake, coiled in the ship, arched his great neck over the stern to gaze down at "the cerulean waves," as Ovid calls them, a pretty phrase to suggest sky and sea mirroring each other in the eyes of the serpent. For six days, the magic ship sailed westward with its strange cargo, like a solemn religious procession wending its way across the sea.

Rounding the heel of Italy, the ship passed through the Sicilian straits and proceeded northward. At Antium, when the sailors had brought the ship into harbor, the serpent uncoiled his great bulk over the side of the ship, slithered across the sands to the temple of Apollo, and with his respects paid to his father, snaked back across the sand and into the ship. Apollo, pleased by his son's reverence, calmed the waves and the ship sailed on toward the Tiber, with the serpent arched at the bow to survey the passing scene. The ship made a triumphant procession up the Tiber, wending a serpentine path through throngs of Romans—elders, matrons, and the Vestal virgins—gathered to cheer the spectacle (O to have seen that Roman holiday!) and to set up altars along the way, whose smoke perfumed the air in the sacred vessel's wake.

At last the ship reached Rome. The serpent, raising his majestic head mast high, swaying to left and right, surveying the scene for the site to mark for his sanctuary, spied a small spit of land where the river divided into two courses—Insula, the Romans called it, the Island—a miniature Earth emerging from the primal waters. There the Apollonian snake, as Ovid calls him, descended from the ship, resumed his celestial form, and restored the Romans to health.

Asclepius is Apollo's ancient enemy, reborn as his son. The terrifying aspects of the serpent are transformed, in Ovid's playful telling, into aspects of beauty to arouse wonder and bring joy to all who witness them. The old enemy's coat of mail is exchanged for gold plate glittering in the sun—the crusty dinosaur transmuted by Brancusi. Even the serpent's hiss is now a caress, the soft sound of animal contentment, a god's blessing. The subtlety for which the serpent was accursed in Eden here becomes suppleness. In the winding path of this genial spirit flowers seems to spring up as if spontaneously. People celebrate this serpent's epiphany, not in fear but in rapture, and in Ovid's tale the snake seems as enraptured as his worshippers. Gliding through city streets like the master of the labyrinth, arched in majesty over the waves like the Doge enthroned on his barge, tracing his elegant signature across the sand, finding a small earth in the midst of the waters for his cloister and garden—this is the god of the old Eden, welcomed back from exile.

In Rome, by Ovid's account, the god resumed his celestial form, and his serpent persona returned to its position as the totem on the god's staff. Thus Asclepius joined the Romans, and from Rome he has traveled westward, in time, to our lands. Today, the god's staff, graced with the double helix, reminds those who with the eyes to see the god in his emblem that the cursed Other lies at the center of our being, and guards the key of our redemption.

4

Herakles: The Hero
of the Anima

Billy the kid was his own father.
—Asa Evan Sherry (age four)

It is not the mother who is the parent of the child.
—Aeschylus, *Eumenides* 658

I: The Paradigm

The gods, in myth, are the signifiers of absolute Being. They live too
exuberantly, perhaps, in the world of the senses to satisfy a philosopher's
definition of Being, but a fault to the philosophical mind may be a virtue to

the imagination. Since the liveliness of mind and body is, to the mythical way of thinking, the clearest evidence of Being, absolute Being is that state, call it Olympos, where the symphony of the senses is given the richest orchestration.

The gods are pure Being both in their capacity for sensuous and sensual delight and in their transcendence of the constraints of time and space, which define human life. Homer gives Apollo the epithet *hekebolos*, which Pharr translates as "the freeshooter," i.e., striking "according to will."[1] Apollo's arrow is his will. Nothing intervenes between intention and act. Such immediacy in the world characterizes the other gods too, who are not subject to gravity, matter, or time. The gods are, in one of Homer's formulas, those "whose being is forever."

While Homer's gods eat *ambrosia*, which is, literally, their nonmortality, humans eat grain and the meat of animals, which is mortal food. Humans, living within the biological cycle, are subject to the same growth and decay that produces (and disposes of) the food they eat.[2] "Of all the beings that breathe and crawl across the earth," Zeus says in the *Iliad*, "none, I think, is more miserable than a man."[3] Why should the human species be more pitiful than any other, if not because humans alone have, in addition to their vegetable and instinctual bodies, the body of consciousness? Humans, embedded in biological becoming, have the vision to project a world of pure Being, yet this is a world unattainable in the body. The hero myths crystallized as the first articulations of this paradox.

The Greek word *hero* began as a cult term, an honorific title accorded by a community to a distant and legendary figure, whom the community venerated as its primordial ancestor.[4] These communal ancestors, who became the heroes celebrated in myth, were situated in a space between the generation of the deathless gods and our own nonheroic times. They lived not exactly *in illo tempore,* as Eliade calls it, that timeless time, in which the gods exist; nor exactly in our chronological period. Theirs was a bracketed time, just as, in their death, they passed into an afterlife in Elysium, bracketed on one side from the deathless state of the gods, and on the other from the chthonic regions to which ordinary mortals are consigned.

Heroes could claim direct descent from the gods, which endowed them with a special relationship to the gods, manifested in feats of superhuman strength and direct epiphanies from the gods. Yet the hero was not a god, since his parentage on one side (more commonly the maternal) was mortal. Despite his access to their numinous power, the hero was condemned like every mortal to biological necessity. In fact, the hero, whether in cult or in the epic tradition derived from local cults, achieved his full heroic status only after death, when he was honored *as if he were a god.* The heroes in the *Iliad* rouse each other to acts of courage by holding before themselves the hope that they may be honored in their own cities "as a god." As ancestors became, in popular culture, the *daimones* of the clan, the hero became the *daimon* of the larger clan, the tutelary deity of the polis.[5]

But such is the paradox that the hero attains a status comparable to that of the deathless gods only by passing through death. The gods, though imaged with bodies and bodily appetites, transcend biology, but the hero achieves transcendence only by fulfilling his biological destiny. The gods are immortal, but the hero is *immortalized.* As Nagy expresses it, "the hero is incorporated (into the permanent and sacred order of the Olympians) through such cultural media as epic in particular and cult in general."[6]

The immortality of the hero is an idealized escape from biological destiny. The rituals honoring the hero reveal the paradox of the heroic paradigm. The hero's bones were buried in his grave, a custom that would point to the finality of the hero's death. Yet, as Nagy points out, "the traditional emphasis on the hero's bones in cult represents a formal commitment to the promise of immortalization."[7] The games celebrated in a hero's honor were, in fact, the ritualized reenactment of his funeral. The Olympic Games opened with a ritual lamentation, which the women of Elis performed in honor of Achilles' death.[8] The hero's bones, while a mute testimony to the disintegration of the hero's physical being in death, gave promise at the same time of his reintegration after death.[9] The great Panhellenic Games at Olympia were both reenactments of the hero's funeral and celebrations of the hero's successful metamorphosis into his idealized body.

The incompatibility of Being and Becoming produced a crisis of consciousness. The hero, image of the ego struggling to emerge from the matrix of unconsciousness, projected a pantheon of gods to function as the ego ideal. The hero creates his own paternity by projecting a pantheon of archetypes to support him and to reflect back to him his ideal self. "Billy the Kid was his own father," young Asa Sherry once said.[10] On the other hand, as counterpoint to the idealized Olympian ego, the hero projects a world of demonic forces obstructing his struggle toward self-idealization.

This polarity was codified at the first level as the combat between the celestial and chthonic powers. The celestial realm is the realm of imagination, accessible to thought alone, whereas the chthonic realm is, by contrast, immediately and continuously accessible to us, as the body. The ancient heroic paradigm records the struggle of the mind to substitute for the deficient biological body an idealized body in the realm of Being. Mt. Olympos, which the heroes championed and strove to attain, rose up in the archaic Greek mind as the ideal landscape of pure act and pure contemplation.[11]

Yet this great feat of the imagination, to invent Mt. Olympos as the ego's asylum from biology, was also the cause of the great schism in the human mind. Mt. Olympos grew only through the negation of biological destiny; the higher its peaks reached into the ether, the greater was the denial of biological being in favor of an idealized Being. If the earth is cast in the role of the demon, our maternal hearth and, indeed, our body itself are negated in favor of an invented father principle, which is always beyond attainment. We become strangers in our own home, and citizens of a kingdom we can never inhabit.

The alienation is even more striking when the hero's adversary is not some monster of the primeval earth but the very god who is, or might be expected to be, the hero's patron and champion on Olympos. *"The hostility of Apollo and Achilles,"* Nagy writes *"has a religious dimension, in which the god and hero function as ritual antagonists."* [12] Nagy goes on to explore how Athena, though she is the protector of Troy, is also Hector's ritual antagonist. She is also the antagonist of Odysseus, the most Athenian of all the Bronze Age warriors, as Clay has discovered, though her antagonism has been largely effaced in the *Odyssey* by the overlay of the ritual antagonism of Poseidon. [13] Nagy sees here "a fundamental principle in Hellenic religion: antagonism between hero and god in myth corresponds to the ritual requirements of symbiosis of hero and god in cult." [14]

The ritual symbiosis and antagonism between god and hero mark the schism that our signifiers themselves create in the human mind. The hero, a schizophrenic, rejects the earth and displaces his own Ground of Being by creating an idealized Being, but every attempt to scale the heights of Olympos only generates greater confusion among the signifiers and places the subject at a further remove. The hero, celebrated for daring to vault beyond the mortal condition, stands as the paradigm of the human tragedy, since the very power of the mind to project its ideal self is also the cause of the mind's alienation.

II: The Hero

Herakles had the good fortune to be born the son of Zeus. Yet this fortune was his great misfortune, since the love that he enjoyed from Zeus was matched by the vindictive hatred of Hera, the wife of Zeus. Herakles lived out to the fullest extent the conflict between the father imago and the mother imago.

Just as his love child was about to be born to Alcmene, Zeus proclaimed that the next child to be born would grow up to be the ruler of all the lands around Argos. Hera, the terrible stepmother and midwife in this myth, seeing here another opportunity to outwit the father, delayed the birth of Alcmene's son and hastened the birth of Eurystheus. Bound by his own oath, Zeus was compelled to grant the lordship of Argos to Eurystheus. Eurystheus grew up to become not only Herakles' rival but also his master, for whom Herakles was compelled to undertake his twelve great Labors. Herakles was the greatest man of his time, and Eurystheus—who remembers anything of him except that he jumped into a great urn in terror when Herakles appeared with the hound of Hades on a leash? The greatest hero, whose abilities marked him as indubitably of the first rank, was forced to accept second place, and the superior man was made servant to the inferior.

Even at birth Herakles was endowed with superlative strength and courage. Yet his advancement was blocked at every turn by some mysterious and invisible force. He was made a bondsman; that is, he was held in bondage to a complex that negated his every achievement. Each of his labors for Eurystheus was an attempt to free himself from this mysterious compulsion; yet, though he succeeded in each specific combat, he still remained in bondage.

The conflict between the Olympian powers, Zeus and Hera, generates the myth of Herakles. At his birth, and at every stage thereafter until his death, the one force propels him forward with magnificent energy, while the other blocks his action, or visits him with some terrible retaliation. The source of Herakles' confusion remains beyond his control or comprehension. As the victim of a quarrel between his signifiers hidden on Mt. Olympos, Herakles conforms to Hegel's paradigm of the divided self, as Taylor explicates it: "The inner self itself is painfully divided, into an ideal immutable and self-identical being on one side and one plunged in a world of confusion and change on the other. This is the stage of the unhappy consciousness, in which the relation of master and slave, which stoicism claimed to have escaped, reappears, but now within the subject, in the relation between these two mutually incompatible sides."[1]

Not content with simple displacement of his divine privileges, Hera sent two snakes to kill Herakles when he was born. But the infant, fresh from his mother's womb, strangled the snakes, and Tiresias confirmed that Amphitryon and Alcmene had been entrusted with an emissary from the realms of light. The infant was a hero not only because he could strangle serpents, but because he was the kind of infant to whom such serpents would gravitate. Even as he was born, Zeus and Hera had both marked him as their elect.

The infant hero proved his divine parentage and won his first victory. But the archetypes are not so easily distracted, nor do they mildly accept the violence done to their emissaries. To strangle the snakes of the snake goddess is to arouse her greater fury. So Herakles' life took its shape. Each exploit manifesting the Zeus-principle provoked a confrontation with the Hera-principle; conversely, every confrontation with the Hera-principle provoked Herakles into proving himself the true son of Zeus. In this myth the God-image splits into an intolerable polar opposition between the archetypal male principle and the archetypal feminine principle. To resolve this contradiction, Herakles acknowledges the archetypal God-image in its one manifestation only, as the father, and disowns its opposite. Herakles, put in bondage to Eurystheus, who is, as it were, Hera's prime minister, labors time after time to overcome the adverse affects of the hidden signifier, but his labors are in vain. The excluded archetype must remain forever subversive: Hera, throughout the myth, is deceitful and malicious; and Herakles goes to his death without discovering why he was named after her.

Herakles was exuberantly male. The serpents that swarmed over him in his cradle were to be replaced with a long series of other monsters—the hydra, lions, centaurs, the serpent Ladon, fire-breathing Cacus, three-headed Geryon, three-headed Cerberus, to name some of the most familiar—and none of them could withstand Herakles' might. Giants and brigands too fell victim to this mighty warrior. Herakles took on even Hades himself, wounding him with an arrow in the shoulder, "at the Gate among the corpses."[2] Of all the human sons of Zeus, Herakles most closely duplicates Zeus himself as the slayer of chaos demons. As a wrestler, hunter, or archer, and for sheer physical strength and stamina, Herakles had no human equal. He was simply invincible.

Herakles was a randy hero; his appetite was ravenous, his libido magnificent. He was twice married, and for three years played the gigolo to Queen Omphale of Lydia. He consorted with Echidna, the snake goddess in one of her forms, and sired the warlike Scythians. Neither male nor female was safe from Herakles's libido. Herakles once undertook to hunt down a lion, which was ravaging the herds of King Thespius. For the fifty days of the hunt Herakles was the guest of King Thespius. Thespius showed himself a grateful and a gracious host by granting Herakles the right to sleep with all fifty of his daughters, a different daughter every night for fifty nights or, in one version, all fifty in one night. Herakles was the phallic hero beyond all others, the projection of the male fantasy of perpetual phallic arousal.[3]

It is conventional to treat Herakles' great Labors as variants on the theme of the triumphs of civilization over chaos.[4] He wrestled with beasts of every sort; he diverted a river's course to provide better irrigation for the land; he cleaned out the stables for King Augeas, a work of sanitation with neither dignity nor reward. When he arrived at the home of his old friend Admetos and found his friend grieving over the death of his wife, Alcestis, Herakles promptly undertook to wrestle with Thanatos to win back Alcestis from the grave. He did the same favor for another old friend, Theseus, and brought him back up to the light on his other expedition to the grave. When he discovered Prometheus chained to a rock in the Caucasus mountains, Herakles killed the eagle that tore at Prometheus's liver and so released Prometheus from his agony. No wonder Herakles was both the popular idol and the philosophers' ideal.

Yet this idol of manhood was tormented like no other pagan hero, given to the *berserker* rage that, as Dumézil has discussed, characterized the warrior-heroes.[5] Herakles killed two of his boyhood teachers—Eurytos, his teacher in archery, and Linos, his music teacher. When King Laomedon of Troy broke his word and refused to give Hesione in marriage to Herakles after he had saved her life, Herakles returned to Troy with an army, sacked the city, and carried off Hesione by force. Augeas, king of Elis, refused to pay the reward that he had promised to Herakles for cleaning out the royal stables. Years later Herakles returned to Elis with an army and killed the king for his treachery.

On another occasion Herakles fell in love with Iole, daughter of King Eurytos. Herakles won in the archery contest, which the king instituted for his daughter's suitors, but Eurytos refused to honor the victor with the prize. Later, when Iphitos, the brother of Iole, passed through Tiryns, Herakles retaliated by throwing him to his death from the citadel wall. Herakles, now guilty of murder, went to Pylos for purification, but Neleus, the king of Pylos, refused to purify him. Herakles went elsewhere for his purification but later made a punitive expedition against both Eurytos and Neleus. He killed Eurytos and carried off Iole to be his concubine. Then, in his expedition against Neleus, he killed Neleus and eleven of his twelve sons, leaving only Nestor (who would later join the Greek expedition to Troy), none of them guilty of any crime against Herakles. The man who went in search of purification for one murder, when his appeal was denied, became a mass murderer.

Herakles is prone to madness. The myths recognize it explicitly as madness when Herakles hurls Iphitos, an innocent man, from the citadel of Tiryns. Tradition has it that Herakles went to Delphi to consult the oracle regarding a cure for the madness that led to the crime, but the Pythian priestess at first refused him an answer. Herakles, not one to brook opposition, seized the god's sacred tripod, intending to set up his own oracle. Herakles wrestled even with Apollo himself for the tripod, until Zeus put a stop to the fracas. Far from discovering the cause of his madness, at the very shrine of understanding Herakles suffered another attack of the disease for which he sought a cure. This incident repeats the theme of Herakles' journey to Pylos for expiation, where he battled not only Neleus but also Poseidon, the tutelary deity of Pylos, committing many times over the very crime for which he had sought cleansing.

When Herakles approaches catharsis, he displaces his still-unspent anger on to his therapist, and suffers an even greater attack of his disease. The Pythian priestess's refusal to give Herakles the answer he sought, and Neleus's refusal to perform the purification rites—are these not the myth's way of saying that Herakles was not willing to take the cure? Herakles' reactions reveal a man dissociated from his rage, who can remain at its effect, and project its cause as an externalized authority figure—a priestess, a king who thwarts his will, a priest-king like Neleus, or the gods themselves. That Herakles should think himself competent to set up as an oracle, when he knew so little of himself, is irony indeed.

The most memorable and tragic instance of Herakles' madness occurred after his long absence from home, when he had been engaged in bringing Cerberus up from the underworld. Herakles returns from the underworld to his home in Thebes to find his earthly father, Amphitryon, his wife, Megara, and their two sons standing terror-stricken outside the house, expecting imminent death at the hands of Lykos, the ruler of Thebes. With his fury aroused, Herakles goes into the house and kills Lykos. After the murder Herakles gathers with his family at the household altar to perform the purification sacrifice. Again, however, at the moment of purification, an attack of madness overwhelms him.

Euripides, in his *Herakles,* personifies this madness in the form of Lyssa (= Madness), whom Hera sends out of her long-standing jealousy at Herakles' successes. As Euripides tells the story, the externalized Lyssa is internalized as a mad inspiration in the mind of Herakles. While his hands are still blood-stained, and his person impure, why should he not set off for Mycenae and kill Eurystheus too, the overlord who has made his life a misery? That way only one purification will be required to remove the stain of two murders. But the mere thought of Eurystheus is enough to activate a manic rage. At first, when Herakles calls for his weapons, the people around him think Herakles must be joking. But this is no jest. When Amphitryon, his human father, remonstrates with him, Herakles takes him for the father of Eurystheus, and he is further enraged. Now, with his hallucination in full spate, Herakles mistakes his own sons for the sons of Eurystheus, and vents on them his anger and his warrior's superhuman strength. He slaughters his wife and both their children, and would have slaughtered Amphitryon too if Athena had not hurled a great rock against him and knocked him senseless. Herakles is truly a *berserker,* the warrior whose murderous energy turns as easily against his friends as his enemies. Most tragic of ironies, in his madness Herakles perpetrates the very murders the tyrant Lykos had intended, taking on himself the blood guilt that would have fallen on his enemy.

Mistaking his family for the enemy is a clear case of psychological displacement. Eurystheus is his real enemy, at least on the earthly plane, but

Eurystheus is the Alpha male in Herakles' life, and his person is tabu. We understand now Herakles' phenomenal success in killing monsters: all of them are targets of an anger displaced from its original target. But none of these displacements is a satisfactory substitute, and the pain increases until one day Herakles vents his rage on the target that is defenseless and close to hand, since the real target is out of reach and too well defended.

We think of Herakles' madness most in connection with this one episode because Euripides has given us, in his *Herakles,* one of the most vivid accounts from antiquity of the tragic confusion of madness. Yet the pattern, which Euripides so well dramatizes in his *Herakles,* is consistent with Herakles' life story. Herakles destroys his second marriage too, not in overt madness but by bringing home Iole as his concubine. To kill his first wife, then to marry a woman named Husband-Destroyer (Deianeira), and then to introduce a young concubine into her household, bespeaks a man woefully unconscious of his own nature.

Two themes are prominent in the Herakles cycle: a man, unable to find relief from an intolerable burden, destroys what is dearest to him in sheer frustration; in addition, he suffers an outbreak of violence whenever he approaches a resolution of his conflicts. Euripides situates Herakles' murder of his wife and children at the end of the Labors imposed upon him by Eurystheus. Bringing Cerberus up from the underworld is Herakles' last and most awesome trial. His wearisome journeys and his days of servitude are over at last, and Herakles can retire to the bosom of his family. The last words that Euripides puts in the mouth of Herakles before madness descends on him are full of tender pathos. Herakles calms his wife's fears and turns to go into the house. He takes the little ones by the hand, like a ship towing small boats in his wake, he says. "I will not neglect the care of my children," Herakles continues, using the word *therapeuma,* with its connotations of nurturing and service. With this eloquent image of fatherhood fresh on his lips, Herakles leads his children indoors and forthwith kills them.

"Did you really go into the house of Hades?" the incredulous Amphitryon asks in Euripides' play, when Herakles returns from his descent into the underworld. "Yes," Herakles replies, "and I brought the three-headed beast into the light." "How did you do it, in a battle or with the gifts of the gods?" "It was a battle," Herakles tersely replies; "I had the blessed fortune to witness the mysteries of the initiated."[6] It was explicitly recognized in antiquity that Herakles' descent into the underworld was an initiation into the Eleusinian mysteries of Persephone.[7] But the initiation, which served his friends so well, and brought back Theseus and Alcestis from the grave, brought no light, alas, to Herakles in his family relationships.

Herakles repeats the pattern of his first marriage in his relationship with his second wife, Deianeira, though the two marriages, on the surface, bear little resemblance to each other. As Sophocles tells the story of Herakles and Deianeira, in his *The Women of Trachis,* again Herakles returns home after a long absence. During this absence he has been a slave to Queen Omphale of Lydia, as expiation for his murder of Iphitos, the brother of Iole. With his period of servitude completed, Herakles can now return home, purified of blood guilt. But no. On his way home he stops off long enough to kill King Eurytos and carry off the king's daughter Iole as his slave. Again Herakles returns home from a pilgrimage abroad, expecting to celebrate the end of his labors. Instead, he himself becomes the sacrificial victim immolated in the blaze of his own victory. Once again, as Herakles approaches the resolution of his conflicts, the persistent dark force entangles his understanding and pulls him again into bondage to the unconscious.

Herakles is all extremes, the mythical paradigm of a manic-depressive, if not in a strict clinical sense, certainly in the sense that his life shows the extreme and violent mood swings that characterize manic-depressive behavior. Herakles goes to Delphi in penitential submission, but seizes the god's tripod instead. He kills the tyrant threatening his family, only to turn immediately on his kin and kill them too. Time and again Herakles descends into the grave, or travels to the farthest extremities of the world, to do battle with Thanatos, or with the serpents and hounds of the underworld; but at the moment of victory elation turns to a manic fury that plunges him back into the depths.

The mysterious power that undermines Herakles' every achievement is, of course, Hera. Simon, seeing Hera's decision to send madness upon Herakles as an irrational prejudice against him, reads Euripides' *Herakles* as the existential tragedy of the human condition in an irrational universe.[8] "In terms of the play," Simon observes, "[Herakles' madness] does not arise out of any *hamartia* [tragic flaw] of Heracles, or because of any crime he has committed. It is a gratuitous affliction, an expression of Hera's cruel jealousy and desire for revenge against Zeus."[9] Simon echoes the interpretation given by Arrowsmith in his introduction to the play.[10] True, for Herakles himself, the catastrophe that befalls him seems irrational. Euripides exaggerates the apparent irrationality of the universe by heightening the contrast between the malice of Hera, on the divine level, and the innocence and fortitude of Herakles, her suffering victim on the human level. Hera is relentlessly inhuman, whereas Euripides arouses our sympathy for Herakles by portraying him as tender toward his children, loyal to his friends, and pious even after catastrophe befalls him.

Herakles' actions in Euripides' play are indeed irrational. But every psychosis is irrational, and Herakles, in Euripides' play, is certainly psychotic. When he awakes from his psychotic episode to discover that he has killed his own wife and children, he can find no reason in his self to account for such an act. Actions, which we cannot match with an objective correlative in our reason, must be attributed to external agents. Since Herakles' destruction of his home is an irrational act, it must emanate from the irrational principle at work in the universe. Herakles is careful to distance himself from such blasphemy, but the syllogism lies implicit in the play as a whole.

It is not true, however, that the world in which Euripides locates his Herakles is irrational; it is incomprehensible to him, but it is motivated, and the motive is Hera's anger, itself a complex of responses to the social structure that produced Hera as one of its principal signifiers. Hera is the consort and sister of Zeus, yet how great is the disparity, in Homer and the tragedians, between Hera's privileged status and her actions. Even in Homer's world, where the heroic code is most highly honored, Hera acts like a savage beast or a shrew, who invites ridicule or contempt. Why should a culture project such a persona onto the supreme goddess if not to reflect the human situation of the wife trapped in matrimony, and compelled by the patriarchal code to exercise her power only through devious and passive provocations? The bickering in the *Iliad* between Zeus and Hera on Mt. Olympos, her sullen acquiescence to the will of Zeus, and her ruses to subvert his will mirror the feud of husband and wife in a thousand Greek homes. Herakles is the son caught in this hostile fire.[11]

Hera is the signifier of the feminine principle, injured by the insults done to her in the name of the father. With the feminine ideologically suppressed, Hera becomes the Jungian Shadow, whose motives always escape the understanding of the conscious mind. The exaggeration of the masculine principle suppresses the feminine until it becomes a violent counterforce in the unconscious, weighing down the conscious mind with inexplicable burdens and frustrating its intentions.

Herakles has a superabundant Animus, but it does not follow that he has a weak Anima. On the contrary, in Herakles Animus and Anima, the masculine and the feminine, are coequal; each has the power to contradict the other, point for point. The result is a life of high achievement matched by catastrophe, of elation followed by depression. The conflict continues without resolution because Herakles can own the masculine principle, but not the feminine. Zeus, the archetypal male energy, though as much a projection as Hera, is never treated as an alien force in the myth. Though Herakles owes his superhuman strength to Zeus, this infusion of energy from the gods in no way reflects an inadequacy in Herakles. On the contrary, the energy of Zeus belongs to Herakles as his birthright. Men do not interpret the favoritism of Zeus as irrational, but only the opposition of Hera. Zeus, the idealized father, enhances what men see in themselves as their natural gifts.

The mother-nature is Herakles' problem. When the Animus is exaggerated to the point of caricature, as it is in the myths of Zeus and Herakles, the suppressed Anima must, by the homeostatic principle that Jung called the law of compensation, appear as alien. In the myth Herakles is at first ignorant of the cause of the recurrent distress in his life. But on the occasion when he goes to Delphi to seek purification for the murder of Iphitos, the oracle, instead of granting him the purification he seeks, names him for the first time *Hera-kles*: "The Glory of Hera." But the meaning of the oracle eludes him, and Herakles falls into a rage at the oracle, and continues to act as if he were the victim of a conspiracy against him among the gods. Even when named "The Glory of Hera," the hero cannot recognize in the oracle's signifier his disowned kinship with the mother.

Herakles, the son who idealizes his father, sees his mother as the enemy.[12] Herakles emerges from the womb fighting. If Hera is the goddess of childbirth, what are the snakes that threaten his birth if not an image of the birth canal, whose contractions constrict the fetus as it moves out into the world? Apollo, who, in the *Eumenides*, defends the paternal principle by arguing that the mother, a mere receptacle, is a stranger in the birth process, sums up the Herakles complex in a single sentence.[13] The father and son are symbiotically joined, whereas the mother and son are estranged from each other and cast as ritual antagonists. With biology so radically revised, is it fanciful to suppose birth to be a life-threatening experience for the infant emerging from a womb ideologically estranged from the mother?

A detail in Diodorus points to the mother-relationship as the source of Herakles' suffering. According to Diodorus, Alcmene, the mother of Herakles, fearing the anger of Hera, exposed her newborn child in a place that came to be called the field of Herakles.[14] Athena and Hera happened to pass by and see the abandoned infant. Athena persuaded Hera to suckle the child. But Herakles took Hera's breast with such violence that she threw him angrily to the ground. Homer preserves another story that expresses the same hostility: "the son of Amphitryon wounded Hera in the right breast with his triple-barbed arrow, and laid upon her a pain beyond endurance."[15] Hera sends snakes to strangle Herakles when he is born, but he strangles them instead. She offers him her breast to suckle, but he assaults it, and she thrusts him to the ground. The mother-nature is Herakles' enemy; he must strangle it, or be strangled by it. The male ego may interpret all Herakles' adversaries as recurrent forms of the chaos demon, but from a medical perspective the hydra, who sprouts a new head for every head Herakles severs, his reptilian enemies, and his several descents into the underworld are repetitions of that original trauma and the psyche's frustrated search for healing.

Man has "an ideological need," Rank writes, "to blot out the mother-origin in order to deny his mortal nature."[16] Bachofen was perhaps the first to perceive the underlying motive as the desire to replace the tellurian body with a Uranian consciousness. "The triumph of paternity," he writes, "brings with it the liberation of the spirit from the manifestations of nature, a sublimation of human existence over the laws of material life. . . . Maternity pertains to the physical side of man, the only thing he shares with the animals: the paternal-spiritual principle belongs to him alone."[17]

This ideology, in which the mother-origin is debased in order to exalt the paternal-spiritual principle, is implicit throughout Greek literature, and becomes one of the pillars of metaphysics in Aristotle. Herakles bears witness to the suffering that such sublimation imposes. If the paternal principle can triumph only through the negation of the mother, then the liberation of the spirit can be maintained only by increasingly repressive measures against the contradictions. The ideology marks as negative everything associated with the mother—the biological mother, mothering, Mother Nature. Both men and women are rendered equally inauthentic; men, because they must plunder biological being to fashion a metaphysical being; and women, because they must be excluded from the discourse, marked as the signifiers of *that which is not*.[18] When the law of the father prescribes the signifiers, nature is inverted. Whatever is of our own nature we call contrary to nature, and the unnatural is called natural. Hera's jealousy is the name of the father seen from the other side. Her vengeance on the warrior son of Zeus takes place where, in Lacan's diagram, the circle of the Signifier eclipses the circle of Being.[19] But if Hera is the Fury who pursues Herakles, the function of the Furies, as Athena says in Aeschylus' *Eumenides*, is "to order human affairs."[20]

Herakles was the great womanizer in ancient Greek myth, yet his relations with women were a disaster. In the tragic episode, which is the subject of Euripides' *Herakles*, Herakles kills his wife, Megara, and their children, mistaking them for his enemies. On the surface the myth is another instance of Hera's vindictive jealousy toward the son of Zeus. But Hera, besides being the mother, is also the wife. Throughout Greek literature the role of the wife is treated as either vicious or comic, whether the wife is Hera, on Mt. Olympos, or any number of human wives, who are cursed on the tragic stage or ridiculed on the comic stage. Domestic responsibilities are an impediment in the warrior ethos. The matrimonial bond of Zeus and Hera, as projected by the warrior ideology, which idolizes the Animus, is a bondage of the male to the female.

In Euripides' play, Herakles speaks fondly of his love for his children, and we should not doubt his sincerity. Herakles loves his children no doubt, but he loves his adventuring more. When Herakles arrives on the scene in Euripides' play, he has been so long absent from home that the tyrant Lykos can expect to kill his family with impunity. His wife has been living as a virtual widow, in a culture where to be a widow is to be defenseless and to live at the mercy of others. It is, on the surface, irrational that Herakles, at the very moment of his reunion with his children, should turn to them and kill them.

But here too we can read the name of the father. Will the warrior, on his rare and brief visits to his home, forget his craft, to become at once the model husband and father? Herakles kills many enemies in the course of his adventures and carries off women and children as his slaves. When all the world lies open for his booty, why should his attitude at home be different from the attitude with which he engages the world? For a hero like Herakles, who must shoulder the ideology of the father, his family is as much the enemy as the hydra lurking in distant bogs.

Euripides emphasizes the irrationality of Hera's decision to induce madness in Herakles. Seneca, whose rhetoric is too bombastic for modern tastes, loses no opportunity to portray Juno as a virago in his *Hercules Furens*. In the long speech that forms the Prologue of the play, Juno complains of Jupiter's many infidelities and expresses her bitter anger at Herakles' successes. Again we have the portrait of irrational female jealousy, conventional in ancient literature. Yet in her angry diatribe is also the suggestion that Juno's motive for inflicting madness on Herakles is to be found in Herakles himself. Inflated by his success, Juno says, this "violent youth" (*violento iuveni*, lines 43–44) threatens to storm heaven itself. "Nor will he take the peaceful path to the stars; no, he will seek a path through ruin," she argues in defense of her action; "he will desire to rule in an empty universe."[21] Seneca's reading of the myth suggests, as Galinsky writes, that the destruction, which Herakles wreaks in his mad delirium, is the logical consequence of his will."[22] As Owen puts it: "His immolation of his family, his mortal connections, is only the logical result of his immortal aspirations. . . . His madness is merely an extension of his sanity."[23] The madness of Herakles and the fury of Hera are the ideology of the father with its golden crown removed.

While Herakles is married to his second wife, Deianeira, a strange episode intervenes, an adventure like nothing else that any other hero in myth was forced to endure. Herakles was sold as a slave to Queen Omphale of Lydia, but for this indignity Herakles had only himself to blame. When Herakles failed to win Iole, of whom he was enamored, he took her father's rejection of his suit as an insult to his manhood, and brooded revenge. He took his revenge later by hurling Iole's brother, Iphitos, from the citadel at Tiryns. Zeus, offended, ordained that Herakles should expiate this crime against an innocent man by serving as a slave for three years (or a single year in Sophocles' *Women of Trachis*) to Omphale, a foreign queen.

To be the slave of Eurystheus was indignity enough, but how much greater the humiliation for the champion of the father to become a woman's plaything. Strange indeed were the rumors that circulated of Herakles' behavior at the court of the Asiatic queen. Omphale demanded, they said, a role reversal for herself and her stalwart slave. Herakles surrendered his lion skin and his manly club in exchange for a woman's dresses and trinkets. Thus the queen and her slave amused themselves, she wielding the club and playing the invincible Herakles, while he played the queen.

According to the myth, Zeus imposed this extraordinary labor upon Herakles, but surely Hera must have been at work behind the scenes. Omphale, the barbarian queen with a taste for the perverse, is none other than Hera herself in one of her allomorphs, the disowned archetype of the feminine. If Zeus decreed this servitude, the myth intimates that, beneath their overt hostility, the Animus and the Anima are in collusion.[24] In venting his frustrated libido on the innocent Iphitos, Herakles carries his personal animus to such an extreme that Zeus, the paternal principle, hands his hero over into the direct control of the feminine principle. If we accept, with all the necessary qualifications, Jung's theory, that for men perfection is a weightier signifier than completeness, while for women completeness outweighs perfection, Hera's function in this myth is to draw the hero of perfection back toward completeness.[25] The Delphic oracle intimates that Herakles must seek the completion of his nature in the suppressed feminine; but such an intimation rouses him to another frenzied grasp for perfection, which he takes to be his birthright from Zeus, the paternal principle. Failing to decipher the oracular warnings, or the meaning of his servitude, Herakles is finally given over directly to the power of feminine principle, sold into unmediated slavery. Even here, however, Herakles misinterprets his signifiers, and submits to being completely feminized, as if mistaking his need for completeness as a punishment.

The murder of Iphitos marks the point in the Herakles cycle where Herakles puts himself into bondage, regardless of the machinations of Zeus and Hera before his birth. According to some accounts, Herakles' servitude to Omphale is the third in a series of his attempts to expiate the murder, but like the others, it too ends in failure. Herakles goes first to Neleus, king of Pylos, for the purification of his blood guilt, but when Neleus refuses to administer the purification rites, Herakles compounds his crime by killing Neleus and eleven of his sons. Even more heinous, he engages the gods themselves in battle, either Hades alone or, in some versions, Hades, Poseidon, and Hera.

In myth Pylos (= "the Gate" in Greek) is the gate to the underworld. Fontenrose argues that Herakles' battle with Hades "among the corpses at the gate," as Homer describes the incident, is a variant of the great combat myth; Neleus (= "the Pitiless One") he interprets as the death god himself.[26] But the myth holds another significance. If Pylos is the Gate, Neleus is the gate-keeper not only of the underworld but of life itself, to whom Herakles is remanded for healing after his murder of Iphitos. If the Keeper of the Gate refuses to administer the purification, this is the myth's way of saying that Herakles is unprepared for the therapy, and Herakles' immediate reaction— to kill the Keeper of the Gate—proves the point. With the gate now thrown open, and no gatekeeper to monitor the traffic, the archetypes come forward in the full panoply of war against the hero, Hera among them. Misinterpreting her meaning, as he mistakes all her surrogates before her, Herakles engages with her as a warrior engages his mortal enemy, and wounds her in the breast with his barbed arrow. Herakles responds to the warnings of the Anima by intensifying his Animus; where completeness is called for, he labors for greater perfection of the father principle.

With the need for purification now intensified, Herakles goes, or is sent, from Pylos to the oracle at Delphi, where Apollo too refuses to grant Herakles the purification he seeks; instead, he signifies the nature of the problem by naming the troubled pilgrim, who until then had been known as the son of Amphitryon, *Hera-kles*: "The Glory of the Mistress," as Fontenrose translates the name.[27] How could the son of Zeus, famed throughout the world for his virility, be named for the goddess whose machinations stripped him of his divine perfection, threatened his birth, forced him into slavery to an unworthy master, and engaged one enemy after another against him?

Fontenrose has argued that in the Herakles myth Hera represents the ancient, chthonic adversary of the archetypal combat myth.[28] Though assimilated to the company of the sky gods on Mt. Olympos by the time the myths appear in our literary records, Hera is the great dragon, or the mother of the dragons, against whom the champion of the gods must wage battle time after time. In the archetypal combat myth the god (or hero) suffers defeats, and even temporary death; in some versions this death is represented as a period of servitude to the adversary, or imprisonment in the dragon's kingdom.

To treat Herakles as "the opponent of the great serpent," as Fontenrose calls him, is to introduce a coherent principle, and to draw the enormous complexity of detail into a single psychological complex. Yet to assimilate the Greek Herakles to an ancestor in the dragon fighters of the Near East does not so much answer our question as thrust the problem back into a more distant history. "The dragoness of the combat myth," Fontenrose argues, "is likely to become Hera in the Herakles legend."[29] How so? How does this explain the hero's name? Other dragon-slayers are not called "The Glory of the Chaos Demon." There was much for the son of Amphitryon to muse on in the Delphic revelation of his hidden name. Until this moment he had been, as it were, the blind victim of an incomprehensible force, but now, for the first time, the oracle brings the problem into the light, like the stain of the unconscious, in Lacan's metaphor, which infiltrates the conscious mind.[30] But Herakles will be no mother's son. Reacting as he did at Pylos, with violent incomprehension, Herakles seizes the oracular tripod, declares war on Apollo, his physician, and thinks to set himself up as the new oracle. Failing to decipher the signifier issuing from the Delphic oracle, the center of understanding, Herakles is now made a slave (by the will of Zeus, we are told) to

Omphale. The champion of the father must now, for a woman's amusement, play the woman's part. One way or another, the offended principle will exact its due.

Fontenrose, who sees the whole Herakles cycle as a heroized version of the cosmogonic combat myth, interprets Herakles' bondage to Omphale as yet another variant of the hero's combat with the death lord: "Omphale appears to be another form of the seductive demoness," Fontenrose argues, and "Herakles' servitude and effeminacy represent his temporary death."[31] But playing the queen is a death in a different form than wrestling with Thanatos, or beheading the hydra, or killing "the Pitiless One" among the corpses at the gate to the underworld. Omphale is the demoness only in the name of the father.

In his other adventures into the death realm Herakles engages as a warrior with the lords and powers of the dead, and returns as the triumphant champion of the father. But Omphale's realm leaves no place for a warrior's might. If *omphalos* is, in Greek, the navel, Omphale is queen of the umbilicus, but Herakles is so alienated that he mistakes his umbilical connection for a tyranny, unable still to understand his imbalance as incompleteness, not imperfection. Omphale invites Herakles to return to his biological being denied in the name of the father. In his other exploits Herakles is the Hegelian hero, who fights with the Other to the death to assert his self-identity. But the animus of the warrior is inconsequential when the hero is drawn by the umbilical cord back to his mother's womb. Omphale's function is to reveal to the hero his suppressed being, but to receive this revelation he must surrender his signifiers; that is, his phallic supremacy, and regress to the pre-oedipal state, where the infant sees himself mirrored in his mother and models himself in her image.[32]

The hero who emerges from his mother's womb fighting Hera's serpents, and later bites her breast, or wounds it with his barbed arrow, is the son traumatized by the ideological exclusion of the maternal principle from the birth process. Confronting the estranged mother, time after time, as the enemy, Herakles is driven at last, by his own excesses, to return to the scene of the crime, to rectify the imbalance by repeating the birth process. Herakles must now be born not of the father alone, but of the mother and the father.

Since Herakles does not comprehend the process, the myth treats this therapeutic regression as if it were a caricature. Herakles and his umbilical mistress act out each other's roles, as if in the nursery, in the polymorphous stage of infancy before gender identities are firmly established. In comic irony, Herakles is made queen of himself, as if his self-identity could be fully realized only when he gives himself completely over into the power of the Other in its most despised form. Herakles does not so much respond as react. Was he a caricature of the masculine before? Now, to compensate, he will caricature the feminine, as if completeness were to substitute one caricature for its opposite. Since he cannot understand the internal dynamic of completeness, this gender reversal comes upon Herakles as a compulsion imposed by a barbarian caprice. Omphale, though her name signifies her true function, is mistaken for the phallic mother, who castrates her son in the name of motherhood. Herakles' bondage to Omphale parodies the birth process, as Herakles impersonates the mother's daughter, and the mother impersonates the swaggering father-principle. Suppression engenders devious forms of compensation.

Herakles makes himself over into the image of the mother, but no healing comes when the mother is still regarded as the enemy, and called a demoness. Herakles leaves Omphale's nursery with his animus more than ever inflamed against Eurytos, whom he can blame both for the frustration of his libido and for his dishonor.[33] Mobilizing an army, Herakles kills Eurytos, sacks his city, and carries off Eurytos' daughter as his slave. He then sends Iole, his sexual prize, ahead of him, to his home in Trachis, where his wife, Deianeira, has been waiting for him.

Sophocles opens his *The Women of Trachis* at this point, with Deianeira lamenting her fate, like Megara in Euripides' *Herakles,* to be the wife of a husband more often absent from home than present. Though Herakles' two marriages differ in their outward circumstances, yet as Sophocles and Euripides tell the story, it is the same husband in both marriages, as little conscious of his nature in his second marriage as he is in the first.

Deianeira, in Sophocles' play, anxiously awaiting her husband's return, thinks back with horror to her courtship, when Herakles and the great river Acheloos competed as her suitors, and remembers her relief when "the glorious son of Zeus and Alcmene" saved her from the embrace of a river of monstrous and inhuman form. But the marriage bed has given her no joy, she says; instead, she nurtures "fear after fear," with each night bringing a new fear for her husband's safety. Herakles is the same father here as he was in Euripides' play, a man whose home is but of peripheral interest. Deianeira puts it bluntly: Herakles sees his children as seldom as a farmer visits his outlying fields—at seed time and at harvesting.[34]

A strange and pitiful sight interrupts Deianeira's lament. A group of women approaches the house, with Iole among them, led by the herald Lichas. They are slaves, Lichas explains, whom Herakles has dedicated "as the first fruits to the gods of his land," to celebrate his victory over Eurytos.[35] The herald goes on to explain that Herakles sacked the city of Oichalia and took the women captive to avenge himself for the reproach that he had been a slave to the barbarian Omphale.[36]

Moments later, however, an informer claims that the herald's story is a fabrication. Not Omphale, he says, but Eros was the motive for Herakle's punitive expedition against Oichalia. Eros alone, the informer claims, be-witched Herakles into taking up arms against the city.[37] When Eurytos refused to surrender his daughter to Herakles, "for his secret bed," as the informer puts it, Herakles invented a pretext to destroy the city and capture the king's daughter. Through the informer, Deianeira discovers that the young captive, whose silence and noble manner have already aroused her compassion, is her husband's concubine. So quick to exact reprisal when his own honor is at stake, Herakles is indifferent to a woman's honor, whether the woman be his wife or his slave. His bondage to Eurystheus and Omphale has given him no understanding and taught him no compassion.

The two versions of Herakles' motives are contradictory, but only on the surface. Enamored of Iole, Herakles takes rejection as an insult, and retaliates by killing her brother Iphitos. Humiliated still more when he must submit to Omphale's caprice, Herakles returns to the site of his original insult with his animus intensified. Yes, it was his libido that drove him to kill first Iphitos, then Eurytos, and then to carry off Iole as his booty. These are the actions of a libido, which turns first to anger and then to sadism, when its impulses are thwarted. Sexual satisfaction, in such a context of desire, demands the de-struction of the sexual object's relations with the world, and then the com-plete subjugation of the sexual object. When, in Sophocles' play, Herakles extracts a promise from his son Hyllos that he will take Iole as his wife after his father's death, the motive is less a concern for Iole's welfare than the male anxiety that his sexual prize may be fondled by alien hands.

When Deianeira is told the truth by the informer, she calls the Eros that holds Herakles in thrall a disease, and she would be mad, she claims, to hold him accountable.[38] She could not be angry with him before, she says, how-ever often he was sick with this chronic condition. But now, she says, he expects her, who had called him good and trustworthy, to share the same bed with his concubine, and lie with her under the same coverlet. Deianeira fears that Herakles will be her husband in name alone, while he plays the husband's part with a younger woman. In her despair Deianeira remembers the occasion when the centaur Nessos had sexually assaulted her as he was carrying her across a river. Herakles had killed the centaur, with an arrow dipped in the hydra's venom. As he was dying the centaur gave Deianeira a secret potion, mixed of his blood and the hydra's venom, which would be an effective an-tidote, he claimed, to prevent Herakles from loving any other woman—the perfect fantasy of any one who has ever hoped to hold his or her lover secure.

Deianeira, mindful of the centaur's warning, had kept the potion a secret all the years of her marriage, and had refrained from experimenting with it, despite Herakles' promiscuity. But now, with her patience at its breaking point, she withdraws into the house, takes a robe, smears it with what she thought (or hoped) was a medication, but was in fact a deadly toxin. Putting the robe in a casket, she hands the casket to Lichas, with instructions to take it to Herakles, who is still at the shore, where he is receiving a victor's triumph from his people. Lichas is to present the robe as gift to Herakles from his wife, and must press him to wear it, for his wife's sake, when he celebrates his victory.

Herakles accepts the gift, albeit with some equivocation, and dons the robe. Then, as he performs his sacrifice of thanksgiving at the altar of Zeus, in the noonday sun, heat and light work to activate the poison, which glues the robe to Herakles' flesh and consumes his body with excruciating pains. Herakles calls this torture that befalls him a disease, but to the end he sees the disease as inflicted on him from without. Stricken with the poison, Herakles addresses his once-mighty hands, his back, and arms, now debilitated, and recalls the victories that his great strength had won in the past. "I proved myself in a thousand labors," Herakles cries, "and no one raised the victory trophy over me. But now, with my joints unhinged, and my flesh torn, I have become the prey of a hidden destroyer." [39] The destroyer, which has now come to light in such a terrible form, is Eros, the disease that Deianeira calls his chronic condition. Juno (i.e., Hera), in Seneca's *Hercules Furens,* invokes on Herakles the most terrible of curses, when she decides to send on him the madness that will lead him to kill his family: "Other enemies he has conquered. Now let his enemy be himself." [40]

Deianeira, as Sophocles portrays her, is innocent of any intentional malice. She affects to accept Herakles' disease as her woman's fate, and her strategy to cure him of his disease seems, on the surface, to have no guile in it. Rather, it reveals a terrible misunderstanding of the centaur's motives when he had given her the potion. This Deianeira, Jebb writes, "has been recognized by general consent as one of the most delicately beautiful creations in literature. She is indeed a perfect type of gentle womanhood; her whole life has been in her home; a winning influence is felt by all who approach her." [41]

Seneca is not so kind to Deianeira. In his *Hercules Oetaeus,* which is modeled on Sophocle's play, Deianeira's nurse describes her, when the new concubine is introduced into the house, as a fury, a tiger, a maenad. [42] Deianeira then appears on stage and invokes Juno (= Hera) as her avenger. She calls on Juno to raise up a serpent "vaster than the marsh," or some other monstrous beast to punish Herakles. If no such beast exists, Deianeira proclaims herself willing to be that monster in heart and mind. [43] This Deianeira scoffs at those grandiose myths of Herakles' triumphs on behalf of civilization. "He is a trifler," she says, "nor does glory spur him on. No, his guest is maiden's chambers. If any is denied to him, she is ravished." [44] This Deianeira bluntly rejects the conventional interpretation that Herakles killed his first wife and their children in a fit of madness. Should she wait, she asks, for him to feign another fit of madness and do away with her? For that, she claims, is Herakles' manner of divorce. And he is always innocent, she continues; for he has made the world believe his stepmother Juno to be the cause of his crimes.[45]

Many will prefer Sophocles' Deianeira, a woman who is compassionate, long-suffering, and well intentioned, if naive, and dismiss Seneca's virago as a symptom, perhaps, of Roman decadence. But are the two Deianeiras so very different? Seneca has made explicit what Fontenrose calls her "demonic origin."[46] Sophocles has given the demon a portrait of more subtle nuance, but in either case Deianeira is true to her name as the Husband-Slayer.

Would "the perfect type of gentle womanhood," as Jebb calls Sophocles' Deianeira, compare her husband's relations to his children to a farmer's visit to his fields at sowing time and harvesting? Would she express her bitter resentment that her husband should expect her to share her marital bed with his concubine? Would she use a secret charm to end her husband's womanizing, and administer it to him with covert means of persuasion?

Myths are full of tragic misunderstandings, in oracles misinterpreted and prophecies ignored or forgotten. As Sophocles shapes his version of the events, the death of Herakles at his wife's hands is certainly an accident. But myth knows nothing of accidents. It was no accident that Oedipus, abandoned by his parents in his infancy, should return to his home to kill his father and claim his mother's bed. It was no more an accident that led Deianeira, as an injured and angry wife, to assume the dying centaur's goodwill and take his poison for a therapy. Sophocles gives us the portrait of a wife who, in struggling to be the model of forbearance, however often she is injured by her husband, reveals the tragic disparity between the latent emotions and the manifest rationale, by which they are disguised and justified. Deianeira's opening speech in Sophocles' play is full of bitterness at her married state, which, as she describes it, is a shell without substance.

When Deianeira first sees the captive women, she is moved by compassion, since their fate is a foreboding paradigm of the common fate of all women, herself included. When she discovers, however, that the silent Iole is her husband's concubine, she delivers a speech full of the anger of a woman whose marriage has been a continual insult. We would be naive to suppose that a woman who declares herself provoked past all tolerance would act with unalloyed goodwill toward her husband. If this Deianeira can assume the purity of her own motives, and the goodwill of the centaur who attempted to rape her, such naiveté only reveals how far her outward person is estranged from her own being.

The tragedy of Sophocles' play is that Herakles and Deianeira live as strangers to each other because they are strangers to themselves. Each destroys the other unwittingly; in doing so the man destroys himself, and the woman, herself. Herakles, though he has endured a life of humiliation (from his overlord Eurystheus, from Neleus, from Apollo's oracle, from Eurytos, who rejected him, and from Omphale), can see no reason for his wife to take offense at his concubine. On the contrary, he expects her to join him in celebrating his latest sexual acquisition. On the other hand, Deianeira, like Megara before her, has long endured her humiliations in silence. What husband would expect his loyal and uncomplaining wife to turn suddenly into his destroyer?

As Herakles sees no offense in his behavior, Deianeira can see none in administering to her husband a secret charm to cure him of his wayward libido. Seneca's Deianeira is consciously duplicitous, but Sophocles' Deianeira is duplicitous because she dare not allow herself to be fully conscious. "Something of the centaur's duplicity . . . speaks through her," Segal writes; "her language too enters into the pattern of double-meaning and deceit which had begun with the appearance of Herakles' emissary on stage."[47] In willing herself to suffer the indignities of her marriage in silence, she becomes so estranged from her own being that she can believe herself to be healing her husband, and securing his love, even as she is destroying him. If Herakles' disease is his wayward libido (his Eros, as Sophocles names it), and the physician is his desperate wife, what else can the cure be but castration?

Herakles and Deianeira, in Sophocles' play, are both alienated from their own being by the social expectations—he by his exaggerated phallicism, and she by her compensating image of the ideal wife who surrenders her identity to enlarge his—and they cannot recognize in their own acts the symptoms of their affliction.[48] The unresolved, and unrecognized, contradiction underlying their public personas leads them inevitably toward self-destruction, since the self in both cases is a hollow construct. Herakles and Deianeira are husband and wife in name alone. They do not live with each other; he visits her on occasion, for the planting and the harvesting, as Deianeira expresses it. She has no share in his life, except to rear his children, since his life is enacted on a stage outside the home. What she, as a woman and wife, thinks or says is outside his frame of reference, since her life unfolds in the seclusion of the home, which is alien territory to the man. This alienation is heightened when we find that, because of the murder of Iphitos, Herakles and Deianeira have been uprooted from their own home and forced into exile in Trachis, where they live as "the guests of a stranger."[49] Even their home is theirs only by the courtesy of someone else.

The Women of Trachis is the story of the reunion of a husband and wife after a long separation. Deianeira has in her possession the tablet on which Herakles had inscribed the oracular message from Dodona years before. This oracular tablet allows her to hope that soon Herakles can become her husband in fact as well as in name. Herakles too relies on the oracle to support his hope that he can retire from the warrior's life to domestic security. But again a signifier misread turns out to be a prophecy of doom.[50]

How could the reunion be anything but doomed when the partners know so little of each other? Throughout the whole play the husband and wife do not once set eyes on each other, nor exchange a single word. Whatever Herakles has to say to his wife, he communicates through his herald, who is his public voice, and through the silent testimony of the newly captured slave women. An informer contradicts the public persona, which Herakles presents through his herald, and reveals to Deianeira a more intimate truth. On her side, Deianeira communicates with her husband only through the herald (his herald, not hers), and with the masquerade of the robe. When the poison has done its fatal work, Deianeira learns of her husband's agony only through their son Hyllos. By the time Herakles appears on stage his wife has withdrawn indoors, to commit suicide, and he learns of her suicide from Hyllos, the hapless son, whose responsibility is to explain and defend his mother and father to each other. Whatever Herakles and Deianeira discover of each other's motives, they learn only through the mediation of some third party. *The Women of Trachis* is the tragedy of two people, joined in the matrimonial bond, who share no intimacy, since they relate to each other only through their public personas.

Even in Sophocles' treatment of the myth Deianeira is not as innocent as Jebb finds her. She has her private misgivings about using the centaur's potion (which she calls "the nurseling of the hydra") as a love charm, and airs these misgivings with the women of Trachis, who form the chorus of the play, to elicit their support. Even when they voice their approval, however, she enjoins secrecy on them: "for even if you do shameful deeds in the darkness, you will never fall into disgrace."[51]

Deianeira informs her women friends in this speech that the centaur had secretly shown her how to draw the hydra's gall from his wound, and had warned her to keep it in a secret place, away from the heat and light of the sun. When she sends the anointed robe to Herakles, she charges Lichas that the robe not be seen by the sun, nor by the sacred enclosure, nor by the sacrificial fire, until Herakles "stands forth conspicuous in the sight of all, and presents it to the gods on the day of the bull-slaying."[52] For so she had promised, Deianeira continues, that when she received Herakles safely in their home, she would present him to the gods, radiant and freshly garbed.[53]

Deianeira's relations with the women, who form the chorus of the play, is conspiratorial throughout. She enlists their sympathy for her pain at receiving into her house "merchandise that will shipwreck my mind."[54] She shares with them her secret shame, her secret fears, her secret anger, and her secret strategy. Darkness, secrecy, and subversion characterize Deianeira's acts and words in this play as much as the sweet femininity, which draws Jebb's admiration. She is practicing occult magic, and she knows it. When she resorts to magic charms, Segal writes, "she enters the dark mythic world of the

Centaur and the Hydra which traps her in the irrational, subliminal violence of her own mind."[55] The play has come down to us aptly named after the chorus—the Trachinian women—being a play about women's work—the whispering conspiracies, and the charms, mysterious and terrible, which women practice on their husbands. What Zeitlin says of Greek tragedy in general holds true for this play: "The house has its many kinds of secrets that men do not share."[56]

When the whole world applauds the champion of the virile force, how could a wife's actions be other than covert? What language would a woman have, even to commune with herself, when the phallus is enthroned as the signifier of civilization, and woman's existence is excluded from, and by, the network of signifiers? "Herakles and Deianeira speak virtually different languages," Segal writes.[57] The truth is even worse. Deianeira is prohibited from possessing a language since the name of the father proscribes woman's very being. "The woman's 'native tongue,' " Rank writes, "has hitherto been unknown or at least unheard."[58] Deianeira can express herself only enigmatically, and Iole, Herakles' slave, is literally speechless.[59]

If Deianeira's motives are obscure because a valid language is denied to her, Herakles too suffers since he must conform to an ideology that dissociates him from his being. "Have I taken a secret bane into my house?" Deianeira asks when the informer reveals the true status of Iole, the woman whom Herakles has raped and offered up as the first fruits of his warrior's exploits.[60] The silent presence of Iole on stage, her anonymity, and the confusion as to whether she is a mere slave or a new sexual partner bear witness to the deep-seated incoherence in Herakles himself. Herakles does not communicate with his wife, nor with Iole, nor indeed with any women. He subjugates them to his will. The only language he possesses is violence. Deianeira takes this kind of language for a deception, which it is, though the herald Lichas claims that Herakles intended no deception, and she retaliates with deception for deception. Deianeira clothes her husband with a robe anointed with a poison that devours him "like the venom of some deadly viper."[61] Herakles and Deianeira are both victims of a semiotic code whose function is to exclude each from the other and from themselves.

The fearlessness for which Herakles is rightly admired is only a persona. Herakles is fearless, provided the signifier remains hidden and alien, inscribed in the register of the chaos demon. When the Other masquerades as wild beasts and demons, Herakles can play out his warrior's role with the greatest conviction, thinking to release the masculine energy from the coils of the feminine. But underneath the phallic hero's bravado is a man's simple fear of being feminized. When Herakles writhes in his death agony, in Sophocles' play, with his great strength undone, he calls to his son to pity him "weeping and shrieking like a girl."[62] No man, he says, had ever seen him act like this before, "but without complaint I was obedient to my evils. But now, though once a man, I have been found a woman."[63] Herakles, in Euripides' play, makes the same lament. Here too the strong hero, who has braved so many terrors, discovers that his greatest calamity is to be reduced to weeping: "I, who was tested in ten thousand labors, have been brought to this state that I never thought would happen, to pour tears from my eyes."[64] The catastrophe, which no enemy could accomplish, falls upon Herakles in his own home.[65]

The warrior's animus may be successful against beasts in the wild, but catastrophic when the enemy is within. At his death Herakles identifies the centaur as his destroyer, but the centaur is only an intermediary. The toxin that destroyed him was "the nurseling of the hydra," which he thought he had killed. The hydra, in turn, was the nurseling of Hera, the mother-origin, against which Herakles waged war all his life. The oracle, which Herakles had received from his father at Dodona, foretold, with an oracle's ironic ambiguity, that Herakles would die at the hands of no living being, but by some dead creature.[66] The dead creature was the feminine principle, which Herakles thought he had killed in the name of the father.

When the feminine is proscribed, its manifestations must conform to the ideology, and become dark and duplicitous in fact. Hera becomes the imago of the cruel stepmother, and Deianeira the modest wife who surreptitiously castrates her husband. The Herakles myth, true to the psychological facts, reveals that the law of the father spells the alienation of the son from the mother, of men from women, of humans from the earth, and of the mind from itself.

Herakles, for all his faults, was a hero because he could claim Zeus for his father, but also, and more important, because he bore the confusion of his signifiers with dignity and courage. In accepting his destiny, to be a brute with words, Herakles becomes the exemplar of the human spirit struggling to achieve consciousness, whatever the cost. Going beyond mere endurance, Herakles courts his destiny as his beloved. She is Megara, Hippolyta, Omphale, Iole, Deianeira, the many-headed hydra, and all the other nurselings of the chthonic mother: the signifier, which Herakles tragically misunderstands.[67]

Whether Herakles was a hero or a god was a question even the ancients could not resolve—he was so fully human in his faults, so fully divine in his daring. The myths show their ambivalence by granting Herakles two forms in the afterlife. In the *Odyssey* Odysseus sees the image of Herakles in the underworld (his *eidolon*), looking baleful, still carrying his bow and wearing his awesome golden baldric.[68] But this was only a phantom. Herakles himself, Homer adds, was on Mt. Olympos, dining with the gods, and married to Hebe, daughter of great Zeus and Hera of the golden sandals.

The apotheosis of Herakles may be a late addition to the myth, but even so, it antedates Hesiod and the *Odyssey*.[69] Elysium was, as Nagy puts it, the place where the hero's body and *psyche* were reintegrated and reanimated by the breezes of Zephyros blowing from Ocean's stream.[70] But some old fabulist, understanding even Elysium to be at best a heroic compromise, spirited Herakles from the Elysian Fields and laid him on Hera's threshold.[71] Hera, the midwife unwilling to see any creature abandoned on the margin of Being, waved her wand, and Herakles woke to find himself on Mt. Olympos, a neophyte to be sure, but a metaphysician nonetheless. Hera endowed him with her own youthfulness, called in the myths Hebe, her daughter; and the old gods smiled to see their hero exchange rings with his eternal youthfulness and grace, meaning and being exactly coinciding at last.

5

The Divine Presence
In Homer's *Iliad*

The gods are terrible if they are seen face to face.
—*Iliad* XX.131 (trans. Samuel Butler)

The ideal of a whole, whether of the whole personal being or of the world, is an imaginative, not a literal idea. The limited world of our observation and reflection becomes the universe only through imaginative extension. It cannot be apprehended in knowledge, nor realized in reflection. Neither observation, thought, nor practical activity can attain that complete unification of the self which is called a whole. The *whole* self is an ideal, an imaginative projection. Hence the idea of a thorough-going and deep-seated harmonizing of the self with the Universe (as a name for the totality of conditions with which the self is connected) operates only through the imagination—which is one reason why this composing of the self is not voluntary in the sense of an act of special volition or resolution. An "adjustment" possesses the will rather than is its express product. Religionists have been right in thinking of it as an influx from sources beyond conscious control—a fact that helps explain, psychologically, why it has so generally been attributed to a supernatural source and that, perhaps, throws some light upon the reference of it by William James to unconscious factors. And it is pertinent to note that the unification of the self throughout the ceaseless flux of what it does, suffers, and achieves, cannot be attained in terms of itself. The self is always directed toward something beyond itself and so its own unification depends upon the idea of the integration of the shifting sense of the world into that imaginative totality we call the Universe.[1]

The sockeye salmon, after spending its first year maturing in a mountain lake, slips from the lake to the river where it was spawned, and from one river to the next, until it reaches the Pacific Ocean three hundred miles away.[2] With three years spent roaming the millions of square miles of ocean, the salmon then regroup at the mouth of the river where they had issued into the ocean, and once assembled, begin their heroic ascent to the same shallow riverbed where they were spawned, there to mate and forthwith die. For the downward journey the smolt, scarcely more substantial than the element in which they move, are carried mostly by the force of gravity. But on the return journey the full-grown salmon is an engineer who must not only resist gravity but use gravity and wave mechanics to propel a body of considerable mass against a hard current, past shoals and rapids, for hundreds of miles. The goal of this heroic effort is sex and death, the one after the other in quick succession.

The salmon's propulsion into life and its steep ascent to its home and grave are the paradigm for the life cycle of all organisms. Biology organizes nature by using the laws of nature against themselves, as it were, to seize some portion of energy from the jaws of universal entropy. Each organism is only a momentary and local reversal of entropy; in time the organism submits to necessity, and passes the rhythm of life to the next generation.

The function of biology being to wrest energy from matter and convert it to organic forms, even the simplest organism is never merely at the effect of its environment. The amoeba must reach out into the environment for the materials necessary to continue biology's inscrutable experiment. In the amoeba, however, biology has so closely assimilated itself to the laws of inorganic matter that, to our eyes, the amoeba seems little more than a reflex response to external stimulus.[3] The salmon smolt, slipping carelessly downstream, seems, again to our eyes, hardly more complex than the amoeba. But in the mature salmon biology makes a bold advance over reflex action, as if it had so penetrated the laws governing matter that it had become their master rather than their slave. If, in our anthropocentrism, we take the amoeba for a simple reflex mechanism, we can hardly deny some kind of intelligence in the salmon. Reflex alone never carried a salmon upstream; here we must assume will and intention, even if we are unwilling to discern them in the first wiggles of the spawn. The salmon must, like us, study nature, both to be in nature and to outwit nature, and no doubt thousands are lost every year who are careless in their studies or overbold in their ambition.[4]

Intelligence in the salmon we call instinct because form and thought are so closely synchronized that there is, or so we think, small room for discourse between the thought and the act. But as biology opened up another avenue, diverging from instinct toward what we call the intellect, a wider space opened up between the biological form and the possible actions of that form upon matter. The space, widening, as Bergson puts it, between representation and action, becomes consciousness.[5]

Other animals share with us, no doubt, the faculty of representing the external forms of the world, the better to act on them, whether for nourishment or defense. But in humans this faculty took yet another turn, and we found ourselves able to represent the world through word and symbol. Language, through which we could articulate perceptions with greater precision, opened up the world for seemingly limitless exploration. But more momentous still, words, at first a vehicle for simple representation, have the power to signify. Humans, discovering significance, opened up a world hitherto unknown, and the revelation reverberates through all ancient myth.

If Achilles commands our greater admiration and compassion than the wordless salmon, it is because he must, in addition, translate his being into meaning. Achilles must inhabit two worlds; two labyrinths overlapping, influencing, and contradicting each other: biological being, marked by the passage of time; and the imagination, where representations of Being proliferate signifiers into infinity. The salmon need not look first for the model (or so we imagine) before each audacious leap, but can trust to instinct to mold his body to the occasion. But Achilles, molding his body to the determinacies of time and matter, and his mind to the determinacies of his signifiers, must search through those signifiers for the signifier that is himself.

The intellect imposes the signifier upon Being, to be the signifier of Being; yet Being, which is life itself for a biological being, always escapes the articulations of the intellect. "There are things that intelligence alone is able to seek, but which, by itself, it will never find. These things instinct alone could find; but it will never seek them."[6] Homer's theology reveals the weight of the paradox on human consciousness.

The gods are the signifiers of Being, yet the Being they signify lies beyond the reach even of the heroes who, godlike though they be, still inhabit biological time with its rhythmic pulsations of coming into and passing out of Being. In the *Phaedrus* Plato, allowing us one of those memorable occasions when the philosopher and the poet in him converse as one master with another, imagines a state of bliss where all desires are fulfilled.[7] Here, Socrates imagines, the gods, marshaled in eleven companies, travel to and fro beneath the vault of heaven, each performing his or her allotted task in the cosmic order. But when they go to their feasts, they move even beyond the vault of heaven, taking their stand on what Socrates calls "the back of Ouranos."[8] We translate Ouranos somewhat weakly as "sky," but, following Worthen's cue, I take Ouranos to be the sky inscribed with signs and signatures.[9]

This region Socrates now attempts to describe, daring to imagine a space never adequately perceived or represented by any poet. The gods, standing beyond representation and metaphor, contemplate the vision of that which has neither color nor figure; the pure, ineffable Being in its very beingness (to paraphrase Plato's almost colloquial Greek). These Socratic gods, Being contemplating Being, erase the signifier, and cancel the space between seer and seen.

Homer's rambunctious gods are too implicated in the world to win Plato's endorsement. Projected by a shame culture, Homer's gods are concerned with form and appearance, for place and position, protocol and ceremony. If they are absolute, they are absolute only, some would say, in matters of etiquette and prerogative.[10] Yet Plato, or Socrates, names his gods after Homer's gods (though by then they were, no doubt, the planets), and in one article at least they meet Plato's definitions of godhood. Homer's sub-Ouranian Olympians may vex themselves over rank and privilege, but never over Being. Indeed, the mystery that they should be related to creatures who slip in and out of Being casts a shadow over their feasts, but the melancholy note is not born of doubts of their own existence. Death, for the gods, is a mystery that grazes their being, but not the annihilation of self and Being.

Homer's heroes, on the other hand, vexed by Being and Nothingness, fashioned two topographies of the imagination to resolve the problem: Olympos and the underworld; the one, the seat of Being; the other, the destiny of beings who, when the radiance of Being has passed over them, disappear from the light. And what could better express the haunting anxiety regarding Being than Homer's iconography of the afterlife? Is death non-Being? No, it is a shadowy kind of Being. The dead are phantoms. But phantoms are real. The Egyptians honored their dead as "an *akh,* an 'effective spirit.' "[11] The shades in Greek myth and literature are certainly as effective as the shades in Egyptian thought; yet, as Anticleia explains to her son Odysseus in the underworld, the dead have neither substance nor vitality.[12] The beings in the underworld, experiencing neither Being nor non-Being, are *eidola*—"images"—mere traces of Being. Odysseus thinks to console the shade of Achilles in the underworld by pointing to the honor Achilles enjoys even in death, but Achilles explains the true situation.[13] The phantom of Achilles, for the moment animated by the blood sacrifice, talks with Odysseus as one person to another, but it is only a shadow, enjoying at most the shadow of a warrior's honor. Honor was a shadow even when Achilles was still alive, a word passed from mouth to mouth, to clothe and sustain his metaphysical body. Most of it he had paid out over the years to his signifiers, to give his life meaning, but what use were they now, if meaning was purchased at the price of life itself?

Only a species haunted by Nothingness could imagine for itself an afterlife marked by Being and Nothingness simultaneously. Homer's Olympians, knowing next to nothing about the determinacies of time, need no afterlife in which to mend themselves; like animals, they can rest confident that Being itself will sustain them forever. His heroes, on the other hand, entranced by Nothingness day in and day out, dared to imagine for themselves an Elysian field, where they could correct the errors of time and arrive at Being. But the templates, which Odysseus observes in the shadows of the underworld— Ajax, implacable in anger; Herakles, prowling for new prey; Achilles, bitter at his sacrifice of life to honor—point to the chasm separating the signifiers on Olympos from even their bravest warriors and creators.

"How soon a psychology of archetypes begins to sound like a mythology of Gods!" Hillman writes.[14]

In the quarrel between Achilles and Agamemnon in *Iliad* I, Achilles is so shamed by Agamemnon's insults that he is tempted to draw his sword and kill him. But Athena, in an epiphany vouchsafed to him alone, advises Achilles to stay his sword, promising him rewards three times over in return for Agamemnon's insults.[15] Rewards? Achilles is bewitched by the word. How can a warrior refuse when his signifiers promise rewards? The chief business of the signifier is to dispense rewards, since the signifiers speak from the center of Being, the source of all rewards. But the reward of the signifier is the eclipse of Being. How could the young Achilles comprehend that life offers no rewards, except life itself? And, since he had already made his choice, in his first man-to-man combat on the plains of Troy, to exchange life for rewards, how could he now refuse the rewards that would give him back a meaning in exchange for his life?

But what reward did Athena mean? Was she referring to the compensation, which Agamemnon would offer to Achilles through his ambassadors in Book IX? If so, why did she not present herself in Achilles' tent that night to persuade him to accept Agamemnon's offer? Surely Athena did not mean the compensation Achilles receives from Agamemnon after the death of Patroclus. Would even a god be so callous as to see significance in those gifts? Perhaps Athena, watching over Achilles' destiny with heavenly eyes, was referring to the honor Achilles would receive in perpetuity in cult and epic song. We shall never know. The god, having given Achilles a sufficient reason to endure his humiliation, passes from view, and no further reference is made to the episode.

"Have you come to witness the hybris of Agamemnon?" Achilles asks, startled by Athena's rude tug on his hair and her eyes, flashing with the presence of Being itself.

"No," Athena replies, "I have come from Ouranos [that is, the vault of signifiers] at Hera's request, who loves you both equally, and cares for you in her heart." [16]

We can infer certain social messages coded in Athena's epiphany. Agamemnon is the Alpha male in the Greek army, whose person is tabu. [17] While it is a mistake for him to rely so heavily on the protection of the tabu, that is a matter between him and his signifiers. Even a commander's hubris will not justify the warrior's revenge. And it is certainly hubris. Insulted in his very manhood, Achilles is so stripped of honor that there is no salvaging his being, at least in a warrior society, where being is identified with honor, except by revenge; yet revenge is tabu. None of the soldiers and commanders stands up to defend Achilles in the assembly. Will they show greater support if Achilles kills Agamemnon? The occasion demands revenge and prohibits it at the same time. While Achilles deliberates, bemused by his signifiers, Athena, herself a signifier, comes with an offer from Being itself to extricate him from disgrace. It was not time for Achilles to hazard his life for mere significance; but it was the moment when Achilles, hedged around by the implications of Being and meaning, first saw the need to find the subject in the gaze of the signifier. [18]

It may seem reductionist for us to translate Athena's vivid epiphany as a thought in the mind of Achilles, yet she is exactly that. Whatever else Homer's gods may be, they are not persons. [19] No human in Homer's world is ignorant of the distinction between gods and humans, though they may be deceived by apparent similarities between the two orders of being, and gods may trade on the similarities for their own inscrutable purposes. Gods may look and act like human persons; they eat, sleep, mate; they have family quarrels and extramarital affairs; they foster the arts; they have territories and hierarchies, tempers and dispositions. Yet woe to any human who mistakes a god's persona for a person. Gods are representations, visible not to human eyes but only to the privileged vision of a seer. Homer's heroes do not witness the gods seated in council, reclining at the table, or making love. Homer grants us to see the gods in their immediacy, but for his heroes the gods' presence must be mediated by some visible sign or persona; if they are attentive, they may detect in the persona's comings or goings some small token of the divine presence.

Athena's epiphany to Achilles lasts but a second, being not a moment of narrative in the ordinary sense, but occupying that space of consciousness, which Bergson posits between representation and action.[20] Her epiphany lasts, in the narrative, exactly as long as it takes for Achilles, with his hand already on the hilt of his sword, to find within himself a reason of sufficient cogency for him to return the sword, half-drawn, to its scabbard. The cogent reason is the promise of rewards in the elusive future, and permission to trade insults with Agamemnon just below the threshold of the tabu surrounding the king's person. Athena is a representation of possible modes of action, and therefore a signifier conveying to Achilles numerous culturally determined meanings. But to call her a signifier is not to take her for a mere mirage. Athena is a direct emissary from the courts of Being, the unconscious if we like, or, in Bergson's image, the fringe of intuition surrounding the intellect, from which a signifier may come forward into a sharp but momentary focus in the intellect.

Athena reminds Achilles of Hera's love, and by her presence proves her own. Of all the heroes at Troy, including Hector and Patroclus, none is loved by the heavenly witnesses as Achilles is. Athena, Hera, Thetis, Zeus, Hephaistos, Achilles' immortal horses—whether observing Achilles from afar, working on his behalf, or in direct conversations with him—all treat Achilles as their beloved, because, as the protagonist, he is the poet's focus, above all others, for the tragedy of consciousness.[21] Achilles consents to Athena's request from a prudent recognition of necessity: "the gods hearken to him who obeys."[22] What alternative is open to Achilles when Being itself reminds him that he is witnessed and loved by Being even when disgraced in the public assembly?

The first function of Homer's gods is to witness the world.[23] The humans, forever doubting their own being, project gods to witness them, and so to validate whatever moments of being are granted to mortal creatures. Ajax, fighting in the mist over the body of Patroclus, prays to Zeus to dispel the mist so that the heroes may witness and be witnessed: "Make bright the air, and grant us to be seen with the eyes. Destroy us in the light if such is your pleasure."[24] Zeus, pitying him, scattered the mist; the sun shone forth, and the battle was revealed to the light.[25] The warrior, even at the moment of his death, claims his right to the I-Thou relationship with his own destiny.

"Father Zeus," Homer says, "had compassion on Ajax as he wept." Even death does not cancel the relationship between the mortals and the Ouranian signifiers. On the contrary, death itself is validated when witnessed by the gods. Homer's witnesses, eternally present, only marginally touched by the past, and not at all by the future, are Dewey's "something beyond the self," which the self projects beyond itself, in whose eyes consciousness can see itself reflected, and so completed. Seeing themselves beloved by eternal Being, Homer's warriors find the courage to love themselves, for all the confusion of their signifiers. Like the beloved in Socrates' parable in the *Phaedrus,* who falls in love with his reflection in his lover's eyes, Homer's warriors love their gods, not quite understanding that, in doing so, they fall in love with themselves.[26]

MacCary calls the mirroring of the lover and his beloved in Plato's *Phaedrus* narcissism, and so it is.[27] Selfhood begins in narcissism. In Hegelian terms, the self requires the Other both to find its own reflection and to complete its unification as a self; paradoxically, therefore, the Other must mirror the self, even while remaining the absolutely Other. We may agree with MacCary that the heroes of the *Iliad* are "de-centered," and that the gods whom they project reveal the nature of their pathology.[28] Yet, without their gods, Homer's heroes might well be not less but more fragmented, if modern literature provides us with any reliable clue. More positively viewed, Homer's gods represent a leap of the imagination to locate the subject, and to recover the wholeness, which, in Aristophanes' myth in the *Symposium,* was our original condition. The gods are, Vivante writes, "reference points for the heroes' highest yearnings."[29]

In the course of the battle, when the Trojans have pressed the Greeks back to their ships, Zeus turns his "light-bearing eyes," as Homer calls them, from the Trojan plain to behold other tribes—the Thracian horsemen, the warlike Mysians, the stalwart milk-drinking Hippomolgoi, and the Abioi, most righteous of all humans—"and he turned his light-bearing eyes not at all towards Troy."[30] Other tribes too need the illumination of the heavenly vision. But the Trojan field did not disappear from view. Seated on the mountain peak in Samothrace, embracing in his vision Mt. Ida, the city of Troy, and the ships of the Achaeans, Poseidon "was amazed at the battle and the fighting, and pitied the Achaeans overwhelmed by the Trojans."[31] Homer's heroes aroused even the gods to amazement and pity.

Poseidon, a heavenly form generated of amazement and pity, takes three strides down the mountain, the ridges and woods trembling beneath his "deathless feet," and with the fourth reaches his home in the depths of the sea at Aigai, "golden, coruscating, imperishable forever."[32] There Poseidon yokes his horses to his chariot and drives it across the sea. The beasts of the sea gambol in the waves, recognizing their master; the sea, rejoicing, makes way for the epiphany; and the chariot skims the waves without so much as wetting the axle.[33]

Being here is pure gold. Poseidon's imperishable home beneath the sea is golden, and golden his horses' manes. Poseidon dresses himself in gold; his lash is golden; and he hobbles his horses with golden hobbles, "not to be broken or unloosed," leaving them to browse on ambrosia while he attends to human affairs.[34] But this vision of purest gold is vouchsafed only to seers and to the creatures of the deep sporting beyond the reach of the signifier. Poseidon, emerging from his seaborn splendor, translates his eternally vigorous being into a signifier, and in the person of Kalchas rouses the two Aiantes to new efforts, using words and his divine scepter, now uniting in himself meaning and Being. His mission accomplished, to touch creatures on the verge of oblivion with Being's own wand, Poseidon takes flight as a hawk lifting off a high escarpment. Ajax, son of Oileus, recognizes that the Kalchas who has just passed in and out of their consciousness was no human, but a signifier from the center of Being. "This was not Kalchas, who divines through bird-lore," the one Ajax says to the other, "for I easily recognized the traces of a god's feet and shins as he was leaving. Gods are very easy to recognize."[35] What would we not give, in these hard times, for even so small a vision of the shanks of deathless Being, seen from behind!

Ajax, hard pressed in battle, catches only a glimpse of the golden epiphany, but even a trace of the divine presence is sufficient for him to become, for the moment, divine. Whitman interprets the image of Poseidon leading the Greeks into battle (in *Iliad* XIV.384–86), with a sword like lightning in his hand, as simply a simile dramatized: "they counter-attacked like fresh men in new armor."[36] Yes, but how pale our poetics, to translate epiphany into simile. Which poet would not give away half his thesaurus, or hers, to see their similes leap, even once, into an epiphany? Ajax, recognizing the god's presence, is for the moment godlike, with his being graced, for the moment, with an adequate meaning. Caught up in the emergencies of combat, Ajax cannot trace the process, which Homer shares with us, whereby his distress, reaching the heights and depths of Being, is transmuted into a vortex of golden energy to surge back to the dispirited warrior. How could the warrior on the battle-line trace the electrical process, complex but instantaneous, by which a judicious disclosure of Being reactivates the failing body by reinvesting it with meaning?

Homer's warriors, to realize their unity in a field that dissolves around them, project celestial beings who, by displacement and transference, become their lovers. Seeing themselves beloved by Being, the humans endure to love themselves. Beheld in the gaze of the gods, as the subject of the gods' thoughts, and the motives for their action, the humans realize themselves, if only in moments, as the subject, having projected the gods precisely to function as their mirrors. The relationship is terrible, of course, between the absolute Subject on Olympos and the humans on the plains of Troy, swept pell-mell under the banners of the signifier, which promise Being but deliver death. Small wonder that the warriors must project their battle onto Olympos, and set one signifier against another, as if to reassure themselves that their labors to find meaning were not only witnessed but mirrored at the heart of Being.[37]

Homer's paradigm of humans defiant of their limits, related to, yet forever separated from, their golden similitudes on Olympos, corresponds more than casually with Freud's myth of the ego and the superego joined in symbiotic antagonism. Freud's lectures to his Viennese colleagues on the role of the sexual drive in psychosomatic disorders would not have mystified, or shocked, the poet who placed that theme at the center of his *Iliad*. The plague that breaks out in the Greek army in *Iliad* I is the first overt symptom of the disease, but when the symptom disappears the pathology remains, to haunt the rest of the poem.[38] Homer's Olympians are as much sexual beings as their human counterparts, and use sex much as humans do, for power and glory. Sex, disguised, manipulated, and confused with honor, is the prize, which distracts even Zeus from his purpose and lures warriors to their death.[39]

Homer's heroes live surrounded and driven by the primitive compulsions that Freud took pains to explicate for his colleagues and patients. They know anger as a gall that seeps into the heart, or envelops a person in a dark cloud. They know *Atē* (which we translate as blind infatuation) as a force that clouds rational judgment.[40] Let Freud label the id, and define it as best he can in objective terms; Homer represents it. It is the unruly Titans in their dungeon in the depths of the underworld, the river Ocean, which circulates around the world, feeding all rivers with its imperishable energy; or the river Styx, by which the gods swear, and whose frigid waters can put even gods into a coma.[41] Why should the gods hold most inviolate the oaths sworn on the Styx if not because, even in the palaces of the intellect, the imperishable signifiers know that they too will topple back to the ground whence they came? The Olympians may pride themselves on their victory over the monstrous Typhon, but they share with him a common mother. They are her energy pressed into thought and culture, and Typhon her magnet drawing their sublimest thoughts back to the dust.

In *Iliad* I the priest Chryses, after his humiliation before the whole Greek army, withdraws to the sea, where he prays to his god for revenge. But this god is two in one: the one is Apollo, ready, with his silver bow, to defend the law of the father; the other, Smintheus—archaic, chthonic, the Rat god, carrier of disease.[42] Celestial god and chthonic rodent are so overlaid in Chryses' prayer that the demon Chryses conjures almost passes notice. Chryses' prayer is a model, beautiful both for its piety and in its image of a celestial being who stalks in majesty around the towns under his protection. Only the cult title *Smintheus*, with which Chryses invokes his god, signifies that his god's work will be far from beautiful.

Chryses, as a priest of the numinous, conjures from the numinous heights and depths a demon, with the protocols proper for such interventions, and charges his demon to punish the Greeks for his humiliation before the assembled Greeks.[43] Though the Greek army applauds Chryses' offer of ransom, when it is heard in the assembly, Chryses' anger now extends to them indiscriminately. Of his daughter, and her response to the bartering of her body, Chryses' prayer says not a word. Insulted and enraged, as a father and as a man, Chryses puts his wizard skills at the service of his rage, to conjure reprisal.

Apollo sweeps down from Olympos in anger, "like the night," with his quiver clanging terribly on his back.[44] His appearance and action are a priest's anger personified, projected to Olympos, whence it returns to earth in the form of a disease. Chryses channels his frustrated libido to the authorities on high, and the suppressed impulse returns both enlarged and sanctified: revenge becomes righteous anger. The ego can take satisfaction that its tabu desires have been given divine approval, and Apollo takes shape, celestial adjudicator and the rodent disseminating disease fused into one.

Homer's gods, like all psychic projections, are replete with unconscious content. As the ego magnified, they are colossal in their desires and in their need for devotion from their worshippers. Like any human ego, they will use deceit, intimidation, or violence to forward their own advantage. The clash of wills on Olympos is not surprising since each god is an aspect of the libido given a name and form. Look at the society on Olympos and see the ego in all its narcissism.[45]

But the superego is both the very image of the ego, enlarged, and its inverted reflection. Homer's gods complete consciousness by being what humans are not. They plunder the ego's illicit desires, and feed on fantasy, never troubled by scarcity, and rarely by regret. Humans die; therefore gods do not. Humans must work for their livelihood; therefore the gods live at ease, with the means to indulge their senses. They may sleep as humans do, but not from fatigue. They sleep for the pleasure of sleep, as they eat, not from hunger but from the pleasure of eating. The gods are pure energy, the pleasure of pure volition. The ego is constrained by time and space; therefore the gods are swift as thought, being thought forms incarnate.

Achilles, as the gods' beloved, has the power to focus the powers of the numinous to his own ends. Yet even the great will of Achilles is successful only temporarily. The ego, sooner or later, comes up against limitation. If the gods are magnified egos, they are also superegos in Freud's sense, the ego's projected *parents,* to whom the ego has surrendered much of its own libidinal energy.[46] The ego, grown to adulthood, learns to fashion tools and even to imagine a world of signifiers supremely alive. Yet all the ego's projectiles of imagination and will meet the limit, marked by the tabu. The gods of the *Iliad* stand as the final authority over the ego, seducing human desires only to bring each to its closure.[47]

The ego develops elaborate strategies for manipulating the superego. Angry when its desires are denied, but forbidden by the tabu surrounding the superego from venting its anger, the ego learns postures of submission, with varying degrees of authenticity. The ego is even willing to surrender a good part of its own narcissism to enlarge the narcissism of the superego.[48] Humans compose hymns of praise to their gods, which graciously overlook their faults and infidelities. They sacrifice the best of their flocks and the first fruits of the harvest to the gods.[49] The superego feasts on the smell of sacrifice; sometimes it rewards the sacrifice, and sometimes it does not. No matter how earnest or frequent the sacrifice, the advantages won are erratic at best, and in any case temporary. With the superego maintaining its right to the choicest of the ego's desires for its own feast, the ego's prayer, even when answered, returns often with some gross distortion. Most of the libidinal energy is levied as a tax to sustain the superego's much-acclaimed, pure volition.

Achilles, insulted by Agamemnon, prays to Thetis; Thetis prays to Zeus, and Achilles wins his advantage over Agamemnon. But he did not know, when he was projecting his desire to his mother imago in the depths of the sea, and to his father imago on the heights of Olympos, that the tax on his revenge would be the death of Patroclus. The signifiers move slowly but surely through the poem, book by book, each casting its predecessors in a new light, but when the light dawns, it is too late, and even the death of Patroclus is not sacrifice enough. The gods do not cancel destiny; they only reveal it.

Homer's gods are certainly infantile, and the infant in us responds to them with the delight of belief or disbelief, depending on our age. We adore them, as Homer's heroes adored them, with a wonder compounded of guilt, envy, and fear. The child in us *knows* the numinous as Homer has imagined it for us: wondrous beings who fly with the speed of thought, and drive their chariots across the waves without wetting the axles; beings with golden bodies and golden palaces, shrouded in mist, yet as brilliant as sunlight; ephemeral and eternal, exuberant, moody, glowing with magical powers, surrounded by awesome tabus, and communicating in codes that only the most cunning wizard can decipher. The child in us loves Homer's gods for their very unconsciousness, being himself or herself a smolt swept along in the flux of direct experience, with boundaries as casual and mobile as the gods themselves. Let the moralist fulminate on the vanity of the ego; the gods of the *Iliad* take us back, with salacious enthusiasm, into the imagination of the child, where the libido is pure pleasure and the ego is king.

The gods of the *Iliad*, where they are demonstrably infantile, can lay the blame on their creators. Infantile egos create infantile superegos. Yet Homer's gods are certainly more than the infant Narcissus magnified. Agamemnon may cling to his illusion that he is not responsible for his actions, but his is not Homer's voice. Homer opens the *Iliad* by invoking the Muse to sing of the anger of Achilles, which sent many heroes to their death, and brought "the plan of Zeus" to fulfillment.[50] But Zeus did not set Achilles and Agamemnon against each other, except insofar as Zeus, as the signifier of supreme power, is the ultimate cause of the quarrel between two human warriors wrestling for power. In the narrative the quarrel breaks out between the two heroes as a result of the plague invoked by Chryses on the Greek army. Apollo, if we like, is responsible for the conflict, but Apollo is a persona, the projection of Chryses' anger. But we cannot lay the blame for the tragedy at Chryses' door since his anger is the direct response to Agamemnon's insults. Did Zeus provoke Agamemnon to insult Apollo's priest? Far from it. The priest approached the king as a respectful suppliant, bearing his god's insignia, which even a foreign king would recognize, and offering a ransom to salve the king's dignity. Chryses' approach gives Agamemnon room to bow gracefully to necessity; but Agamemnon, with his infantile dignity, takes the slightest compromise for surrender; and the Olympian signifiers, reacting to human insecurities, are thrown into disorder.

One priest's anger conjures the rodent demon to devastate a whole army. This is not realism in our modern sense since, for us, rodents and disease stand on one side, as the real; and the gods on the other, as the unreal. But Homer uses the same formula, *aeikea loigon*—"ugly plague"—for the disease sent by Apollo, and for the war itself, which is the concatenation of many angers. Anger, disease, and war are points on the same continuum in Homer's cosmology, or moments in the same complex. The *Iliad* opens onto the scene of an army almost broken by long years of failure and attrition, encamped on a foreign soil made more hostile by the army's rape and pillage. If the sanitary conditions in the camp were appalling, even worse must have been the morale of the soldiers confronting death day in and day out, and each day watching hope crumble into despair. The immune system, exhausted, was ripe for epidemic. As the events after the epidemic reveal (specifically, the quarrel between Agamemnon and Achilles, and the confusions in Book II), the rodent is only the most immediate cause for the collapse. Chryses' ego, the most recent but by no means the last of many egos equally humiliated and frustrated, is the provocation that brings the system to its breaking point.

A wiser leader than Agamemnon might have heard in Chryses' appeal a warning that the disease infecting the Greek army was close to explosion. But Agamemnon, made overconfident by the tabus surrounding the king, heard only a harmless old priest, and saw in the priest's submission another opportunity for exploitation. Woe to the person who sees Homer's gods as merely infantile! They are the guardians also of natural law, each an aspect of nature translated into a signifier. If Agamemnon can attribute his losses to the will of Zeus, while insulting the insignia of the gods, we can see what he will not, that an army that desecrates its environment, feeds on injustice, and squanders its resources is a society diseased. The rodent and the healer unite in Apollo's person to bring the disease to light and restore the balance.

Homer himself is no child, and the *Iliad* is more than a child's fantasy.[51] If Achilles is a mere boy when the *Iliad* begins, with his head full of boyish dreams, he becomes a man in the moment when he receives the news of Patroclus's death. Until then death itself was no more than a word, which Achilles could lightly exchange for glory. After the death of Patroclus Achilles has no choice but to return to the battle; what else is the warrior's path than to meet his destiny face to face?

Achilles is no boy when he and Priam look upon each other in Achilles' tent at the end of the *Iliad*, each realizing the other in a gaze of wonder. He is no boy to whom Priam says: "I have dared what no other mortal has dared—to stretch my hand to the mouth of the man who has killed his son."[52] The paradoxes are exquisite. Achilles looks on the enemy who could be his father, and Priam looks on the enemy who could be his son. Priam, seeing Achilles, grieves for the son he has lost; Achilles, seeing Priam, grieves for the father he has lost. Each grieves for his own loss, seeing in the other the cause of his grief.

But a transformation occurs in Achilles' tent like nothing else in the poem. After the two men have satisfied their longing (as Homer calls it) for grief, Achilles rises from his seat and reaches out to raise the old man from the ground. Earlier, when Priam had first entered the tent, Achilles had thrust him to the ground, but now Achilles "had compassion on his grey hair and his grey beard."[53] Achilles invites Priam to sit, but Priam will not sit, as if in a friend's house, while Hector's body lies desecrated outside. Achilles goes out and, with his companions and slave women, lays out the corpse of his enemy as if it were the corpse of his dearest friend. So close is the assimilation that Achilles is moved to cry out to the dead Patroclus to pardon him for releasing Hector's body to Priam.[54] With the corpse dressed, Achilles and Priam sit down to dinner together as guest and host.

As the two men weep together each weeps for his own loss, yet in their weeping the two become one. One grief binds them together, one destiny. Priam becomes father to Achilles, and Achilles Priam's son. Hector, Patroclus, and Achilles are fused into the single figure of the son, whom the father sends to his early death. Peleus and Priam fuse into the father, whom the young warrior will not see again once he sets out for war. Priam for Achilles, and Achilles for Priam—each is for each the Other in its most terrible form, each the cause of the other's imminent death. In this, the most profound of the many mirrors in the *Iliad*, the Other, remaining the Other, melts into the self. Joined in a common destiny, the two warriors forget the boundaries of their signifiers, and each sees in the other himself.

Such an extraordinary transformation is, of course, the work of the gods. Once again, while the human actors comprehend some of the workings of the gods, Homer takes us deeper into the council chambers of Being. At this point Olympos is still in disarray. Poseidon is fixated still on the destruction of Troy; Hera and Athena are fixated on their grievance against Paris for preferring the gifts of Aphrodite over theirs.[55] Fixation on the Olympian plane translates back into the fixation of Achilles on his anger and revenge.

But compassion too is from the gods, the symbiosis of instinct, translated into social codes in the field of the signifier and emerging beyond signifiers as an intuition of organic unity. Other gods feel the desecration of Hector's corpse, and are horrified by Achilles' unmitigated savagery. "He has destroyed pity, and there is no shame in him," Apollo says, in the last council of the gods in the poem.[56] Compassion was the part of himself Achilles had given to Patroclus, mistaking it for effeminacy when he had sent Patroclus out on his twofold mission, to take Achilles' place as the defense of the Greeks, while saving Achilles' honor from the least taint of compromise. When Apollo felled Patroclus at the city wall, Achilles was parted not only from his armor but from his compassion.[57]

Apollo puts the meaning of this loss in the plainest terms: the mind of Achilles is not aligned with the divine order; he has lost the flexibility of reason; and he is no longer human, but an animal. Apollo concludes with the warning that Achilles, in disfiguring the "mute earth," risks the *nemesis* of the gods.[58] If by the "blunt, inarticulate" earth Apollo means Hector's corpse, the equation of earth and body is doubly significant.[59] The earth too has its signifiers, not the least of which is the corpse; and an insult done to a vessel, which once has housed a moment of Being, is a violence as much to heaven as to earth. The metaphysical body, which is all that is left to Achilles, cannot be perfected by the degradation of the physical body; even the spent shell, crumbling back to dust, is to be reverenced. In fact, only through its proper monument and memorial can the warrior's corpse be transmuted into the regenerative *agathos daimon* of the hero cults or given its status, in epic, as the signifier of the victory of the metaphysical over the physical.[60]

Achilles is now psychotic, beyond justice and sanity, and his gods must take it in hand to dissolve his psychosis; first Apollo; then Zeus, who bends the mind of Hera not by threats, which are his more common form of persuasion, but by persuading her that Achilles, in honoring Hector's corpse, will lose no honor of his own. Hera raises no further protest, as if understanding that, with Achilles' honor assured, hers is no longer at risk; and Athena and Poseidon by their silence give implicit assent, as if they too were coming to their senses, reminded that even their imperishable palaces could be toppled by a human catastrophe. The Parnassians must have their footmen, to borrow from Merrill's poem, for "without our common meanings" their meanings "would have slid headlong to apocalypse."[61]

For the first time in the *Iliad* we hear it put that one man can win honor without dishonoring another, and see the discordant signifiers reach a common purpose. Gods too have their halcyon days. The covenant radiates swiftly through the ether to Trojan and Achaean alike that neither will lose, but both will gain, from preferring the other's honor to his own.

The gods too are changed by this perception, if we can talk of change in eternal beings, as if Being had come upon its need for meaning in the human register, the Parnassians finding "theirs was a language within ours."[62] They had hitherto, in their heedless way, thought the current ran only vice versa. Apollo understands Hera's need to implicate herself in human affairs; and she, his. From gazing so long at the human carnage, had the gods glimpsed at last that they too would figure in the tapestry on Helen's loom? Once the gods concur in their common need for their human signifiers, even those lying as corpses on the battlefield, the intuition goes forth from Mt. Olympos into human consciousness, relayed by Thetis, Iris, and Hermes, swift shuttles between the high throne of Being and human huts.

When Priam dares to decline Achilles' hospitality until Achilles shows honor to Hector's corpse, Achilles bridles, taking Priam's request for an implicit criticism of his sense of ceremony. Achilles already intends to release the body, he says, not of his own volition but because his mother has transmitted to him a command from Being itself. Achilles knows too, he says, that Priam, advanced in years, would not have dared of his own volition to come to the Greek ships, nor slipped past the guards, without some god guiding him.[63]

The gods here are Dewey's "influx from sources beyond conscious deliberation and purpose," which imagination requires for the completion of the self. Through much of the *Iliad* the gods are narcissistic, as projections of the ego's will to individuation. But when the ego perceives that death overrides all its constructions, it must find another function for its signifiers. Achilles and Priam could have not reached reconciliation by conscious will, but by what Dewey calls an adjustment to the will. No person could dissolve Achilles' anger, which is not directed at any person, but at death, which plunders first a warrior's meanings, and then his being.

The relations between the gods and the humans in the *Iliad* are far different from those of the puppet master and his puppets.[64] The gods require Achilles to return Hector's corpse to his people. But this requirement is not to preserve some arbitrary tabu; it issues from deep-seated human codes bonding the living and the dead, and includes even an enemy's corpse within the field of significance. Achilles could meet the gods' command, sullenly and without ceremony, as a slave might obey his master, honoring the command to the letter only. The gods do not demand that Achilles invite Priam to share his table, nor that Priam should spend the night under his enemy's roof, trusting to the bonds of friendship. They do not ask Achilles to commiserate with Priam in the death of his son and the loss of his fabled power, nor Priam to commiserate with Achilles.

Or rather, this is exactly the gods' request. The gods ask Achilles to honor the corpse of his enemy, and in doing so to find in himself a place for death, first his enemy's, and then his own. But an ego hardened by its grievance against the world can find no place for any honor but its own. Priam must transcend his ego to venture beyond the walls of Troy to Achilles' tent, as Achilles must transcend his to welcome his enemy into his own house. The transformation, when it occurs, is a miracle. As the two men weep, each for his own grief, the separate egos dissolve: Priam becomes Peleus, and Achilles becomes Hector. When the ego becomes conscious of its absolute limit and its supreme loss, it discovers compassion. The compassion with which Being embraces its darling finally dissolves his ego, and the grace of Being touches his heart.[65] Achilles goes beyond the gods' command to find in himself a grace that ego alone could never reach. The meal, to which he invites his enemy, becomes the eucharist joining one man and another, and reconciling humans and their signifiers, which, even when creating differences, refer all difference back to the unified field of Being.[66]

Some may think Achilles most heroic when he goes forth to battle blazing as a star, wearing armor forged by a god and driving his immortal horses, like a god himself, transcending human reference altogether. But superhuman rage is not godhood; rather, it is the image of godhood, what Diel calls *"false and imaginative exaltation, the seductive monster."*[67] The anger of Achilles returning to the battlefield is the explosion of an ego betrayed by its passion for rewards. But compassion is more divine than ego-possessed fury. Achilles and Priam, becoming autonomous themselves, as the compassionate gaze of the gods dissolves the boundaries between self and Other, meet at the crossing between meaning and Being, where they can touch the pain on the other side. Here Achilles learns the meaning of sublimation, which was the theme, obscurely intimated, of Athena's first epiphany.[68]

"True address from God," Buber writes, "directs man into the place of lived speech, where the voices of the creatures grope past one another, and in their very missing of one another succeed in reaching the eternal partner."[69]

Oh, to have been Achilles or Priam that night, like gods, on the verge of meaning. No, not Achilles, but the poet present at their funeral supper, to draw the strands together, and show us king and warrior, seated on their rude thrones, gazing across the divide, to find each his meaning in the other's being.

6

Hamlet's Hungry Ghost

Well may it sort that this portentous figure
Comes arméd through our watch so like the king
That was and is the question of these wars.
                                    Hamlet I.i.109–11[1]

BERNARDO. *Who's there?*
FRANCISCO. *Nay, answer me. Stand and unfold yourself.*
BERNARDO. *Long live the king!*
FRANCISCO. *Bernardo?*
BERNARDO. *He.*

                                    Hamlet I.i.1–5

Claudius, the new king of Denmark, has posted a nightly watch on the battlements of the royal castle at Elsinore, and we quickly learn the reason. Young Fortinbras threatens to mount an attack on Denmark to reclaim the territories from which he was dispossessed when his father was killed by King Hamlet. Claudius, as yet unproven in the royal arts of war and diplomacy, holds a precarious position, as the king of a commonwealth destabilized by the sudden death of the previous king. A king who has acquired the throne in a sudden turn of fortune does well to post guards on the battlements. But Claudius has a more pressing reason for anxiety. Norway's territorial ambitions are a convenient coincidence to screen Claudius's deeper fear that he may be discovered as the assassin of the late king, who was, we are told, the popular idol. "Long live the king!" Bernardo's password is the time-honored exclamation of allegiance to the new king, but here, exchanged between guards who move like phantoms in the dark, it is as much a question as an affirmation. Long live which king? The first scene of *Hamlet* quickly unfolds the answer. Hamlet senior, thought dead, is very much alive and, in fact, the prime mover of the play. Though the loyal guards may signify Claudius with their "Long live the King!", the first scene of *Hamlet* shows their thoughts centered on the dead king, who has already revealed himself to them as uncomfortably alive.

The ghost has received much less than his due in studies and interpretations of the play. His appearance in the play prompts scholars to discuss the belief in ghosts in Elizabethan England. Did Shakespeare, or his Elizabethan audiences, believe in ghosts? Of course Shakespeare and his contemporaries believed in ghosts, or they would not have allowed themselves to become engrossed in the tragedy of a ghost's power to subvert a political state and a man's soul. Hamlet's ghost is as credible today as it was in Shakespeare's time, as proven by the general consensus that Hamlet demonstrated some moral or intellectual flaw in toying with the ghost's instructions, when a dutiful son would have fallen into the ghostly trap without resistance. We are a ghost-ridden species.

Interpreters, busy searching for the mote in Hamlet's character, miss the point. A ghost is a problematic phenomenon, less substantial than flesh and blood, but much more powerful. Disturbed itself, this ghost creates a profound disturbance in all who see it. Even invisible, it creates a queasy unease in the land. The old sources of the legend, Saxo Grammaticus and Belleforest (whose versions are included in the Norton edition of the play), tell nothing of a ghost. Perhaps Thomas Kyd's now-lost *Hamlet,* which appeared on the London stage a few years before Shakespeare's play, introduced the ghost into the legend; or perhaps the ghost was Shakespeare's invention. In any case, the motivation for Hamlet's bizarre behavior, which was only implicit in the old tale, becomes explicit with the appearance of the ghost. If the old History of Hamlet was a revenge play, Shakespeare's *Hamlet* is a study in ghost-possession.

The difficult, even dangerous, mission that this ghost will entrust to his son is to commit murder without regard for the social consequences. The man to be killed is the young man's uncle, and also the monarch of the state. Murder of a kinsman, and political assassination—this is an initiation ordeal of the severest kind. Yet many, who talk of Hamlet's moral flaw, act as if ghosts were commonplace, and assassination of the head of state on the orders of a ghost entirely normal. Under this ghost's influence otherwise sober and law-abiding citizens become bloodhounds salivating for the kill.

How will the ghost persuade young Hamlet to undertake a mission so fool-hardy? The ghost must appeal to Hamlet's love, which must be so strong that it will sacrifice everything—logic, sanity, life itself if necessary—to carry the burden placed upon it. The curtain opens on the tragic story of a young man in love with his father's ghost. "If thou didst ever thy dear father love." So speaks the ghost to Hamlet, when he has drawn Hamlet into his net, and the moment is ripe for Hamlet to shoulder the burden of his destiny. And the burden is revenge—the condition the father requires as proof of his son's love, and the test the son must pass to earn his father's love. The father's equation of love and revenge is picked up immediately by the son:

> Haste me to know't, that I, with wings as swift
> As meditation or the thoughts of love,
> May sweep to my revenge.
>> (I.v.29–31)

"I find thee apt," the ghost replies.

In what form does this fatherly ghost choose to make his appeal for his son's unconditional love? He comes in armor, armed from head to foot. Horatio, seeing the ghost, addresses it:

> What art thou that usurp'st this time of night
> Together with that fair and warlike form
> In which the majesty of buried Denmark
> Did sometimes march?
>> (I.i.46–49)

After the ghost has disappeared Horatio agrees with his friends that the ghost was in the very likeness of the dead king:

> Such was the very armor he had on
> When he the ambitious Norway combated.
> So frowned he once when, in an angry parle,
> He smote the sledded Polacks on the ice.
>> (I.i.60–63)

Horatio later describes the ghost to Hamlet as "armed at point exactly, cap-a-pe," and adds that the guards were distilled "almost to jelly with the act of fear" by the apparition. Hamlet muses, in particular, on the ghost's mode of dress:

> HAMLET.   Armed, say you?
> ALL.   Armed, my lord.
> HAMLET.   From top to toe?
> ALL.   From head to foot.
>   (I.ii.224–27)

That fair and warlike form: this father will not risk failure by appeals to mere sentiment. What form more persuasive than the uniform of the general marching to war, frowning as he frowned when he smote his enemies? Hamlet, seeing the ghost, is awestruck:

> What may this mean
> That thou, dead corse, again in complete steel
> Revisits thus the glimpses of the moon,
> Making night hideous, and we fools of nature
> So horridly to shake our disposition
> With thoughts beyond the reaches of our souls?
>   (I.iv.51–56)

This ghost, breathing war, is the very form of anger, and the love he demands from his son is complete submission. For such a father even his son is the enemy, unless he agrees to play the slave.

Not satisfied with a warlike appearance alone, this ghost elicits his son's compassion with hints of the tortures he is suffering in the sulphurous flames of the other world:

> I could a tale unfold whose lightest word
> Would harrow up thy soul, freeze thy young blood,
> Make thy two eyes like stars start from their spheres,
> Thy knotted and combinéd locks to part,
> And each particular hair to stand on end,
> Like quills upon the fretful porpentine.
>   (I.v.15–20)

Hamlet's young soul is harrowed sufficiently by the vision before his eyes; he needs no further details of what the ghost calls "the secrets of my prison house." What son, as sensitive as Hamlet, can refuse the ghost's imperative, if by his refusal he dooms his father's soul to eternal torment in the fires of hell? The pliable ego, unable to withstand an assault from a signifier so massively armed, collapses.

The martial stalk of the ghost in the first scene of the play reflects the customary behavior of the king when he was alive. To his countrymen the king was valiant, heroic, majestic, if Horatio's words reflect the general opinion. In Horatio's patriotic fervor we have the portrait of the conventional monarch, engaged in conventional wars with his neighbors, quick to stand on his honor, or to seize new territories by diplomacy or war. The deceased Hamlet was a good son of the warrior caste: a supercharged animus; a stranger to any dress but armor, to any form of communication but offense and counteroffense; indifferent to anyone's honor but his own. If Claudius killed Hamlet and seized his lands, Hamlet did the same to old Fortinbras. The military relations between the two old pirates, Fortinbras and Hamlet, should caution us against total credence in the pious portrait of the ideal monarch, which old Hamlet's subjects gives us.

Hamlet, the father, was a pirate plain and simple, and in the course of his piracy killed Koll, king of Norway, and took his throne. Belleforest puts it bluntly: "Now the greatest honor that men of noble birth could at that time win and obtaine, was in exercising the art of Piracie upon the seas; assayling their neighbours, & the countries bordering upon them: and how much the more they vsed to rob, pill, and spoyle other Provinces, and Ilands farre adiacent, so much the more their honours and reputation increased and augmented: wherein Horuendile [Hamlet senior] obtained the highest place in his time, beeing the most renouned Pirate that in those dayes scoured the seas."[2] In both Saxo's and Belleforest's accounts King Hamlet's marriage was an act of political diplomacy. This stalwart pirate, in the old accounts, so ingratiated himself with Rorik, King of Denmark, with handsome spoils from his piracy, that King Rorik gave Horwendile [Hamlet senior] his daughter Gerutha [Gertrude] in marriage. Shakespeare plays down the most blatant aspects of King Hamlet's piratical character, but enough still remains of Horwendile in Shakespeare's ghostly king. Shakespeare gives the old pirate a semblance of respectability, and with good dramatic reason, since the ghost takes the form of the old king as he was remembered by those completely submissive to his charisma. "Our valiant Hamlet," Horatio calls him, and adds, diplomatically, "for so this side of our known world esteemed him" (I.i.84–85). The ghost's confession of his eternal damnation reveals the king, whom it impersonates, to be still the unregenerate pirate of the medieval legend.

King Hamlet lived by the sword and died by poison. The warrior code makes a distinction between poison and the sword, but the difference is not as great as the warrior ideology claims. Absolute monarchs have courtiers aplenty, who are willing to carry out the monarch's designs by unscrupulous means, while saving the monarch's reputation for chivalry and fair dealing. The warrior ideology, dividing the world into the conqueror and the con- quered, counts only the despoiling of other egos as success.

The ghost of the father demands that the son prove his manhood, by taking up his sword against his father's enemies, exacting reprisal for reprisal. "My father's spirit in arms? All is not well," Hamlet says (I.iii.252). Hamlet is correct, and Marcellus too, when he surmises that "something is rotten in the state of Denmark" (I.v.90). But the rot did not begin with Claudius. As Clau- dius has a covert anxiety, which can be conveniently masked under a political concern, so the ghost cloaks his private enterprise under the persona of the *pater patriae,* the monarch dressed in the accoutrements of war. The ghost in this play is the warrior ideology, and Hamlet's burden is that he must now assume the ideology in his own person, or repudiate it.

The late king, someone will object, was more than a military man. He was a loving husband, we are told. But what is our source? The ghost himself, who else? In describing his end the ghost shows his indifference to nuance, and his preference for hyperbole. He calls Claudius, who enjoys his throne, an incestuous and an adulterate beast. Fair enough, perhaps. Whether inces- tuous or adulterous by the strict letter of the law, Claudius is certainly a villain. Here is the ghost's high-minded comparison of himself with his rival:

> O Hamlet, what a falling off was there,
> From me, whose love was of that dignity
> That it went hand in hand even with the vow
> I made to her in marriage, and to decline
> Upon a wretch whose natural gifts were poor
> To those of mine!
>
> (I.v.47–52)

Amplifying on this theme, the ghost talks of virtue, heaven, radiant angels, and a celestial bed, all on one side—his side; and, on the villain's side, lust and lewdness preying on garbage. O happy Gertrude, to have been courted and loved by an angel sent from heaven!

If King Hamlet was, in his mortal days, as angelic as his ghost pretends, why did he leave behind a ghost doomed, as he says, "to fast in fires," to purge "the foul crimes done in my days of nature" (I.v.10–13)? The torments, which the ghost puts past the imagination of the living to endure, give the lie to his claims of purity and integrity. To invoke the doctrine of purgatory here would be entirely inappropriate. This ghost is not in purgatory, whatever our definition of purgatory. We need only compare him with the persons in Dante's *Purgatorio* to see the difference; they are not burning in the fires of the damned.

We have a second witness to the dead king's high principles: the king's son, young Hamlet. Hamlet muses, in his first soliloquy, on the contrast between his dead father and the new king:

> So excellent a king, that was to this
> Hyperion to a satyr.
>
> (I.ii.139ff.)

He remembers the flawless love between his father and mother—

> so loving to my mother,
> That he might not beteem the winds of heaven
> Visit her face too roughly. Heaven and earth,
> Must I remember? Why, she would hang on him
> As if increase of appetite had grown
> By what it fed on—.

Should we doubt this son's idyllic memory of his parent's matrimonial concord? Even mindful of the cautions against the biographical fallacy in literary interpretations, we cannot avoid the suspicion that this is the idealized portrait of marriage. If Hamlet senior was in his days of nature as chivalrous as Hamlet remembers him, and his parents' love so rich and full, are we to believe that Gertrude would have transferred her affections so immediately to the man said to be so much her first husband's inferior? A widowed queen must protect her position by remarriage; such is the necessity of monarchies. But Queen Gertrude gives every sign, except in one confessional scene with her son, of enjoying life with her new spouse. Hamlet's memory of his parents' pure love sounds like a son's nostalgia for both his ideal father imago and his ideal mother imago. The language Hamlet uses to recall his dead father's perfections is more than hyperbole; it is mythical, archetypal. King Hamlet is to Claudius as *Hyperion to a satyr.*

If Hamlet senior was so much the paragon of the lover as to induce in his son thoughts of angels in celestial beds, why his need to steel himself in armor for his epiphany to his son? Was this man tender only with his wife, but never with his son? Is armor the prescribed dress for fathers in their relations with their sons? We can accept Hamlet's account of his father's chivalry. The warrior ideology expects the warrior to be a paragon of chivalry in the home. Aggressive and violent outside the home, the warrior must be gentle, affectionate, and courteous within the home. Homer's Hector is this kind of warrior, but how great the difference between Hector and Hamlet's departed father. Hector removes his helmet when it terrifies his young son; the ghost of King Hamlet wears his to induce terror.

A warrior, who lived by violence and died by violence, appears in ghostly form, arrayed in steel, and commands his son to become an assassin for love. Hamlet vacillates. Given occasions to commit the murder, he passes them up. He invents a scheme of great plausibility to test the validity of the ghost, only to recognize the scheme as a delaying tactic. He berates himself for his own vacillation, and discovers several good reasons to hate himself; unable to decipher the ghostly signifier, he accuses himself of cowardice and insufficient love for his father. But if he were to murder his uncle, though he might survive the initiation, one villain would have replaced another on Denmark's throne. Hamlet would owe his throne to the same violence and duplicity that his father and uncle had used before him, and would sit only until another usurper used the same methods to depose him.

Critics have been quick to add their judgments to Hamlet's self-abuse, as we can see abundantly repeated in the essays in the Norton edition of *Hamlet*. MacKenzie speaks of Hamlet's weakness and irresolution.[3] Goethe talks of the play as depicting "a great action laid upon a soul unfit for the performance of it. . . . A lovely, pure, noble, and most moral nature, without the strength of nerve which forms a hero."[4] But what is the great action? Schlegel is less sympathetic: "He [Hamlet] has a natural inclination for crooked ways; he is a hypocrite towards himself; his far-fetched scruples are often pretexts to cover his want of determination."[5] Far-fetched scruples? As if Hamlet's ways were more crooked than those of a ghost who hides his motives in the hugger mugger of darkness. Schlegel's voice rises in a crescendo: "A voice from another world, commissioned it would appear, by heaven, demands vengeance for a monstrous enormity, and the demand remains without effect."[6] A voice from heaven? Who, reading *Hamlet,* could take the apparition of the father, swollen with self-righteousness, as a messenger from heaven? Hamlet, to give him his due, recognizes ghosts as signifiers of terrible ambiguity, but some of his critics write as if ghostly epiphanies present no hermeneutic problem at all. The law of the father casts a long shadow.

Here is Coleridge, in the same vein: in Hamlet he finds "great, enormous, intellectual activity, and a consequent proportionate aversion to real action."[7] Hamlet vacillates, true; and his outward vacillation manifests a confusion in his mind. But let those who call him coward tell us first of the ghosts who haunt their midnight watch, and teach us the prescripts for interpreting their nocturnal imperatives. Ernest Jones, who derives Hamlet's paralysis "not from physical or moral cowardice, but from the intellectual cowardice, that reluctance to dare the exploration of his inmost soul, which Hamlet shares with the rest of the human race," at least brings Hamlet back from ostracism, and invites us to see the ghost as ours, as much as Hamlet's, as we struggle to find ourselves in the shadow play of our signifiers.[8]

Have the critics forgotten that heaven has declared a prohibition against murder? If murder is tabu, the murder of a kinsman more so; and the most potent tabu is placed around the person of the king. Hamlet is caught in the crossfire between two commandments. The first reads: "Thou shalt not kill." The second, which takes precedence over the first in the view of many critics, reads: "Thou shalt obey the ghost of the father." Talk of Hamlet's weakness is misplaced. The greater fault lies in the contradictions in the law of the father, which permits the son no independence, except at the risk of losing his father's love. Ghosts prosper on confusion and contradiction. This ghost, so persuasively armed, has young Hamlet believing he will find his manhood in submitting to the will of the ghost, but the opposite is true; Hamlet, in obeying the ghost, would certainly lose his manhood.

We cannot expect in a revenge play, some might argue, the same moral code that we honor in our own modern lives. But we read *Hamlet* not as a quaint period piece; Hamlet is our contemporary. Moral imperatives blocked by tabus, contradictions in the law of the father, the hermeneutics of ghosts, the loss of self in the maze of the signifier, are as much the themes of our modern consciousness as they were in Elizabethan or medieval times.

Hamlet makes no explicit recognition of the prohibition against murder, and never uses the prohibition as an argument to justify his own procrastination. On the contrary, he accepts his responsibility to honor his father's ghost with passionate enthusiasm. Yet his hesitations betray his deep-seated aversion to murder, distinguishing him, in this respect, from his father and uncle, for whom murder comes easily. Coming up against his quite normal aversion to taking another's life, Hamlet can see it only as his weakness, since it conflicts with the more powerful ghost of the father, which clouds the moral issues by laying down revenge as the fundamental law governing ego relations. By becoming the instrument of his father's vengeance, Hamlet would prove himself a loyal son, but less of a man; he might find his manhood only in refusing the ghost's demands, but the ghost's intimidation makes this option almost impossible to see. Trapped in the contradictions. Hamlet turns to thoughts of "self-slaughter," and such thoughts give him further grounds for self-hatred, since he has not even the courage to take his life. But suicide is the real commandment laid upon the youth by the ghost of his father. Hamlet is called upon to kill his independent self, and damn his soul, to satisfy a never-to-be-satisfied ghost.[9]

Wherein lies the power of this ghost, to bind the young prince in sophistries, from which he cannot extricate himself, and in expectations, which he cannot satisfy? The authority of steel blinds the prince and blurs the distinctions between father and ghost, father and son. "Hamlet, king, father, royal Dane": dressed in the compelling insignia of war, the ghost assumes all identities—father, son, monarch, and the very ground of Denmark. By contrast, the enemies of the king are terrorists. In King Hamlet's days of nature King

Fortinbras was "pricked on" by ambition to wage war against Hamlet. But "our valiant Hamlet," as Horatio calls him, killed Fortinbras, and seized his lands by a compact "well ratified by law and heraldry." Now Fortinbras, the dispossessed son, of "unimproved mettle hot and full," has "sharked up a list of lawless resolutes" to march on Denmark.[10] Horatio reinforces the identity of king and father when he tells Hamlet that he has seen "the king your father," which Hamlet echoes in his response: "The king my father?"[11] *Hamlet* takes place in that moment in the psychic history of the son when the father is the absolute monarch, and his word absolute law.[12]

"*Mana* inheres in an object or person in direct proportion to the ability of that object or person to recapture the illusion of infantile narcissistic omnipotence."[13] A leader must have protective power, Slater argues, if he is to satisfy the dependency needs of his followers. "Since leaders are mortal," Slater writes, "ways must be sought to exaggerate this power psychologically, and the most common method is to increase his 'mana' in the sense used above; in other words, to create a situation in which the leader approximates as much as possible, in his orientation to the world, the primary narcissism of the infant."[14] The thinking of the followers, who endow their leader with *mana,* Slater expresses thus: "I know I can depend on this person to protect and guide me, because he is omnipotent; and I know that he is omnipotent because he has the narcissistic orientation that I had in the golden era when *I* was omnipotent.[15] Slater goes on to talk of hereditary monarchs, who "must be trained from birth to adopt a life-long attitude of primary narcissism. In the most extreme cases the king is simply kept in an infantile state by constant admiration, flattery, compulsory exhibitionism, and by refusing to permit him to satisfy any of his own needs without help."[16]

What better exemplar of primary narcissism elevated to absolute monarchy than the ghost of Hamlet's father? Omnipotent when alive, King Hamlet was all things to all men: the perfect soldier in battle; the perfect diplomat at court; the perfect lover, husband, and father at home. He had the volatile temper, which we would expect in His Majesty the Infant when his wishes are not immediately gratified. Do we hear one word, in his several appearances, to indicate his interest in his son's well-being, or see one gesture that, by the broadest definition, could be construed as affection for the son whose love he commandeers to his own ends? Love for another is, to this ghost, a state of mind unknown; his one purpose is to feed his own narcissism.

The love, which this ghost demands, is the obedience of the slave; his methods are intimidation and terror, and guilt is the penalty inflicted upon a recalcitrant follower. Since the monarch and the state are identical in the ghost's paradigm, the most infantile of the king's needs must be treated as the gravest matter of state. Wrapped in the flags of war, the king's ghost convinces the guards Marcellus and Bernardo, Horatio, Hamlet—all who see him—that obedience to his narcissism is to serve God and country.

Though Claudius is the living monarch in this play, and his courtiers observe all proper forms of allegiance, the *mana* emanates all from the dead king. The new king is vulnerable because he has not yet succeeded in transferring the *mana* of the old king to himself. Politics, at the highest level, is a game begun in the nursery; narcissism is its name, and the plays are the acquisition and distribution of *mana*. One infant narcissus will not lightly surrender his *mana* to another, *mana* being the life force itself, or its signifiers, at least in the nursery, where we first learn to color our actions with meanings.

Buddhist tradition recognizes several classes of sentient beings, among them the class called hungry ghosts. Hungry ghosts are not, of course, unknown in our Western tradition, ghosts being, by definition, hungry. The ghosts, which rise up out of the trench that Odysseus digs on the shore of Ocean, are hungry for the warm blood of the living or, like Achilles, for some scrap of news of the living. The ghosts, which creep out of their graves during the ancient Athenian festival of the Anthesteria, or during our own Halloween, are hungry for food and affection. The ghosts in Dante's *Inferno* are hungry for the lives they led in their days of nature or, failing that, at least a moment's simulated life through conversation with Dante, a living being. Hungry ghosts departed this life with desires still unsatisfied; such beings, who were at best shadows even in their lifetime, prowl the earth after death, searching for the victim whose life they can appropriate as compensation for the life they never had when alive. So the ghost of Hamlet's father complains:

> Thus was I sleeping by a brother's hand
> Of life, of crown, of queen at once dispatched,
> Cut off even in the blossoms of my sin,
> Unhouseled, disappointed, unaneled,
> No reck'ning made, but sent to my account
> With all my imperfections on my head.
> O horrible! O, horrible! most horrible!
>
> (I.v.74–80)

Shakespeare was not a theologian, but a psychologist. Specific Christian doctrines regarding sin, venial or mortal, or the sacrament of extreme unction, or punishments in the next life for sins committed in this life, are irrelevant here except insofar as theology codifies propositions growing out of psychological experience. The souls of the damned are, in any theology, those damned by their own choice to live forever with frustrated desire. "The blossoms of my sin," as the ghost of Hamlet's father calls them, are the bitterness and rage of the imperial ego left with only its desires, but without the

means to satisfy them. The "sulph'rous and tormenting flames," with which
the ghost harrows young Hamlet's soul, are the sufferings of a soul unable to
make peace with its own destiny. The ghosts of the heroes, which Homer's
Odysseus sees in the underworld, are frustrated to be cut off from life, yet
bitter at the life destiny gave them. The ghost of Agamemnon carries still his
hatred for his treacherous Klytemnestra. The ghost of Ajax is speechless with
rage at the treachery of fate, which awarded the arms of Achilles to Odysseus, and not to him. The ghost of Achilles resents the life he had, even while
mourning its loss. The ghost of Herakles, stalking with club in hand, glowers
as Herakles glowered in life, still expecting enemies at every turn, who might
deprive him of his goods.

If the king is His Majesty the Infant, we understand the depth of his rage
at being cut off from life. Imperial narcissism cannot tolerate the slightest
brake on its desires. What is it to be a king but to enjoy the omnipotence of
desire, never to experience the gap between desire and its satisfaction? Death
is the greatest outrage of all to His Majesty. Engrossed in his own reflection,
which is polished by others willing to surrender to him their own narcissism,
the king must view any impediment to his will as an offense against heaven
itself. The monarch learns—and in this education he has the support of his
followers—to identify his will with the law and the commonwealth.

Haunted themselves, ghosts look to alleviate their burden by finding someone else's life to expropriate, and who better than a son with an idealistic and
still impressionable ego?

> GHOST.   If thou didst ever thy dear father love—
> HAMLET. O God!
> GHOST.   Revenge his foul and most unnatural murder.
>   . . .
> HAMLET. Haste me to know't, that I, with wings as swift
>   As meditation or the thoughts of love,
>   May sweep to my revenge.
>   (I.v.23–25; 29–31)

Thy dear father . . . love . . . revenge . . . thoughts of love . . . revenge.
Love is revenge; revenge, love. Narcissistic love is insatiable; revenge is,
therefore, its natural companion, even its natural expression. The son, in this
arrangement, owes the father unconditional love; the father owes the son
nothing.

"Remember me." With these words the ghost takes leave of his son, and
his haunted son responds:

> Remember thee?
> Ay, thou poor ghost, whiles memory holds a seat

In this distracted globe. Remember thee?
Yea, from the table of my memory
I'll wipe away all trivial fond records,
All saws of books, all forms, all pressures past
That youth and observation copied there,
And thy commandment all alone shall live
Within the book and volume of my brain.

(I.v.95–103)

Here we watch the catastrophe of a young mind's collapse under the weight of a signifier, which, though only a shadow, pulverizes Hamlet's being. This scene, in Elizabethan dramaturgy, is equivalent to the moment of surrender to divine possession in ancient tragedy, as in Euripides' *Bacchae,* when the energy of Dionysus passes into Pentheus, a human unprepared for direct contact with full, numinous Being, or in his *Herakles,* when Hera takes possession of Herakles' mind through Lyssa, her shadowlike allomorph. Hamlet, erasing his own records, clears the ground for a ghost to inscribe its angry will, as the mind of Herakles, in Euripides' play, is opened to Hera's hallucinations. Euripides makes the surrender in the cases of Pentheus and Herakles unconscious; Shakespeare has Hamlet make the choice consciously, yet without any true understanding of its consequences. Hamlet, erasing his own signifiers, surrenders memory, mind, and life itself to the ghost's influence; henceforth, deprived of his soul, Hamlet is more an automaton than a living, independent being. In his pithy wit, his ingenious schemes, and his private meditations, we see a mind, once functional, become ghost-ridden, seeking its function but unable to find it, since it has lost its center and its ground of Being:

O, what a noble mind is here o'erthrown!
. . . .
Now see that noble and most sovereign reason
Like sweet bells jangled, out of time and harsh;
That unmatched form and feature of blown youth
Blasted with ecstasy.

(III.i.146, 153–56)

T. S. Eliot judged the play *Hamlet* an artistic failure for its lack of an objective correlative adequate for Hamlet's turbulent emotions and behavior: "Hamlet's bafflement at the absence of objective equivalent to his feelings is a prolongation of the bafflement of his creator in the face of his artistic problem."[17] True, Hamlet is baffled by his inability to find the center of his being, or the spring of action, or a sufficient reason for his inaction. But whether a play that represents a soul so damaged is itself a dramatic failure is another question. The ghost, surely, is a sufficient correlative for Hamlet's confusion.[18] Ghosts are elusive; they do their damage and vanish into the thinnest air. Of course Hamlet cannot find the objective correlative for his inner confusion; thinking to erase only his personal signifiers, he surrenders his whole being to the ghost at the same time, to allow the ghost a blank slate for its obscure purposes.

Hamlet, with his reason and soul undermined by the ghost, becomes ghost-like himself. He is a haunted figure even before he sees the ghost, standing out in the first court scene as though from an alien world, in "inky cloak," and with melancholy on his face. He is obsessed, as his first soliloquy reveals, with his mother's infidelity to his father's memory, but we, who have already witnessed the ghost, can see deeper into Hamlet's melancholy than he can himself. Here we must imagine ourselves into a young mind, perhaps even, as Jones does, into the mind of an infant. The father, from whom the son derives his own significance, has departed, taking significance with him, and leaving the son with only half his being, the other half (or more) being mortgaged to keep a ghost alive.

Hamlet's first soliloquy intimates that Hamlet, even before the ghost's epiphany, has already surrendered much of his being to sustain his obsession with his idealized father image—"who was so excellent a king" (1.ii.139). Hamlet's soliloquy breaks off when his friends arrive to tell him of his father's ghost. But before they can divulge their news Hamlet is distracted for a moment by a vision, which anticipates and reads, as it were, their very thoughts:

> HAMLET. My father—methinks I see my father.
> HORATIO. Where, my lord?
> HAMLET.   In my mind's eye, Horatio.
>   (I.ii.183–85)

Whereupon Horatio reveals that, by coincidence, he too, and the trusted guards, have just seen the same phenomenon, which he had earlier described as "so like the king that was and is the question of these wars" (I.i.110–11).

Later, with almost the whole of his being now deeded to the ghost, Hamlet appears to Ophelia as a ghost himself:

> with his doublet all unbraced,
> No hat upon his head, his stockings fouled,
> Ungartered and down-gyvéd to his ankle,
> Pale as his shirt, his knees knocking each other,
> And with a look so piteous in purport

As if he had been loosed out of hell
To speak of horrors.

(II.i.78–84)

On other occasions Hamlet's ghostlike character shows more in his repartee, the signifiers of a mind possessing wit but to no purpose, spinning intentions and meanings to disguise, as best it can, the vortex of its own disintegration. All who see Hamlet or talk to him find him as disturbed as he is disturbing. Hamlet is the ghost at every gathering. The hazard of trafficking with ghosts is that they consume the life of their victims, and so render their victims ghosts too.

HAMLET.   Be thou a spirit of health or goblin damned,
              Bring with thee airs from heaven or blasts from hell,
              Be thy intents wicked or charitable,
              Thou com'st in such a questionable shape
              That I will speak to thee.

(I.iv.40–44)

Is the ghost a spirit of health? The answer is obvious. This ghost brings no airs from heaven, but reeks with the anger of the damned. The ghost confesses as much, and by intimidation implies the same damnation for Hamlet if he disobeys. If Hamlet repudiates the ghost, he will, so the ghost implies, condemn the ghost to eternal frustration, and his own soul to eternal guilt. But will the ghost be laid to rest by Hamlet's obedience? Will the son's obedience alleviate his father's suffering and release his father's soul from its prison? The question is absurd. To the degree that Hamlet complies with the ghost's orders, his compliance accomplishes only an increase in suffering, adding several new victims to the number of the damned. In his lust for revenge, his indifference to his son's welfare, his coercive means for extracting a son's submission to a father's ego—in look, word, and gesture, the ghost reveals itself as the spirit of hatred loosed from hell.

With good reason to suspect the ghost's motives, Hamlet conceives a test of the ghost's veracity:

                        The spirit that I have seen
              May be a devil, and the devil hath power
              T' assume a pleasing shape, yea, and perhaps
              Out of weakness and melancholy,
              As he is very potent with such spirits,
              Abuses me to damn me.

(II.ii.565–70)

Hamlet's play-within-the-play catches the conscience of King Claudius, but the revelation only tangles the issue in tighter knots, making it more difficult than ever for Hamlet to recognize in the ghost a diabolical spirit playing on his weakness and melancholy.

"Try the spirits," St. John instructs us.[19] How do we distinguish a good spirit from an evil spirit? Good ghosts are not hungry for other lives to feed on. They are satisfied with whatever destiny has given them, as we see in Dante's *Purgatorio* and *Paradiso*. If they return to the living, they come as helpers and teachers. Good ghosts—let us rather call them angels—are on the side of life. A messenger from heaven would be concerned more for Hamlet's health and safety at a corrupt court than in maintaining revenge as the mainspring of political action. Does this ghost ask once after Hamlet's health? And if, for the sake of public morality, Hamlet must bring Claudius to justice, has the ghost no means to ease Hamlet's burden? Does the ghost recall so much as one hour when father and son had enjoyed each other's company? No; instead, the ghost overwhelms Hamlet's will and robs him of his mind, leaving him only so much as will allow him to play the fool.

Buffoonery, Slater points out, is one of the strategies open to a weak ego threatened by the absolutism of the father. A little girl, Slater suggests, may win her father's affection by a display of girlish charm, but what is the son's equivalent strategy? "Shall he give a corresponding display of manly strength and athletic prowess? Will it produce the same affectionate reaction? Clearly it might; but even more clearly, it is less likely to, human vanity being what it is. For just as the daughter's performance contains an element of flattery, so the son's cannot avoid being inherently a little competitive—is he not, after all, striving to equal the father's masculinity and power, as he perceives it?"[20] It is a double bind: a good son is a submissive son, but a submissive son, to the degree that he is less of a man, is less his father's son. Buffoonery is a compromise solution: "If the father lacks this maturity, or if for any reason the son feels uncertain of his tolerance and love, the only role left to him . . . is to play the role of buffoon."[21] Slater goes on to talk of the wide latitude allowed the son, once he has adopted this strategy of self-castration. "The Fool," as Slater says, "can insult the King."[22]

Hamlet is trapped by the demands of a ghostly superego, which are so contradictory that they can in no way be satisfied. If the ghost cannot satisfy his desires, how can he expect his son to satisfy them? To show himself a man, with an ego secure in its sense of itself, Hamlet could politely decline the ghost's invitation to join in its dance of death, bidding the ghost a sad adieu, with profound regrets for the ghost's sorry plight. One soul cannot satisfy another's desires, and no soul is surrogate for another. "Since you, my dear ghost," Hamlet might say, "have the power to materialize yourself from the grave, and to turn grown men's hearts to jelly, clearly you do not need my

humble services. Excuse me, dear father, but I must return to my studies."
As the perfect diplomat, refraining from vulgarities, but using only courtly
flourishes in the best baroque style, prince Hamlet could disengage himself
from the ghost's shadow play, adding such flatteries as the king had thrived
on in his days of nature.

What son would dare an act of such insubordination to the ghost of his
father? Hamlet, idealistic himself, is easily confused by the false image of
idealism, by the ghost's perversion of the father image. More generous than
his father, Hamlet gives away his soul without hesitation, but in his obedience
he betrays himself. What course is left to him but to go mad and play the
fool?

There is method in his madness. By playing the fool, Hamlet can shield
his vulnerable being from the ghost's imperium and, at the same time, exercise a degree of control over his father's fate, insofar as the mouse can work
the cat. In his first encounter with the ghost Hamlet moves, with surprising
speed, from fear to jocular familiarity:

> *Ghost cries under the stage.*
>
> GHOST.   Swear.
> HAMLET   Ha, ha, boy, say'st thou so? Are thou there, truepenny?
>   Come on. You hear this fellow in the cellarage.
>   Consent to swear. . . .
> GHOST.   [*Beneath.*] Swear.
> HAMLET.   Hic et ubique? Then we'll shift our ground.
> ....
> GHOST.   [*Beneath.*] Swear by his sword.
> HAMLET.   Well said, old mole! Canst work i' th' earth so fast?
>   A worthy pioneer! Once more remove, good friends.
>   (I.v.149–62)

Boy? This fellow in the cellarage? Old mole? Is this the same Hamlet who,
only moments earlier, was addressing the dreaded apparition as "king, father,
royal Dane"? We are witnesses to a remarkable transformation. The roles are
reversed when the son discovers that his father's happiness is beholden to the
will of the son. "We'll shift our ground": Hamlet discovers the pleasure of
eluding his father's will while acting the obedient son. "Rest, rest, perturbéd
spirit": the son is now father to his father, with the power to pacify his father's
spirit, or to keep it in perpetual disturbance.

The antic style Hamlet adopts first toward the ghost, and then with others,
is Hamlet's best compromise, but this comic persona is itself a double bind.
The one arrow left to the son overwhelmed by his father's ego is to scramble
the orders, and botch his life. But this arrow fells, alas, the archer, not his

prey. Change the names and the historical dress and we have the same paradigm in the *Iliad*. Achilles is effectively paralyzed by the contradictions in the law of the father, vested in Agamemnon's scepter, with its power to distribute meanings according to the arbitrary will whether of Agamemnon, the surrogate father in the social ranks, or of Zeus, the protector of paternal privilege on the ethereal plane.[23] Befuddled by Agamemnon's contradictory exercise of his authority, to grant or withhold significance at will, Achilles chooses independence, but independence proves to be his self-destruction. In the same way, in attempting to integrate the contradictions of the father into his own being, Hamlet becomes a walking oxymoron: wise in his madness, dangerous in his innocence, intelligent in his stupidity. As Hamlet himself confesses: "His madness is poor Hamlet's enemy" (V.ii.218).

Yorick is the good ghost in this tale. How sweet is Yorick's appearance in the play, even if the form he takes is a grinning skull shoveled out of a grave. Yorick and Hamlet are brothers, two sons who sacrifice their egos to the greater glory of the father, and play the fool to salvage what they can of themselves from annihilation.[24]

Yorick is Hamlet's true father, or the closest resemblance to a father in this complicated play of father images. Seeing Yorick's skull transports Hamlet, for the first and only time, to scenes of his childhood, and to what we must accept as genuine memories of a bygone happiness, not simply idealized fantasies: "He hath bore me on his back a thousand times. . . . Here hung those lips that I have kissed I know not how oft. Where be your gibes now, your gambols, your songs, your flashes of merriment that were wont to set the table on a roar?" (V.i.164–68). No memory of kisses, of songs and jokes, of affectionate horseplay between child and man, rise to mind in Hamlet's encounter with the ghost of his father. Through a play dominated by the image of the father, Hamlet never recalls a single gesture of his father's love (except his portrait of his father as his mother's ideal lover) that would justify the sacrifice of his own life and happiness. From the graveyard scene we learn (if coincidence has any meaning) that when Hamlet was born his biological father was at the battlefront, killing King Fortinbras of Norway. In the clowning in the graveyard we hear for the first time of a surrogate paternal love Hamlet had enjoyed as a child. Yorick was Hamlet's nursemaid, companion, playmate, father and mother, all in one.

Hamlet grows up as more Yorick's son than Hamlet's. Like Yorick, Hamlet too is "a fellow of infinite jest, of most excellent fancy," though with his wit clouded over by his guilt. Hamlet's natural bent is not for his father's ideology of murder and reprisal, but for humor, art, and self-conscious thought. With Yorick's skull in his hand, Hamlet stands on the brink of consciousness. Memories of a healthier, and more generous, love, rising up from the jester's grave, open onto a vision of another road Hamlet might have taken. But the

jester's way, or the philosopher's (and the jester is the philosopher in traditional monarchies), is not open to the prince of the realm. The ghost of the
destructive father is more compelling than the spirit, which Yorick's skull
invokes, of the loving and joyful father. Love that nurtures, amuses, and aims
at the joy of the beloved, is taken for a lesser good than the love that aims at
the annihilation of the beloved. In Yorick's grave lies buried the promise of
Hamlet's autonomous identity.

As Hamlet stands on the brink of self-realization, the funeral procession
enters the graveyard to bury Ophelia, and Hamlet is swept back into the
vortex of events. Hamlet is the prince, not the jester, haunted by a ghost that
knows no peace and allows none to others. The hungry ghost, who feeds on
chaos and destruction, has his way, and eight victims in all are crushed beneath his juggernaut.

Schlegel notes that "the criminals are at last punished, but, as it were, by
an accidental blow, and not in the solemn way requisite to convey to the world
a warning example of justice; irresolute foresight, cunning treachery, and
impetuous rage, hurry on to a common destruction; the less guilty and the
innocent are equally involved in the general ruin."[25] True, but we should not
say that the play conveys no "warning example of justice." Since the ghost of
the father determines the course of the action, the cunning, treachery, and
rage, which Schlegel finds operative in the play, must be posted to the ghost's
account. This ghost cares nothing for the commonwealth, nor for fine distinctions between the innocent and the guilty; it is the spirit of ruin.

Yet, as a tragic protagonist, Hamlet is responsible for the ruin that engulfs
his kingdom, his family, and himself. But his fault lies less in his philoso-
phizing than in his sacrifice of himself in the name of the father. Until we
have made peace with our ghosts, we would do better to temper our condem-
nation with compassion for a noble soul who, from generosity, agrees to trade
his being for a weightless and nearly insubstantial signifier.

> Good night, sweet prince,
> And flights of angels sing thee to thy rest!
> (V.ii.344–45)

How different his destiny would have been if the little prince had heard this
goodnight in the nursery from his father's lips. But the prince grew up unblest
and unloved, and the blessing, when it is spoken at last, is spoken to a corpse.

7

The Empirical Stranger

"Mother died today." So runs, in Gilbert's translation, the first sentence of Albert Camus's novel, *The Stranger,* a sentence now famous among memorable literary first lines.[1] *Aujourd'hui, maman est morte:* the sentence is as stoic as an ancient epitaph, as modern as the telegram. We respond sympathetically to this speaker, who speaks without the mask and gestures of tragedy, but as the ordinary man, whose humdrum day leaves no space for operatic stances, even when the fabric of the day is torn by the intrusion of the extraordinary. Our aged parents end their days in a nursing home, comfortable perhaps, but almost anonymous. Death notices arrive typed and delivered by anonymous hands, and things continue exactly as before. Death, in modern times, calls for a certain minimal ceremony, per- haps a day or two off work. The first sentence of *The Stranger* records an event almost banal. Yet a merely ordinary man might affect an emotion, be- lieving emotions to be expected of him at such a moment. Meursault will not falsify the record, and for that he gains our admiration. We sense in him the noble Roman fiber.

"Or, maybe, yesterday. I can't be sure." So runs the second sentence of the austere first paragraph of *The Stranger*. Let others affect an emotion. Let the anonymous dispatch from The Home for Aged Persons express its "deep sympathy." Society expects sons to grieve at the death of their mothers, but our protagonist shuns mere social expectations. If it is callous for a son, receiving the telegram announcing his mother's death, to muse on a trivial detail, so be it. Integrity is more to be valued than social approval. In his willingness to acknowledge his flat response to his mother's death, Meursault displays a quality almost heroic.

Meursault will not ascribe motives to his killing of the Arab not present to his consciousness when he committed the crime. He will not fabricate a defense for himself. He is almost a Socrates, so scrupulous is he to avoid even the semblance of improving his chances of acquittal by some strategy, however acceptable it might be in the eyes of the law. If the court links the hearsay evidence of Meursault's callousness toward his mother with his shooting of the Arab, Meursault gains in stature by refusing to participate in a game where the rewards go to the insincere. Let the magistrate or the chaplain talk of God; even threatened with execution, Meursault will not capitulate to social expectations and feign adherence to beliefs imposed on him by others. He makes no excuses for his crime, and offers no defense; condemned to death, he refuses the consolation of religion.

A man of such integrity we are tempted to call a hero. This is not the protagonist of ancient tragedy, the king or warrior on whom the destinies of cities or nations depend, but the modern hero, the existentialist, able to accept with serenity his utter insignificance in a universe devoid of consciousness. No ghosts haunt this man's dreams; no god looms over him, either to inspire him to heroic achievements or to plunge him to his destruction. In this man's cosmology are no ideals, no values, neither good nor evil. His universe is irrational and directionless, but Meursault is willing to accept its vacancy. If it is heroic to meet destiny with courage and clear vision, then Meursault, ordinary clerk though he be, seems to have the qualities that entitle him to a place in the company of the ancient heroes. Camus himself looked on Meursault as a new Christ, and many modern commentators have agreed. If the universe is truly random, and all social values mere human artifacts, the modern Christ might indeed be a person who could endure both the false values of society and the unconsciousness of the universe.

Before we too quickly call Meursault, who kills a man without regret, a modern Socrates, we do well to examine his integrity more closely. The first paragraph of the novel runs thus:

"Mother died today. Or, maybe, yesterday; I can't be sure. The telegram from the Home says: YOUR MOTHER PASSED AWAY. FUNERAL TO-MORROW. DEEP SYMPATHY." Which leaves the matter doubtful; it could have been yesterday" (p.1).

If the first sentence speaks with an almost Roman gravity, the second sentence was spoken by no ancient Stoic. In a crisis, it seems, Meursault falls back on a certain kind of exactitude, fastening on indefiniteness in the telegram as if to reassure himself of his own definiteness. "Which leaves the matter doubtful; it could have been yesterday." So Meursault sums up his response to the announcement of his mother's death. Callous? Perhaps, but a welter of emotions can produce a tone of apparent callousness. What is the emotion appropriate to death? Acculturated to banality, who of us has not been nonplussed when the numinous touches the deepest chords of our being? Words, if any come, are inadequate, platitudes sufficient for the ordinary day, but mere echolalia when the abyss opens up at our feet. Grief wears many faces, but the absolutism of death mocks them all.

We accept the first paragraph of *The Stranger* as the honest response of a man who, unable to comprehend the fact of his mother's death, retreats into a stoic calm. But the first paragraph, with its seven terse sentences, contains Meursault's total emotional response to his mother's death (or seems to). The next paragraph talks of Meursault's mental calculations as to the effect of the funeral on his daily routine, and how his boss will react to his request for a leave of absence to attend the funeral. In the next paragraph Meursault admits that the death hasn't really registered; he expects "the funeral will bring it home to me, put an official seal on it, so to speak . . ." (p. 2).

It does. The officials at the Home for the Aged give the event its place in the social register: they conduct the bereaved son to the corpse when he arrives at the Home; they arrange for the all-night vigil by the corpse; they provide the mourners; they have the coffin lid screwed in place; they make up the funeral procession. A priest and acolytes carry out the registration in the religious sphere. The death is given its due, registered in all the official forms; everywhere, in fact, except in the heart of the bereaved son. In the whole first chapter, in which we are given the announcement of the death and the attendant funeral rites, Meursault shows scarcely a flicker of an emotional response. Throughout the funeral rites he remains an observer; everything happens around him in a choreography designed by others, in which he is expected to make certain moves. It is all so distant from him that he is less a participant than a spectator observing some alien social rite. Death must have some arcane meaning for other humans; our narrator will observe and record their behavior, doing his best not to offend their sensibilities, but it is a business in which he has no feelings one way or another.

The first chapter of *The Stranger* shows us a character devoid of feelings but with a kind of curiosity, if we can call it that, his sporadic attentiveness to the peculiar mannerisms of others. Meursault has, in place of feelings, sensations. He is hypersensitive. The silent presence of the mourners who joined him in the vigil by his mother's corpse, he says, "was telling on my nerves." The vigil leaves him aware of his fatigue and the aching in his limbs. The walk to the cemetery in the morning heat "blurs" his thoughts; he is aware of the throbbing in his temples. Meursault is sensitive to the white-washed walls of the mortuary, the nickel-coated screws in his mother's coffin, the heat of the day, the glare of the road, the smell of gasoline fumes; to color, light, sound; to moustaches, scarves, furniture, body odors, facial expressions; to almost anything—provided it is not an emotion. Emotions puzzle him. When a woman begins weeping during the vigil by his mother's corpse, our narrator is, as he says, "rather surprised" (p. 11).

Meursault is so assiduous in calibrating his sensations that he has fooled many into taking him for a man of feeling. On the contrary, he records not feelings but sense data, being the truly modern, who takes only sense data for primary realities, and feelings for subjective impressions. Throughout his visit to the Home for the Aged, in his dealings with the officials and residents there, in his vigil by the corpse, in his deportment at the burial, Meursault records only sense data, except for those expressions of irritation or surprise that even a dispassionate scientist might permit himself when a minor inconvenience impedes the experiment. The feelings Meursault expresses, such as they are, are trivial. Once or twice he apologizes, or affects a vaguely apologetic attitude, for causing some inconvenience. He worries, slightly, about the propriety of smoking a cigarette in the presence of a corpse. He is partial to *café au lait*. The mannerisms of the old folks keeping vigil with him irritate his nerves, slightly.

Under the guise of the detached observer is a man dissociated from his feelings. From the moment when he receives the telegram with its news of his mother's death until his return to the city of Algiers after the funeral, no real feelings intrude into Meursault's record. The first paragraph says it all: ". . . today. Or, maybe, yesterday. Which leaves the matter doubtful; it could have been yesterday." What matter? The matter of his mother's death? No, the only matter in doubt is the precise moment of her death.[2] This is quibbling, but any of us might do the same. In the face of death, we too might fasten on some inconsequential detail, as if to stave off chaos by rearranging a twig or two. But Meursault fastens only on inconsequential details from start to finish. The quibbling in the first paragraph of the novel is the behavior of a mind habituated to evasion.

A small feeling glimmers on the morning after the vigil by the corpse. Meursault, standing outside the mortuary, feels the morning breeze, with its salty tang. "There was the promise of a very fine day," Meursault notes, and catches himself thinking "what an agreeable walk I could have had, if it hadn't been for Mother" (p. 14). This agreeable event, first provided, but then thwarted, by his mother's inconvenient death looms all the larger when we read in the next paragraph that the morning hour, when Meursault would normally be preparing to go to work, was always "the worst hour of the day" for him (ibid.). Mornings, with their promise of renewal, mean for Meursault only a deadening of his spirit, since all he has to look forward to is the dull mechanical routine at the office. In an almost inadvertent slip Meursault admits that his mother's death opens up the prospect of at least one pleasurable morning in his life, but such a thought is unseemly, and the man who is so studiously unconventional shows himself quite conventional in censoring the thought. Psychoanalysts have much to ponder in this brief passage, in which the death of a mother gives the son his first agreeable sensation, bordering on an emotion, which he must forthwith suppress.

After this small revelation of the inner dynamics of his mind, Meursault allows himself one more expression of genuine feeling in chapter 1. As he sums up, in the final paragraph of the first chapter, his impressions of the day of the funeral, he remembers "my little thrill of pleasure when we entered the first brightly lit streets of Algiers, and I pictured myself going straight to bed and sleeping twelve hours at a stretch" (p. 22).[3] With the inconvenience and irritation of the funeral subsiding and the official seals duly affixed to the event, Meursault can return to his sleep. It is not much, this little pleasure, but in the emotionally anesthetized the smallest emotion speaks volumes. Death is so disagreeable to our narrator—a fact that becomes progressively clearer through the novel—that he will do anything to avoid responding to, or thinking about, it. He will quibble about details, or fasten on minutiae like a biologist examining an unfamiliar organism; he will, whenever possible, doze off. The prospect of a long, uninterrupted sleep is one of the few thoughts that can arouse in him a "thrill of pleasure."

Meursault, we may say, had no particular affection for his mother. So be it. Not every mother is the Madonna. Later in the novel, when the magistrate asks him whether he loved his mother, Meursault replies: "Yes, like everybody else" (p. 83). Earlier, however, Meursault admits that when his mother was living with him, before he arranged for her move to the Home for the Aged, they scarcely had a relationship: "Mother was always watching me, but we hardly ever talked" (p. 3). While the novel implies that Meursault is superior to conventional mores, in fact he is thoroughly conventional, at least in his relations with his mother. He observes all the proprieties expected of the son, but with no warmth, friendship, or pleasure. All Meursault can remember of his mother by way of personal connection is that she stared at him while she was alive, and inconvenienced him in her death.

Meursault is honest enough to admit his merely tepid feelings for his mother, and at his trial this honesty is brought against him. It is unfair, we may say, as indeed we are encouraged by the novel itself to say, to drag his relations with his mother into his trial on a charge of murder. No man is obliged to love his mother. Meursault at least saw that his mother was decently provided for, and what more can society demand? Meursault, an artful dramaturge, persuades us to join him in placing the judicial system itself on trial. He would have us believe that the trial proceedings, in bringing forward considerations of motive, are hopelessly corrupt. By the time the verdict of guilty is handed down, we have almost been convinced that Meursault is condemned to death for callousness rather than for murder.

Meursault's attitude toward his mother is, in fact, germane to the trial since considerations of character and motive are society's mechanism, however imperfect, for tempering blind justice with mercy. If Meursault were emotionally tepid only in his relations with his mother, or if his behavior at her funeral were the major pieces of circumstantial evidence on which he was convicted, we should certainly protest the inequity of the judicial system. The question of his guilt, however, is never in doubt. The prosecution probes to find whether, behind the act of murder, is a man with any kind of emotion at all. The narrator, who is also our only witness to the proceedings, replays his trial in such a way as to make us believe that the judicial system rendered him invisible. The truth is that the accused resists every attempt by the court to bring him forward into visibility; instead, he retreats into a self-imposed invisibility, from which he can sneer with polite contempt at his fellows as they perform an irrelevant drama, starring an imaginary person, whom they call Monsieur Meursault.

Meursault is emotionally anesthetized in every aspect of his life, and here again he is our chief witness. He likes Marie. He likes going for a swim with her; he likes her body, and having sex with her. But when she asks him if he would marry her, he says he "didn't mind; if she was keen on it, we'd get married" (p. 53). Probing for a vestige of an emotion from her lover, Marie asks him, for the second time, if he loves her. He replies "much as before, that her question meant nothing or next to nothing—but I supposed I didn't" (p. 52). Marie continues to probe, but all her probes produce the same noncommittal response. Marie's body produces pleasurable sensations in Meursault's body. One body enjoys conjunction with another. But when Marie interjects her person into the lovemaking and looks for a relationship instead of a sensation, Meursault retreats into his objectivity, which is his refuge from the world.

Perhaps Meursault's problem is women. But no, it's the same everywhere we look. Meursault has his little pleasures. He enjoys his cigarettes; on his day off he reads the newspaper, and clips out amusing items for his scrapbook; he sits on his balcony to watch the Sunday afternoon promenade. At one point, Meursault's employer, with plans to open an office in Paris, asks if Meursault would like the opportunity to develop his career there? No, Meursault has no interest in changing his life, though we have already heard him confess that his mornings are hateful to him. Once, Meursault tells his employer, he had ambition, but now he realizes the futility of such desires. One life is as good as another, Meursault claims (pp. 51–52).

This would be a noble resignation if genuine, but Meursault's resignation is a mask to cover the emotional void in his relations with his mother, his girlfriend, his work, his daily routines in his apartment, his leisure time, his play, his friends. This is not philosophical detachment but an attitude, which, when it comes up against something demanding more than attitude, is revealed for what it is—a persona masking a pathological state of emotional dissociation. Meursault is a somnambulist.

Until his trial we are convinced that he is a man incapable of emotion. As his trial proceeds, however, stronger and more genuine emotions begin to surface. At the conclusion of the first day's hearings, as Meursault is being driven from the courtroom back to the prison, he hears outside the police van "all the characteristic sounds of a town I'd loved" (p. 122). Loved? Nothing in the narrative up to this point suggests that Meursault is capable of love. Meursault likes his cigarette, his café au lait, his Sunday paper, a swim in the sea. He enjoys his girlfriend's breasts, her teasing pout, the sea smell in her hair, but love? Now he talks of love, the man who has presented his life as a tedious and meaningless routine, and himself wrapped in ennui. If the word *love* at this point in the novel strikes a false note, we accept it, as a promise of emotional healing; perhaps, under the threat of execution, he is willing to lift his guard and acknowledge his deeper feelings.

After the trial is over, and the verdict delivered, Meursault is confined to his prison cell where he awaits the guillotine. This is, for any convict, a period of hideous emotional confusion, when the condemned, ignorant of the time appointed for his execution, knows only that it will take place some morning at dawn. That dawn when Meursault, after a night's vigil by his mother's corpse, steps into the fresh breezes outside the mortuary, and those loathed mornings, which pull Meursault from sleep to his sleep-walking routines at the office, now take on a special poignancy. Meursault, no longer able to slip into the comfort of unconsciousness, keeps vigil every night over his own death.[4] Every morning becomes both a relief from the night's disturbed vigil and a torture, since each dawn may be his last. For a man awaiting his execution all forms of expectancy are perverted, until he knows not whether he fears or yearns for the guillotine. When the dawn passes, the prisoner knows not whether to believe himself given a special grace or a greater torture.

Under such conditions Meursault experiences even stronger emotions. So ingrained is his habit of evasion, however, that the emotions are masked, refused their place, or translated wherever possible into mere sensations. Eavesdropping on his thoughts, as Meursault lives out his final days in his jail cell, we might think we were listening to an ordinary man musing randomly on an ordinary life, pondering idly this or that more-or-less trivial project. Under the mind's casual chatter, however, we discern a man listening to the "faint throbbing" of his own heart (p. 141). Faint indeed. Hitherto Meursault's heart had been virtually an obsolete organ. Now, as his heart becomes functional, under the threat of execution, the throbbing grows louder, stronger, more insistent. We see him hurrying to the door of his cell every time he hears a sound outside, listening so intently that he hears his breathing "quick and hoarse like a dog's panting" (p. 142). He dreams now of escape; he dreams that his appeal is successful; the thought sends "a rush of joy" through his body and brings tears to his eyes (p. 143). But his emotions are tabu, and must be suppressed. He compels himself to calm down: "It was up to me to bring my nerves to heel and steady my mind; for, even in considering this possibility, I had to keep some order in my thoughts" (ibid.). Successful in routing the unruly emotions, our protagonist takes pride in his work, glad to have "earned a good hour's peace of mind" (p. 144). Meursault will do almost anything to gain an hour's peace of mind, and long practice has developed into a fine proficiency. He can sit through his trial, and hear himself condemned to execution, without the testimony of the witnesses, the arguments of the prosecution, or the cross-examination causing more than a ripple of boredom and impatience across his peace of mind.

We are led to believe that we are eavesdropping on a man's dialogue with his deepest, most intimate self, when Meursault reveals the drift of his mind in those final days of his life between his trial and the execution. In fact, the self Meursault communicates with is nothing more than a surface self, since he has excluded so much of himself from conscious recognition that he hardly has a self to communicate with, or a language in which to communicate. But he is clever enough to persuade us, almost, that the equanimity he achieves in his prison cell expresses an enlightened detachment.

Meursault certainly has himself persuaded until the chaplain walks in on him unexpectedly. Meursault lies on his cot in his cell, musing on his girlfriend Marie, and in his somnambulistic fashion thinking that, without their physical conjunction, nothing now remains to remind either of them of the other. The priest, breaking in on Meursault's thoughts, begins to speak of God. Meursault responds as we would expect; he has no belief in God, nor any interest in other people's thoughts on the subject. A man who denies a real existence to his emotions will certainly give no credence to some metaphysical abstraction in the sky. The priest continues to probe, and Meursault's boredom turns to mild interest as he perceives the priest's increasing emotional agitation. Suddenly, in a reversal almost as momentous as the *peripeteia* in ancient tragedy, the agitation shifts from the priest to the condemned man. At first Meursault finds the priest's interrogation merely irksome, and his pronouncements about God, guilt, and the afterlife irrelevant. Then something in Meursault breaks. Meursault begins screaming. Grabbing the priest's cassock, Meursault pours out all his rationalizations "in a sort of ecstasy of joy and rage" (p. 151). A storm of self-righteousness erupts in the prison cell, so violent that the guards come in to release the chaplain from the prisoner's grip.

Meursault claims that his ecstasy was prompted by the priest's cocksure attitude, but the opposite is true. The explosion detonates when Meursault's own self-righteousness is threatened. "Actually, I was sure of myself," Meursault says, "sure about everything, far surer than he [the chaplain]; sure of my present life and of the death that was coming. . . . I'd been right, I was still right, I was always right" (ibid.). True, Camus has staged the scene to prejudice us against the priest. The priest, given to sanctimonious platitudes, confuses the issue by talking of the afterlife, bringing in at least implicitly the machinery of punishments and rewards that any modern person would be justified in rejecting as medieval sentimentality. But, with his shibboleths, his tearful gaze, and his fondness for playing surrogate father, the priest is only the manifest provocation. The truth is that Meursault's cosmology, so rigorously constructed, and daily rehearsed, proves inadequate to the ultimate test, and years of suppressed emotions burst the dam and flood the prison cell.

If Camus had allowed a psychotherapist to visit Meursault at this moment, a true therapist of the soul, Meursault's liberation might have been complete. The therapist might have baptized the condemned man in that flood of emotion, and transformed the liberated anger into the grace of the Eumenides. But no, Camus would not grant his prisoner that grace, nor us. His priest must be a cliché, a voice canting outmoded ideologies. So the baptism is proscribed, and Meursault must die with a specious understanding, tragically unreconciled.

Meursault himself takes his explosion for a true catharsis. The rush of anger cleansed him, he says, and emptied him of hope; "gazing up at the dark sky spangled with its signs and stars," Meursault says, "for the first time, the first, I laid my heart open to the benign indifference of the universe. To feel it so like myself, indeed, so brotherly, made me realize that I'd been happy, and that I was happy still" (p. 154). Meursault falls asleep after his outburst, and when he wakes he sees the stars shining, hears the sounds of the countryside, feels the cool night air moving in his cell, hears a steamer's siren in the distance. For the first time in the novel Meursault even shows some understanding of his mother, and experiences empathetically her feelings as she faced her own death in the Home for the Aged.

Yet, despite the lyricism of the final paragraph of the novel, Meursault is not a reliable witness. True, Meursault has experienced a high emotional state, and for one moment moves beyond his alienation to experience the bond between him and the universe. But in the next moment, in his last utterance in the novel, Meursault states that all that remains for him ("so that I might feel less alone," as he puts it in a pregnant clause) is to hope that a large crowd of spectators will gather to witness his execution, and "that they should greet me with howls of execration" (ibid.). Such is his last will and testament. Poor heart, it opens, but the shock is too great, and Meursault retreats into the habit of his alienation. The curses Meursault invokes on himself are the cries of a man locked in the lazaret of his own making.

Until the priest's appeals unloose Meursault's pent-up anger, the novel is situated in a world where emotions are virtually banished, or appear as the curious mannerisms of beings whom the protagonist cannot comprehend. After the priest's visit to Meursault in his prison cell the last few pages of the novel—four, in Gilbert's translation—are vivid with emotion, but the emotions are fear, anger, and hate. Where is humor in his cosmology, or joy? Why are so many emotions tabu? By what impulses was Meursault directed to build his lazaret to quarantine him from life?

Under the priest's probing Meursault admits to feeling fear so intense that it blocks out any other feeling. Meursault describes eloquently the source of his fear: "from the dark horizon of my future a sort of slow, persistent breeze had been blowing toward me, all my life long, from the years that were to come. And on its way the breeze had leveled out all the ideas that people had tried to foist on me in the equally unreal years I was then living through" (p. 152).[5] Knowledge of his own death is the only valid idea in Meursault's cosmology, which negates all other ideas, and his fear of death the emotion that negates all other emotions. Holding to his consciousness of his own death as the only certainty, Meursault falls into the fallacy of our age, and takes everything else for illusion, elaborations spun by the mind to veil its own fear. *Almost* everything else, we should say, since, as a modern, Meursault grants validity to one set of mental operations—immediate sense impressions. In our modern cosmology, which takes sensations for objective data, emotions, seen as unreal themselves, lead to unreal ideas—the soul, conscience, the collective welfare, guilt and responsibility, ideas that Meursault claims other people foisted on him in his earlier years before he saw through their pretense. He will have none of them. Meursault lives only in the moment, but here too he only simulates enlightenment. He assumes that sense data provide unmediated knowledge, and that they are thus truer than the webs of cognitive structures that the history of the human psyche reveals. But the unmediated sense datum is a fiction, and the separation of sensations from emotions rests on an arbitrary decision. The moment-by-moment sensations by which Meursault registers his own existence are carefully circumscribed to conform to his own definition of both moment and sensation. Meursault has never experienced Blake's discovery of all Eternity in a grain of sand. Meursault has not transcended human ideas and emotions; he simply represses most of them.

Meursault invites our collaboration by affecting an integrity free of the claptrap of several thousand years of human cogitation. Meursault goes to a martyr's death, so Camus would suggest, as the heroic victim of the claptrap he has chosen to reject. But his is a spurious integrity. Our sympathy is carefully managed in the events surrounding the trial, in the proceedings of the trial, in Meursault's confinement in the prison cell, and in his encounters with the magistrate and the priest—the two mouthpieces for society, secular and spiritual. Throughout these events Meursault presents his customary persona as the slightly quizzical observer of folkways foreign to him. He finds it difficult to comprehend that he is indeed the person on trial; that strangers are accusing him of murder; that he is the prisoner, the defendant, the criminal. Who of us could recognize himself or herself if we were to eavesdrop on discussions held by strangers, in which we were the object of their remarks, criticisms, or hypotheses? When Meursault complains that the legal system functions "to exclude me from the case, to put me off the map, so to speak, by substituting the lawyer for myself," we nod in agreement (p. 130). Who among us have not stood with Meursault, in our minds, seeing ourselves on trial for our individuality, with a hostile society as the judge and jury? Orchestrating such feelings, which lie deep in our souls, Camus stages the trial to appear a travesty of justice. Meursault's presence in the courtroom is made irrelevant to the case. Judgments are based on innuendo, flagrant manipulation of circumstantial evidence, and by direct appeals to sentiment and prejudice. The trial is made to seem the juggernaut of the herd instinct.

At one point in the trial, irked by what he sees as a "conspiracy" to exclude him from the proceedings, Meursault has the urge to break in to announce that he is the man on trial and that he has "something really important" to say (p. 124). On second thought, he realizes that he has "nothing to say." Ironically, tragically, he is correct on both counts. By deliberate intent he has nothing to say to the court, having excluded himself as a participant in the trial, as he had excluded himself from the murder under discussion in the court. In his silence Meursault maintains his customary persona, as the man with no deep convictions or ideas, and no strong desire to articulate them even if he had them. In fact, he has much to say, at least to us, who are privy to his more intimate thoughts. His record of the trial is an exercise in self-justification. When the verdict is delivered, we have almost forgotten that the charge was murder, and have been led to believe that Meursault is convicted for having no soul, for showing no remorse after the crime, for his nonconformity. Meursault gives us to believe that the prosecution manipulated the trial; in fact, Meursault is the manipulator, who assumes the pose of silent resignation, all the while constructing the case for himself as the innocent scapegoat for society's hypocrisy.

Always the innocent, Meursault is a man to whom things happen. In all the arrangements for his mother's funeral Meursault does nothing except what is assigned to him, or expected of him. The authorities at the Home take care of the legal and practical details, and the priest fulfills the religious obligations. Meursault goes along with the arrangements, though he is an atheist and claims that his mother was one also. He attends the body as expected; he walks with the funeral procession; he attends the burial. In all these rites Meursault makes no gesture toward the deceased that is authentically his own, except to muse that he might have had a pleasant morning, but for his mother's death. With Marie he is the same emotionally passive person, whose indifference cuts to the bone.

A symptom of Meursault's pathology is that he frequently dozes off, or wishes to do so, to escape the pressures of the moment. He is frequently tired, overcome by the heat, dazed by the light; he is easily bored, even by his own trial—an event that he finds "tedious." At one point in the trial, when a sound from outside the courtroom opens him up to a rush of memories, Meursault has "only one idea: to get it over, to go back to my cell, and sleep . . . and sleep" (p. 132). Whenever life calls for Meursault to participate, Meursault retreats into nonchalance, boredom, or sleep.

Meursault's attitude, as always the object of others' action and never the subject, culminates in his murder of the Arab. When Meursault takes his walk along the beach to the fatal encounter, he has already engaged in one fight with the Arabs, and his friend Raymond has already been wounded. Despite the obvious danger, and the prior hostilities, Meursault chooses to take his walk alone, carrying a loaded revolver, to the very place where the hostile engagement has just taken place. His excuse is that he wants to get away from the emotional turbulence in his friend's house; he wants some peace and quiet. But, to find his peace, he goes to the very rock and stream where he and Raymond have just seen the Arabs.

The only explanation Meursault can offer in his own trial for the shooting is that "it was because of the sun" (p. 130). Camus's description of the moment of the shooting is one of the most extraordinary paeans to the sun's violence in literature. The heat and light on the beach that day were like superhuman agencies, pressing in on Meursault relentlessly. Meursault clenches his fist and keys up his nerves, to fend off "the dark befuddlement" the sun was pouring into him. The sun scorches Meursault's skin; his forehead threatens to burst from internal pressure; the sky is a sea of molten steel; Meursault's eyes are blinded by tears; the light reflected off the Arab's knife scars his eyelashes and gouges his eyeballs: "Then everything began to reel before my eyes, a fiery gust came from the sea, while the sky cracked in two, from end to end, and a great sheet of flame poured down through the rift. Every nerve in my body was a steel spring, and my grip closed on the revolver. The trigger gave, and the smooth underbelly of the butt jogged my palm" (p. 76). Hypnotized by his eloquence, we overlook the real cataclysm, which is Meursault's retreat from responsibility.

Meursault is prone to befuddlement. The sun befuddles his mind when he confronts the Arab on the beach, as it had befuddled him during the walk to his mother's grave. His mind blurs over when he kills the Arab, as it blurs in the trial, when he is forced to sit through the interminable drone of others discussing his "soul" (to use his quotes). In many small ways Meursault displays the same inclination to retreat to a perplexed ignorance. This pose, which Meursault maintains with studied rigor, reaches its extreme when Meursault admits to feeling little regret for committing the murder. A man not responsible for his actions need be troubled by no regrets. During the trial Meursault wishes he could explain to the prosecutor, "in a quite friendly, almost affectionate way, that I had never been able really to regret anything in all my life" (p. 127). How could an automaton experience regret?

In the behaviorist paradigm, which is the foundation of Meursault's cosmology, the universe is a random spin of unconscious matter, and the human, the microcosmic reflection, is a collection of reflex responses. If humans like to believe themselves endowed by some Creator with ideas, emotions, or purposes, that is the ultimate absurdity in an absurd world. Meaningless itself, the universe is indifferent to all human constructions of meaning. Volition and motivation being, for this philosophy, archaisms, intellectual honesty calls us to repudiate meaning in our existence, or direction in the universe at large. But the universe is mindless, provided we remove our minds from consideration. If the same forces that produce protein molecules have also produced our consciousness, what is our evidence that the universe is indifferent to consciousness? If we experience significance, by what argument do we deny significance to the natural order? We construct a universe without meaning only by disenfranchising ourselves.

The ideology of *The Stranger* represents the universe as a blank, emotionally and spiritually: a cosmos where inanimate matter is the prime element, and coincidence substitutes for cause. The protagonist, moulding himself to this ideology, erases from his mind any ideas contaminated by the mythical or theological bias, which interprets the world in terms of agent and cause. Yet, despite its rejection of the imagination, *The Stranger* is the modern version of the ancient myth of a hero's combat with the primeval powers. The hero of ancient myth was defined by a relationship to a deity, which was both symbiotic and adversarial. Ovid's *Metamorphoses* is a long recital of catastrophic meetings of humans and their gods. Pentheus was destroyed in his encounter with Dionysos. Actaeon, the hunter, was felled by the anger of Artemis, his goddess, when he came upon her naked. Semele, following Hera's blandishments, was burned to ash when her lover Zeus revealed himself to her in his full being. Arachne, best of weavers, was transformed to a spider by Athena, goddess of weaving, for daring to call herself Athena's equal. The musician Marsyas was flayed alive for competing with the god of music. Phaethon was destroyed by Helios, his father, for driving the solar chariot beyond its appointed course. Such myths, of heroes blasted when they trespass on the numinous, tell of the grandiose ego that has overreached itself.[6]

In *The Stranger* the numinous adversary is Helios, whom we recognize as the divine adversary in many ancient myths, and the encounter is as elemental as the meeting of god and human in any ancient tragedy. In a spare, modern style, without recourse to the personas and machinery of ancient myth, Camus presents a myth as tragic as Euripides' drama of Pentheus. As the ancient hero's mind was unhinged by the provocative Dionysus, so Meursault's mind is unhinged by the naked power of Helios. Like the heroes of old, Meursault goes about his mundane business, but suddenly, as in ancient tragedies, the numinous breaks through the mundane and shatters his life. The sun alone is the cause, Meursault claims, which made him pull the trigger of the revolver in his hands and release the bullet. As in the ancient myths, the protagonist in this antimythical myth is both victim and unsuspecting agent of forces beyond his control or comprehension.

The hero's adversary in the ancient myths was, of course, a god, who was assumed to act from some kind of motive—injured honor, jealousy, or anger. The sun, in Camus's novel, is devoid of anthropomorphic motives, being the novelist's engine to destroy all considerations of motive or character. Meursault is a set of reflexes, like the salmon smolt slipping mindlessly downstream, except that, in this case, the reflexes reached for a revolver, took precise aim, and fired one bullet, then four more, point blank into a man's body. But any talk of motive here is construction after the fact. To convict the unwitting carrier of those reflexes of a criminal offense is an absurdity. It was "pure chance," Meursault says, which led him to walk, with a revolver in hand, to the stream where the hostile encounter with the Arabs had just taken place (p. 110). Crimes presume agents and motives, and here there are neither.

Camus will have none of the old mythical agents of human destiny, but, paradoxically, by denying any reality to the gods of myth, with their subtle interchanges on the theme of Being, Camus effaces the ego too as the locus of thought and action. Meursault had no thoughts of murder when the bullets left the revolver in his hand, nor any afterwards. The event, which holds the attention of so many people in the courtroom, is a nonevent (in Meursault's mind), there being no one present to plan the shooting, to perform the killing, or to reflect on it afterwards. The judicial process becomes a windy ramble about nothing.

In Meursault's cosmology the sun is simply a material body of enormous and, in this instance, fatal power. Yet like the deities of myth, even here the sun is the archetypal signifier of understanding. Meursault's encounter with the sun is the climax in a series of signifiers, tending all in the same direction. Meursault, who cannot see himself a murderer when the bullets from his revolver pierce another man's body, will assume no responsibility for any other action in his so-called life. His mother's funeral, Marie's feelings, his participation in the shady affairs of his friend Raymond, the loaded revolver in his hands, the walk up the beach, the blinding sun: everywhere we see, through the changing scenes, the same protagonist, and always disclaiming his responsibility. How could Meursault be responsible if his only defense is that a man is at the mercy of his reflexes? But where does that put the mind and its signifiers?

Meursault's cosmology grows from an intention, which is covert and far from scientific. By stripping the world of its mythical icons, those final witnesses of Being, Meursault pretends to erase his own ego from the canvas at the same time. Suffering neither the gaze of the Almighty nor his own, Meursault presents himself as a fair imitation of a man with no investment in the world. Trial, defense, conviction, and, finally, execution—let others handle such matters who have an investment in them, even as Meursault leaves his mother's death to those likely to profit from the event. Meursault reserves only the right to mutter a mild complaint in our ear, of his exclusion from the legal process, as if his person were being made over into an object by some nonsensical social code. The truth is the opposite. Meursault objects to the court's determination to make sense of the Arab's death, and resents most of all others investing his being with their meanings when he has declared all being meaningless. Having made himself into an object, he will not have himself personified, as if he were a subject acting of his own free will.

Meursault first depersonalizes himself as a ruse for psychic survival, and then, in a more cunning and desperate ruse, charges society with the crime; society, after all, coins the signifiers, and calls reflex action a crime. Meursault achieves, in the eyes of some, a kind of sainthood for transcending the ego, but his rage at the prison chaplain tells a more convincing truth: "I'd been right, I was still right, I was always right" (p. 151)—this is the voice of an ego so displaced that it will commit murder to justify its displacement. This man has his signifiers too, to which he is passionately attached, even while denying their significance. "I was questioned several times immediately after my arrest," Meursault says, never thinking to question himself (p. 77). How can there be sainthood without self-examination, and how can there be an examination when the self has been spirited away? Pretending to have neither preferences nor choices, Meursault chooses solipsism, granting no reality to any signifiers but his own, and then, reversing himself, denying reality even to them.

Meursault, standing with his friend Raymond on the beach, confronting the hostile Arabs, revolver in hand, has a moment of insight: "Just then it crossed my mind that one might fire, or not fire—and it would come to absolutely the same thing" (p. 72). Soon Meursault is back at the same place on the beach, the loaded revolver again in his hand, confronting the same Arabs who had just wounded his friend. The trigger is pulled; five bullets ejected; the Arab killed with the precision of coincidence, as if some proposition were being put to the test; and we have the perfect alibi: the blinding sun. "C'était le hasard," Meursault says of his rendezvous with destiny.[7] If the reflexes alone are responsible, the signifier is deposed, and unconscious instinct crowned in its place.

But who is this person, whose instincts so coincided with intention that not so much as a hairline intervened for consciousness, who cannot discriminate between killing and not killing? A man who cannot say whether he loves or not, or keep his mind on the arguments presented in his trial, but must inform us of his ennui, has hardly proven himself the master at deciphering the signifiers of the universe. Is the decision to kill or not the same for the killer and the killed alike? Do the Arab's family and friends count for nothing? Brutes may not count, but we do; once evolved into the species that differentiates, we have no path back to unity but through the gates of the signifier.[8] Meursault, though he claims to make no distinctions, is himself adept at discrimination, at least when emotions must be placed under quarantine.

Alienated from his own feelings, Meursault reads alienation as the universal condition. His case is as baffling as it is tragic. He is so acute in his observations, so scrupulous in recording minute-by-minute data, and noting his restlessness, drowsiness, or boredom, that we are convinced of his superior vision. After his catharsis we are all the more ready to be convinced, but we are fooled; even after catharsis he is tangled, tragically, in his signifiers. A man who insists on his right to kill, with reflex action and coincidence as his defense, is, in a curious and tragic way, enlightened and unenlightened at the same time. Like the heroes of myth, Meursault is blinded by the narrow slit of his personal consciousness, which he equates with universal vision.

Meursault, in the litany of self-justification that he recites to us and the prison chaplain, says that nothing has the least importance to him. "What difference could they make to me, the deaths of others, or a mother's love, or his [the priest's] God; or the way man decides to live, the fate he thinks he chooses, since one and the same fate was bound to 'choose' not only me but thousands of millions of privileged people who, like him, called themselves my brothers. Surely, surely he must see that?" (p. 152). The logic here is of the intellect using signifiers to cancel signifiers, without canceling them, until, wearied of its crosspurposes, it drowses back into unconsciousness.

Protestations notwithstanding, Meursault is far from indifferent to his own fate. The anger of the last pages, betraying the novel's stance of clinical objectivity, reveals Meursault as, in fact, a man of passion, who cloaks his passion in indifference to protect his own vulnerability. But so beholden is he to the confusion of his signifiers that death, not life, is his passion, as he admits while awaiting his execution. Meursault, fixated on death, generates a plot to revolve around three deaths: the death of his mother from old age; the death of the Arab from a bullet wound; and finally his own execution, following the Arab's death sequentially but not causally, cause and effect being excluded by the rules of the plot and replaced by coincidence. The common feature in all three is Meursault's disclaimer of his personal investment in any of them, yet this is the same man who talks, with haunting eloquence, of "the dark horizon of my future," from which "a sort of slow, persistent breeze had been blowing toward me, all my life long, from the years that were to come" (ibid.). His obsession with his own death blinds him to any deaths but his own.

Death, which ridicules every initiative, in Meursault's cosmology, is the objective fact that reduces the world to an object and all relations to object relations. Meursault, believing himself a mere object in the path of faceless, impersonal forces, dedicates himself to becoming as unconscious as the forces that he believes determine his fate. Nothing in the novel indicates that Meursault has experienced more than object relations with anyone in his life. He never saw his father. His mother was only an object to him, as much when she was alive as when she was a corpse, as he assumes that he, likewise, was no more than an object for her. With Marie, his neighbors, his friends, the magistrate, the court, the jailer, the prison chaplain, Meursault maintains the same depersonalized relations. The man killed by the bullets from his revolver is also an object, no more significant than bullets or revolvers. Obsessed with his own death, Meursault will not risk an authentic relationship, since he needs all his resources to keep his fears at bay and maintain his objectivity. But Meursault's depersonalized relations with others are a symptomatic reflection of a deeper malaise: to escape consciousness, Meursault must maintain only an object relationship with himself. Meursault first depersonalizes himself, then others; finally, he depersonalizes the universe to reflect back to him the emptiness he has inscribed in his heart.[9]

Meursault is devoted to death like the ancient warrior dedicated to his war god. In his final days in his prison cell, while musing on his impending execution, Meursault recalls a story his mother had told him about the father he had never known. His father, according to his mother's story, once witnessing a public execution, had returned home, and was "violently sick" (p. 138). This fourth death, mentioned almost in parenthesis, as a memory of a memory, is the seed from which the novel grows. How strange, for the psychoanalyst, that this story makes the only reference in the novel to the protagonist's father; strange, too, that the only connection made between father and son is the story, passed on to the child, of his father's reaction to a public execution. But strangest of all, the child grows up to become a murderer condemned to execution. Thus the son, engineering his own execution, creates his relationship with his father. On first hearing the story, Meursault remembers, he had thought his father's conduct disgusting. "But now I understood; it was so natural. How had I failed to recognize that nothing was more important than an execution; that, viewed from one angle, it's the only thing that can genuinely interest a man?" (p. 35).[10]

Hypnotized by the story of a public execution, Meursault relives the story by becoming the criminal, whom he had so long imagined, and the executioner, and by one further projection joins the crowd to shower curses on the condemned man in his final moments. So numbed by fear that he can neither find meaning in his life nor experience his authentic being, Meursault stages a tragedy to invest his life with meaning and feeling. This overzealous ego must play dramatist, protagonist, the chorus of keen-eyed reporters, and jeering audience, to be all parts—the murderer, the murdered, witness, and judge, all in one. The innocent martyr becomes the focus of attention: magistrate, judges, friends, the jailer, the Arabs, the chaplain—all are drawn to the fateful precipice, to witness Icarus plunge to his death.

Meursault takes some interest in the presence of the reporters in the courtroom, when they are pointed out to him, and feels something akin to gratitude at first when he grasps their function, to be his ears and eyes, and broadcast his story to the world. Then his eyes are drawn to the eyes of the one reporter who, with his pencil laid aside, fixes his gaze on the defendant with a compelling force. *Et j'ai eu l'impression bizarre d'être regardé par moi-même:* "I had the bizarre impression of being observed by myself."[11] Meursault confesses himself disoriented, and with good reason, since the secret rises here almost to consciousness, that narcissism may contrive murder, to justify its objectivity; and suicide, to find, past objectivity, its real being.[12]

Meursault's universe is neither indifferent nor benign, and to kill a man is by no means a neutral act. Meursault creates his drama both to confirm and to engender his anger. He will be heartless to prove the universe heartless. He makes himself into a murderer to reveal the murderous intent at the heart of the universe; he has himself placed behind bars to signify his quarantine; he is remorseless, to himself no less than to others, to take his revenge on a universe without remorse.

Like Narcissus, Meursault is doomed in all his relations with the world. Though the drama places him at the center of attention, he is still only object, not person, since he refuses to acknowledge his intention. Significance must exist only for others, not for Meursault, who had removed himself to some hallowed ground beyond the reach of significance, and the significance our hero dies for is itself canceled. Narcissism negates all other egos and then, bereft of witnesses, it negates itself. Staging a tragedy, in which to play all the parts, Meursault dismisses it as an absurd fiction, performed and witnessed by persons equally absurd. The revelation, glimpsed in the exchange between the eyes of the criminal and the eyes of his reporter, fades before it can be deciphered, leaving Meursault confused, as if returned suddenly from deep hypnosis. The numinous signifier quickly blurs in the hubbub of the court, and our protagonist regains his habitual insignificance.

Meursault is a vortex of contradiction. Contemptuous of all ideas, he prides himself on his own. Absenting himself from human relations, he accuses society of investing his life with a significance he refuses to accept, while registering his complaint against society for treating him as a nonperson: objectivity cancels itself. Indifferent to death, he permits in his consciousness almost no space for any thoughts except of his own death. In his contradictions Meursault conforms exactly to Hegel's portrait of the skeptic. Skepticism, Hegel writes, "announces the nullity of seeing, hearing, and so on, while *itself* sees and hears. It proclaims the nothingness of essential ethical principles, and makes those very truths the sinews of its conduct. Its deeds and its words belie each other continually. . . . But it keeps asunder the poles of this contradiction within itself." [13] Consciousness lights on one impression after another in this novel, with no consciousness to mediate between them, since the protagonist, while proud of his superior consciousness, uses consciousness to deny consciousness. This flickering consciousness is mystified at the traces of a more extended consciousness in others, as Meursault is nonplussed at anyone's expression of grief or love.

This consciousness differentiates even as it repudiates differentiation; it despises others for their emotions while permitting anger in itself; it claims clarity of vision while repudiating perception; it fairly boasts of its integrity and denies the value of integrity. Such a consciousness is, as Hegel describes it, "an absolutely fortuitous embroglio, the giddy whirl of a perpetually self-creating disorder. This is what it takes itself to be; for itself maintains and produces this self-impelling confusion. Hence it even confesses the fact; it owns to being an entirely fortuitous *individual* consciousness—a consciousness which is empirical, which is directed upon what admittedly has no reality for it, which obeys what, in its regard, has no essential being, which realizes and does what it knows to have no truth. . . . This form of consciousness is, therefore, aimless fickleness and instability of going to and fro, hither and thither." [14]

Meursault, having cut away his Ground of Being, in the name of Being, has nothing left, after reducing his trial to insignificance, but to reduce his death to the same insignificance. But, by a puzzling inversion, the signifier marking death's insignificance emerges as a curse, like an arrow sprung from the archer's bow, which is deflected back upon the archer. Even the curse is not authentic, there being no consciousness present to utter it, but it must reach the protagonist as though projected from a host of witnesses, whose hatred, returning his, will enhance his pain (p. 154). But the evil eye, which Meursault invokes to make his dying less lonely, has no more significance than anything else in his life, and the curtain closes on the protagonist marking his imprisoned being with one final, inconclusive signifier.

Holding all myths to be meaningless, Meursault tells a myth as old as Eden, of the mind blinding itself to hide from the gaze of its signifiers.

8

The Universal Self

Every action is an effort towards vision. Compulsive
action drags vision more toward the external. What is
called voluntary action is less concerned with externals;
nevertheless, it too arises from the desire for vision.
— Plotinus, *Enneads* III.8.1

"So God created man in his own image, in the image of God he created
him; male and female he created them."[1] With a single leap, from
representation to self-representation, the human imagination opened the
space for consciousness. Has the human mind contrived any thought more
audacious than this simple declaration recorded in the Book of Genesis? And
if this God, whose being we mirror, is beyond representation, what is it to be
a human, made in the image of that which cannot be imaged?

Bergson talks of an intuition at the base of every philosopher's metaphysics, the simplicity of which resists articulation, though philosophers will seek

to fix the elusive intuition with ever greater refinement of their metaphysics.[2] Perhaps the intuition is the old maxim that appears in one form or another in every religion and philosophy: the microcosm reflects the macrocosm. The very breadth of the axiom defeats articulation: supposing it to be true, we would need libraries as large as the universe to house the data and the differential equations. The salmon, thrashing from one pool to the next, neatly articulates the coincidence between macrocosm and microcosm by instinct; but we articulate the same electric currents into strings of signifiers, which first propose possible modes of action in the world, and then shape purposes and causes to fit the actions, stitching a metaphysical body to replicate the instinctual body given by nature. Here myth stands with its semaphore flags, to guide the soul's ascent from physics into metaphysics. The world itself, personified, is given metaphysical form: nature's multiple appearances are studied as matter imprinted with mind's intentions; and the mind, reading intention in nature, dares to signify its own intentions. Anthropomorphism is consciousness first reflecting upon itself.

If the correspondence of macrocosm and microcosm is one essential principle of myth, the breach between the two is the second. Consciousness, the ancient myths tirelessly repeat, alienated humans from the animals on one side and from the gods on the other. The gods of myth are paradigms of consciousness; yet, as paradigms of Being, in many ways as mindless as animals, they mark the distance separating consciousness from Being.

The correspondence of macrocosm and microcosm and their mutual incompatability, taken together, summarize the myth of consciousness threading its way through instinct into significance. Ancient mythologies concur that consciousness, when it made its appearance in the world, was a cataclysm, and its seismic waves have sheared through time, transmitting the original disturbance even into our modern literature. Instinct is at one with nature, but the intellect must arrange its signifiers in endless equations, searching for the same unanimity. Yet those same signifiers, which intellect extends into the field of the Other, only widen the chasm between the two. The gods retreat into the deeper recesses of Being, as the intellect extends its meanings, until the intellect collapses in despair.

Believing itself the paradigm of coherence, the intellect reflects upon the world, but under its inspection the world disintegrates into its parts, which cannot be restored to the whole again but disintegrate into finer particles the more the intellect works upon them. Banished from Eden, where intellect and instinct were one, consciousness wanders in a desolate place, searching for itself but finding only the Other. Consciousness, the myths tell us, is nature's crown, and yet for us the crown is all thorns.

Yet the intellect is not mistaken in reading its laws on the bark of nature. Our technology has proven the intellect's power to replicate, with signifiers, the engineering principles that remain instinctual in other animals. Daedalus meditates in his labyrinth for several thousand years, until the secret is perfected, and the two American brothers take to the skies. The metaphysical body is aerodynamic, even if the body given to us by nature is not, and metaphysics, working hand in hand with physics, proves more potent than physics alone. The ancient myth of superior beings with the magic of Māyā at their fingertips is no fiction: for better or worse, we are those astronauts, who travel faster than sound and communicate across the planet with electrical speed.

If instinct is eclipsed by the intellect, it emerges from behind the eclipse as what Bergson calls "a super-intellectual intuition."[3] Here the gods have their second station, where they gather the separate strands together, implicating instinct in intellect and intellect in intuition. Homer invokes the Muses to speak, through him, the long roll call of the Greek heroes mustered on the Trojan plain: "For you are gods, ever present; and you have witnessed everything. But we hear only the report, and have seen nothing."[4] We identify these Muses as the signifiers of tradition in an oral culture. Tradition has many branches, which have become organized, in our schools, as history, anthropology, political science, psychology. All these Homer gathers into his Muses, together with the formulas and themes from his bardic inheritance. The Muses are his projected witnesses of events outside his memory, and the invisible relay transmitting the story from poet to poet, until it comes to the ears of Homer, living half a millennium or more after the Trojan War.

But the daughters of Memory are more than the tribal archivists, or the repository of an oral poet's formulas and themes. Signifiers also of Homer's personal vision, the Muses reach into the poet's genetic code for the instinctual knowledge below the waterline, and when intellect has hardened this clay into persons and plot, their intuition graces the work with the persuasion of life itself. Circling the throne of Being, to witness and reflect its eternal presence, the Muses weave into their strophes reverberations of human significance, and breathe into the blind poet's ears, name by name, phrase by phrase, intimations of the universal Being, embracing and transcending significance.

Notes

Introduction

1. Lacan (1978) 45.

2. Freud gave such prominence to the Oedipus myth that for almost fifty years it seemed the dominant myth of our time. In recent years, however, a remarkable shift has taken place, which has instated the myth of Narcissus as even more seminal in the human psyche. The essays in Layton and Shapiro (1986) give a good indication of this shift.

3. Bergson (1911) 143ff.

4. See Rank (1958.1) for a discussion of this spiritualizing process.

5. I find confirmation for this interpretation in the essay by Eugene Holland, in Layton and Shapiro (1986) 149–69, on the narcissism in the modern existentialism hero. "When today we reread *Nausea* or *The Stranger*," Holland writes (p. 150), "what we see is in fact a proto-typical narcissistic hero."

Chapter 1: The Numinous Ground

1. Langer (1957) 78–102.
2. Milton, *Paradise Lost* 5.487–88.
3. Barfield (1977) 22–31.
4. Ayer (1946) 35.
5. Ayer (1946) 37.
6. Ibid.
7. Whitehead (1929) 17.
8. Whitehead (1929) 472.
9. Lacan (1978) 211.
10. Ibid.
11. See Buber (1947) 11–13. See also Buber (1970). The two modes of thought translate, in Buber's thinking, into two modes of relating to the world, which he calls the I-Thou and the I-It.
12. Cf. Lacan (1978) 22: "The Freudian unconscious is situated at that point, where, between cause and that which it affects, there is always something wrong." Cf. also Lacan (1978) 25: "Discontinuity, then, is the essential form in which the unconscious first appears to us as a phenomenon."
13. Jung (1959) 30.
14. Heraclitus, fr. 247, Kirk and Raven.
15. Cf. Lacan (1978) 236: "The signifier is that which represents a subject for another signifier."
16. See Lacan (1978) 25.
17. Lacan (1978) 35.
18. Cf. Lacan (1978) 44: "Freud addresses the subject in order to say to him the following, which is new—*Here, in the field of the dream, you are at home.*"
19. Cf. *Iliad* XXIV.306ff., where Nestor acknowledges that Zeus and Poseidon have taught his son Antilochos horsemanship; even so, Nestor advises his son to be mindful of his own skill; the woodcutter, he says, is better for skill than for sheer strength; by skill the captain steers his course across the wine-faced sea; and by skill one charioteer surpasses another.
20. Langer (1953) 188. Cf. Frankfort (1949) 29: "Natural phenomena, whether or not they were personified and became gods, confronted ancient man with a living presence, a significant 'Thou', which, again, exceeded the scope of conceptual definition."
21. Hillman (1975) 15.
22. Hillman (1972) 1xiii.
23. See Lévy-Bruhl (1923), chap. 3, pp. 97–121, for a lengthy discussion of this topic.
24. Cf. Schelling, quoted by Cassirer (1955) 8: "The mythological process deals

not only with natural *objects* but with the pure creative potencies whose original product is consciousness itself."

25. Lévy-Bruhl (1923) 106–7.

26. Lévy-Bruhl (1923) 107.

27. Frankfort (1949) 11.

28. Frankfort (1949) 13.

29. Cassirer (1955) 35.

30. See Frankfort (1949) 27.

31. See Lacan (1978) 212–13 for a pointed discussion of the human dilemma. If the choice is between life and freedom, to choose freedom is to choose death, since only by choosing death can we demonstrate our freedom. The alienating factor, as Lacan calls it, permeates ancient myths; it is not the product of some modern anxiety.

32. Lacan (1978) 26.

33. Lacan (1978) 23.

34. See Lacan (1978), esp. pp. 67–119, "On the Gaze as *Objet Petit a,*" where he articulates the quandary of self-consciousness, that the gaze of the subject, which gives us the certainty of our existence, is located in the field of the other.

35. Buber (1947) 12.

36. Genesis 11:1.

37. Cf. J. S. Mill, quoted in Whitehead (1929) 17–18, on the impasse in Greek philosophy: the Greeks "had great difficulty in distinguishing between things which their language confounded, or in putting mentally together things which it distinguished. . . . They thought that by determining the meaning of words they could become acquainted with facts."

38. Lacan (1978) 185.

39. Lacan (1978) 198.

40. Freud (1953), chap. 4, "Distortion in Dreams," posits a censor in the conscious mind, which permits illicit material from the unconscious to surface only after it has been so sanitized that it is no longer recognizable as illicit. Girard (1977) takes Freud's thinking one step farther, to argue that the function of religion, ritual, (and therefore myth), is to camouflage the universal violence by transferring it onto a surrogate victim. He writes of the Oedipus myth (77): "In the myth, the fearful transgression of a single individual is substituted for the universal onslaught of reciprocal violence." Though Girard argues against Freud's emphasis on the incest motif, as being merely one instance of a more generalized violence, Freud and Girard are not so far apart, in seeing the role of the conscious mind (whether in dreams or in collective rituals) as camouflaging violence, even while propagating it.

41. Homer, *Iliad* 6.311.

42. See Girard (1977) for an acute discussion, from the sociological perspective, of the problematic function of sacrifice in human culture.

43. See Homer, *Iliad* XXIV.54.

44. Homer, *Iliad* XXIV.54.

45. Whitehead (1929) 524.

46. Homer, *Odyssey* XI.602–4.

47. Vergil, *Bucolics,* ed. T. E. Page (1891), note on *Eclogues* 4.62.

48. On the *Puer* archetype, see Jung (1959.1) 151–81: "The Psychology of the Child Archetype."

49. See Jung (1959.2) 104.

50. For an eloquent essay on the relations between this child-wizard and the giants, see Alain (1934), esp. 23–27.

51. Coleridge, *BL,* XIII.167. Jung calls this the "active imagination." See Jung (1960) 67ff.

52. See Gould (1977) 70–75.

53. Lacan (1978), 115, 119, is bemused by the universality of the evil eye, balanced by "no trace anywhere of a good eye, of an eye that blesses." It is a pity that he did not extend his discussion of the function of the gaze to include the benevolent smile; for example, Athena's smile, by which she acknowledges her pleasure in her favorite hero's intelligence (Homer, *Odyssey* XIII.287). See also Freud (1947) for his now-famous discussion of the influence of the mother's smile on Leonardo's creative life.

54. Whitehead (1929) 525.

Chapter 2: Job's Noble Euphemism

1. Job 1:5, Revised Standard Version.

2. Kluger (1967), 29, argues that the primal meaning of the Hebrew verb *satan,* from which Satan derives his name, is "*persecution by hindering free forward movement;* i.e., it means 'to hinder, to oppose, an existing intention.'" Following Jung's lead, she interprets Satan as God's doubt of himself. See Jung (1954) 19: "Yahweh, quite without reason, has let himself be influenced by one of his sons, *a doubting thought,* and made unsure of Job's faithfulness."

3. Job 1:8.

4. Job 1:9–10.

5. Job 1:11.

6. Job 1:12.

7. Job 3–20, 23.

8. My colleague William Mullen has shared many of his ideas on catastrophism with me, whose suggestions I am happy to acknowledge here, though the confines of this study prevent me from treating them with the full elaboration they deserve.

9. Job 1:21.

10. Job 2:3.

11. Job 2:5.

12. Job 2:6.

13. Job 2:9.

14. Job 2:10.
15. Soleri (1981) 32.
16. Dewey (1934) 18.
17. Job 3:3–10.
18. Job 8:4–6.
19. Job 6:4.
20. Job 9:2–3.
21. Job 9:19.
22. Job 11:4, 6.
23. Job 12:2–3.
24. Job 23:3, 8–9.
25. Job 19:25.
26. Job 38:3–4.
27. Job 42:5–6.

28. Cf. Jung (1954) 7: Job "knows that he is confronted with a superhuman being who is personally most easily provoked." Jung's understanding of the dynamics in the Book of Job is very supple, but to call the voice in the whirlwind a superhuman being can be misleading. The voice speaks not for any single being, human or otherwise, but as Being itself, which overrides any considerations of meaning; hence its removal of the argument from Job's specific case to images suggestive, in mythical form, of universal Being.

29. See *The Anchor Bible,* commentary on Job 1:5.

30. See *The Interpreter's Bible,* vol. 3 (*Job*), p. 918, on Job 1:20–22.

31. Job 1.21.

32. Bergson (1911) 99.

33. Eliade (1963) 141.

34. For a clear presentation of the dynamics for materializing a god, see Callimachus's *Hymn to Apollo* (No.2). The chorus in Euripides' *Bacchae* (lines 68–70) calls for every mouth to welcome the approaching presence of Dionysus with holy euphemism; i.e., silence. Cf. also *Iliad* 1.22, where the Greek army *euphemizes* Chryses' offer of ransom, thus making Agamemnon's rejection of the offer more heinous; cf. also the pregnant use at *Iliad* 9.171–72, when Nestor calls for *euphemizing* rituals to invoke the blessing of Zeus on the embassy, before it sets out to carry Agamemnon's offer of restitutions to Achilles.

35. For examples of euphemism in ancient Greek thought, see Cook (1925) 1112; Halliday (1913) 33. Cook cites an example in modern Greek: smallpox is *eulogia,* "the blessing"—the same word the Septuagint uses in the phrase our translations so blithely render as "curse God." I have included the Book of Job in this study as one of the most dramatic representations of the close connection between tabu and euphemism in myth. Psychoanalysis has provided us with many instances of their connection and their significance even in the most modern mind. For the classic modern studies, see Freud *ID* (passim), *MM* (1913); Steiner (1956).

36. Dewey (1934) 19.

37. Job 40:15.

38. Job 41:1, 4–6, 31–34.

39. Day (1985), 4, gives the etymology: Leviathan = Hebrew *ltn;* i.e., *litan,* "the twisting one."

40. Day (1985), 62–87, argues that neither Behemoth nor Leviathan is a biological creature, but both are names for Jehovah's archetypal antagonist, the primordial sea serpent, which was defeated at Creation. See Dumézil (1942), 345, for the correspondence of the serpent and Satan, and for what he calls "the dialectical role" of Satan in the Book of Job. See also Forsyth (1987). I cannot agree with Jung (1954), p. 27, that Satan disappears at the end of the drama, and remains "unmentioned and unconscious." The Adversary retires as Satan, "the doubting thought," only to manifest itself in other primeval bodies, as "the twisting one." Anthropomorphic images, with which the drama opens, are exchanged for theriomorphic, as if to turn consciousness aside from the debilitating warfare among its signifiers to deeper intuitions, through which it can glean the dynamics of resistance and opposition at the instinctual level, and return from wrestling in the pleroma with meaning and Being more sinuously knit.

41. Forsyth (19870 114: "The Satan of Job is certainly no 'fallen angel.'"

42. Job 42:7–8.

43. *The Interpreter's Bible,* vol. 3, p. 886.

44. See *The Jerusalem Bible* at Job. 13:6.

45. See Terrien's exegesis at Job 13:15.

46. Whitehead (1926) 48.

47. Cf. Jung (1954) 10: "Yahweh is not split but is an *antinomy*—a totality of inner opposites—and this is the indispensable condition for his tremendous dynamism, his omniscience and omnipotence." Jung's study of Job is a classic, and I should be pleased if my interpretation of Job were read as an addendum to his. To elucidate the psychological processes, however, Jung anthropomorphizes Jahweh and the Satan in ways that I find distracting, and I prefer to shift the locus of consciousness from God's mind to Job's. But we are both agreed that the drama takes place in consciousness, wherever we, for convenience, choose to locate it.

48. Edinger (1973) 76–96.

49. Hegel (1910) 226.

50. Otto (1910) 80.

51. Job 40:21–22.

Chapter 3: Hesiod's Archaic Cosmology

I: The Prime Elements

1. Jung (1959.1) 4.
2. Quoted in Heisenberg (1974) 182.

3. Köhler (1972) 82.

4. Ibid.

5. Heisenberg (1974) 116.

6. Pauli (1952) 152. Quoted in Heisenberg (1974) 179–80. Bergson (1911), taking issue with Plato's theory of Forms, as blueprints either in the past or in the future, gives an eloquent account of the inadequacy of logic (which always works on inert material) to encompass the ever-variable and creative life force.

7. Pauli (1952) 153.

8. Hegel (1907) 225.

9. Dewey (1934) 18.

10. Neumann (1949) 5–38.

11. Here I follow Brown (1973), 1–4, in applying his same laws of form to consciousness.

12. Gould (1977) 72.

13. Fränkel (1962), 166ff., is sensitive to the abstractions implicit in Hesiod's concept of Chaos, and indeed to Hesiod's whole cosmogonic process as an exercise in abstract thought.

14. Brown (1973) 1.

15. Hesiod's succession myth is worthy of a full-length study in itself, but I touch only on some of its major themes. For further discussions of the social and psychological themes in the myth, see the translations and commentaries by Norman Brown and Richard Caldwell.

16. Brown (1973) 1–4.

17. See Lacan (1973) 26.

18. See Caldwell's translation, pp. 18–20, 109–110, for a fuller discussion of Kronos's ingestion of his children as a strategy to avoid the fate he had inflicted on his father, Ouranos.

19. Lacan (1973) 67–119.

20. Hegel (1907) 211.

21. Camus (1955) 51.

22. Soleri (1981) 31–32.

23. Camus (1955) 50.

24. Soleri (1981) 32.

25. Soleri (1981) 30.

II: Pandora and the Revenge of the Mind

1. Lacan (1982) 168.

2. Freud, *ID* (1900) 351.

3. See Vernant (1980), 184, on the ambiguity of Hope in this myth.

4. Freud, *ID* (1900) 151. See also chapter 3 of the same work for a fuller discussion of dreams as wish-fulfillment.

5. The passage has several textual problems. I have, for the most part, followed the readings of West's edition, but cf. also Lattimore's translation.

6. Freud, *MM* (1939) 95–96.

7. Freud, *MM* (1939) 93.

8. Hesiod (1966), note on line 535.

9. Vernant (1980) concentrates his analysis primarily on this aspect of the myth. See also Burkert (1983) for the complex psychology that surrounds and motivates the rituals of animal sacrifice.

10. Burkert (1983) 16ff., but the thesis gains its cogency from the full array of evidence presented through his book as a whole.

11. For fuller discussions of this aspect of Hesiod's myth of Pandora, see Fontenrose (1974); von Fritz (1947).

12. Hesiod (1959) 25.

13. See Lacan (1978) 196–99.

14. See Widengren (1967) 21–55.

15. Freud, *ID* (1900) 619, says of dreams that their normal role is to be "the *guardian* of sleep."

16. See Paul Radin (1956) on the trickster in American Indian myth and folklore; also Jung (1959.1) 255–72, "On the Psychology of the Trickster-Figure."

17. Kerényi (1967) 3–17.

18. Lacan (1978), 197, in his image of the libido as an amoebalike lamella, gives me the confidence to call Prometheus in this myth the signifier of the libido.

19. See Detienne and Vernant (1978) for their comprehensive study of the meaning of *metis* in early Greek thought. See pp. 57–105 for the prominence of *metis* in the struggle between Zeus and Prometheus.

20. Cf. Lacan (1978), 211, who puts this alienation in terms of the incompatibility of the circles of "Being" and "Meaning."

21. *Theogony* 511–12.

22. See Vernant (1980), 183, on the ambiguity of Pandora.

23. McCary (1982) 102.

24. McCary (1982) 103.

25. Harrison (1900) 99–114.

26. Gardner (1901) 4–9. On the identification in antiquity of Pandora and Gaia, see also Smith (1890) 278–83.

27. Gonda (1959) 126.

28. *RV* 3.53.8; see Gonda (1959) 128ff.

29. Reyna (1962).

30. Zimmer (1938) 78. See also Zimmer (1936).

31. Zeitlin (1985) 79. See also 92 n. 39, for her discussion of Pandora as the cunningly wrought "object." Woman as the signifer of the Other in the patriarchal order has become a commonplace since Beauvoir's pioneering study (1953). See esp. her introduction, and pp. 1–96.

32. Lacan (1978) 185.

33. Pucci (1977) 95.

34. *Theogony* 527–28.

35. Hesiod, *fragment* 25 (Merkelbach and West), 30–34.

III: The Serpent in the Garden

1. Worthen (1988) argues that Olympos and Ouranos (i.e., sky) became synonymous in archaic Greek thought.

2. Hesiod, *Theogony* 720ff., for the classical description of Tartaros.

3. Hesiod, *Theogony* 742–43, trans. Brown.

4. *Theogony* 736–38.

5. Fontenrose (1959). See also West's commentary on *Theogony* 820–80 for his bibliography and his discussion of Near Eastern parallels to the Typhon myth; and Forsyth (1989).

6. *Rg Veda* 1.32.3; see Fontenrose (1959) 194.

7. Homeric Hymn 3.182–387; see Fontenrose (1959) 13–27.

8. I am grateful to Gregory Nagy for this suggestion.

9. *Hom. Hymn to Apollo* 305–55.

10. *Iliad* 18.607ff.

11. Fontenrose (1959) 236.

12. Fontenrose (1959) 230–36.

13. Fontenrose (1959) 231.

14. Fontenrose (1959) 374.

15. Ibid.

16. For the evidence of the cult of Python at Delphi, see Fontenrose (1959) 374–75, and 375 n. 12.

17. Ovid, *Metamorphoses* 4.618–22.

18. See Ovid, *Metamorphoses* 3.1–137.

19. Fontenrose (1959) 307.

20. Fontenrose (1959) 219.

21. Nilsson (1925) 13.

22. Gimbutas (1982) 93.

23. Nonnus, *Dionysiaca* 12.293–362. Kerényi (1976) 58–60.

24. Kerényi (1976) 60ff.

25. Athenagoras, *Libellus pro Christianis* 20. Kerényi (1976) 112.

26. Ovid, *Metamorphoses* 6.117; Nonnus, *Dionysiaca* 6.90–168.

27. Kerényi (1976) 113.

28. Cook (1925) 1108–10, figs. 944–46; Harrison (1903) 19; Campbell (1964) 18; Kerényi (1976) 123. See Harrison (1912), 260ff., for a lengthy discussion of the snake as originally the *agathos daimon*.

29. *Māhā-vagga* 1.3.1–3; quoted by Campbell (1964) 16.

30. *Homeric Hymn to Pythian Apollo* 371–73.

31. Róheim (1930) 303.

32. See Fontenrose (1959), 374–89, for a discussion of the equivalence in myth and cult of Dionysos and Python.

33. Harrison (1903) passim; Cook (1914), 1111 n. 1, gives a short bibliography on studies of serpent worship among the ancient Semitic peoples. Campbell (1959), 30, reminds us that the Israelites continued to venerate the bronze serpent which Moses had made until the time of King Hezekiah (719–691 B.C.); see II Kings 18:4.

34. Apollonios Rhodius, *Argonautica* 1.496–511; Fontenrose (1959) 230. Cf. Eliade (1965) 40 n. 70, who notes that the dragon frequently symbolizes "the preformal modality, of the universe, the undivided 'One' of pre-Creation. . . . This is why snakes and dragons are nearly everywhere identified with the 'masters of the ground.'"

35. Campbell (1964) 9.

36. See Day (1985), 4, for the meaning of the name "Leviathan." He argues (62–87) that Leviathan and Behemoth were never natural animals but were embodiments of that original chaos demon whom Jahweh conquered at Creation.

37. Harrison (1903) 19; cf. also Harrison (1912), 434, for the bifurcation of the original unity of snake and *daimon* into the antagonism of snake and Olympian gods.

38. Aelian, *De natura animalium* XI.2; Harrison (1912) 429; Campbell (1964) 20.

39. Campbell (1959) 21; cf. also Harrison (1912) 445ff.

40. Harrison (1912) 451.

41. Campbell (1964) 21.

42. Fontenrose (1959) 219.

43. A point made at length by Bergson (1911).

44. Genesis 1:31.

45. Genesis 3:14.

46. Róheim (1930), esp. 303–7.

47. Job 40:19.

48. Job 41:12; 33–34.

49. Genesis 3:5.

50. I am grateful to Jane Brown of Oakland, California, for making this understanding fundamental to all her dance studies.

51. MacLean (1973) 7.

52. MacLean (1973) 8.

53. Ibid.

54. MacLean (1973) 10.

55. MacLean (1973) 8.

56. Sagan (1977) 82.

57. MacLean (1973) 54.

58. MacLean (1973) 18.

59. Ibid.

60. MacLean (1973) 41.

61. Henderson (1963), whose title I have incorporated into this chapter, has little to say about serpents specifically, but uses the serpent as the mythical image to represent the process of psychic death and rebirth, which is necessary for all who wish to experience health and wholeness.

62. See II Kings 18:4; Campbell (1964) 30.

63. Ovid, *Metamorphoses* 15.626–744.

Chapter 4: Herakles: The Hero of the Anima

I: The Paradigm

1. Pharr (1920) 16.
2. It is a commonplace in Homer to compare the human life cycle to the vegetal cycle of birth, growth, and decay. See *Iliad* 6.145–49; 21.463–66; and Nagy (1979) 178–79.
3. Homer, *Iliad* 17.446–47.
4. See Nagy (1979) 115; Rohde (1894) I, 108–10; and Harrison (1912) 261ff. on the cult hero as the *genius loci*.
5. Nagy (1979) traces this development in exemplary detail.
6. Nagy (1979) 189.
7. Nagy (1979) 208.
8. See Nagy (1979) 114–17.
9. On the theme of the disintegration of the hero and the reintegration of his body and *psyche* after death, in Elysium, see Nagy (1979) 208.
10. Asa Sherry, the son of my colleague Charles Sherry, was four years old when he solved the mystery of Billy the Kid's parentage.
11. On this point, see Rank (1958.2).
12. Nagy (1979) 62.
13. Odysseus has at least three ritual antagonists in the *Odyssey:* Athena, Poseidon, and Helios. Each antagonism exerts its own pressure on the development of the poem's structure. See Clay (1983).
14. Nagy (1979) 121.

II: The Hero

1. Taylor (1975) 159.
2. *Iliad* 5.396–400.
3. For a detailed study of the primary status of the phallic hero in classical myth, see Keuls (1985).
4. See, for example, Fontenrose (1959) passim. Segal (1977 and 1981) treats Herakles in Sophocles' *Women of Trachis* as the champion of civilization swept to his doom by the irrational and elemental powers of the universe.
5. See Dumézil (1970) passim. See Nagy (1979), 135–37, for a discussion of a similar kind of latent savagery in the character of Achilles.
6. Euripides, *Herakles* 610–13.

7. See Kerényi (1967) 52–60.

8. Simon (1978) 130ff. Simon sees the plays as indicating a shift "from the heroic and mythic ethos to the more tragic and existential" (134).

9. Simon (1979) 136.

10. See Arrowsmith (1956) 266–81.

11. See Slater (1968), who traces the destructive effect of this conflict in Greek society in great detail.

12. For the ambivalence, and overt hostility, of the mother-son relationship, particularly as it was expressed in the myth of Herakles, see Slater (1968) 337–88.

13. Aeschylus, *Eumenides* 658–62.

14. Diodorus Siculus IV.9.

15. Homer, *Iliad* 5.392–94.

16. Rank (1958.2) 236.

17. Bachofen (1967) 109.

18. Simone de Beauvoir (1953) was the first to articulate how women are deprived of their being by this patriarchal ideology.

19. Lacan (1978) 211; see my chapter 1, page 12.

20. Aeschylus, *Eumenides* 603.

21. Seneca, *Hercules Furens* 66–68.

22. Galinsky (1972) 170.

23. Owen (1968) 304–5.

24. For further evidence of this collusion, see *Iliad* VIII.362–68, where Athena recalls (in conversation with Hera) the many times she brought assistance to Herakles in his labors for Eurystheus, including the occasion when he brought Kerberos back from the underworld. The feminine was acceptable to Herakles when it took the form of the warlike daughter of the father.

25. See Jung (1954) 52: "*Perfection* is a masculine desideratum, while woman inclines by nature to *completeness*." I would treat both qualities as signifiers rather than natural attributes, each with a relative weight determined by the social code at any particular historical moment.

26. Fontenrose (1959) 327ff. For Homer's allusion to the battle, see *Iliad* 5.394–404.

27. Fontenrose (1959) 322.

28. Fontenrose (1959) 321–64.

29. Fontenrose (1959) 307.

30. Lacan (1978) 38.

31. Fontenrose (1959) 108.

32. Harrison (1912), 506, suggests that the myth of Herakles compelled to wear women's dress at Omphale's court represents an ancient puberty rite of the *kouros*. If so, the meaning remains the same: the youth must return to the mother, so that the mother and father archetype may be better integrated, before he enters into his manhood.

33. Sophocles stresses the humiliation of Herakles at Omphale's court as one of the motives for Herakles' assault on Oichalia and his rape of Iole; see *The Women of Trachis* 254ff.

34. Sophocles, *WT* 31–33.

35. Sophocles, *WT* 183.
36. Sophocles, *WT* 254ff.
37. Sophocles, *WT* 351–58.
38. Sophocles, *WT* 445. Disease is a recurrent theme throughout the play. At lines 234–35 Lichas, in reporting the news of Herakles' safe return, tells Deianeira that her husband is "alive, strong, flourishing, and unburdened by disease." On this theme, see Segal (1977) 113–15.
39. Sophocles, *WT* 1089–1104. Jebb's translation gives the full rhetorical flourish of this speech.
40. Seneca, *HF* 84–85. Galinsky (1972), 50, has a good discussion of the external disease in this play as the manifestation of Herakles' internal disease, but goes no farther to relate it to the myth of Herakles as a whole, or with Hera's presence in his life.
41. See Jebb's edition, xxxi–xxxii.
42. Seneca, *HO* 240–45.
43. Seneca, *HO* 258–65.
44. Seneca, *HO* 410–20.
45. Seneca, *HO* 428–34.
46. Fontenrose (1959) 109.
47. Segal (1977) 127.
48. Cf. Rank (1958.2), 248, on the masculine ideology: "Civilization means increasing rationalization whereby man's importance and power is augmented at the expense of woman's right to herself."
49. Sophocles, *WT* 40.
50. See Sophocles, *WT* 46–48, for Deianeira's use of the oracular tablet, and lines 1164–73 for Herakles' understanding of its message.
51. Sophocles, *WT* 596–97.
52. Sophocles, *WT* 606–9.
53. Sophocles, *WT* 610–13.
54. Sophocles, *WT* 536–37.
55. Segal (1981) 88.
56. Zeitlin (1985) 74. Cf. also Keuls (1985) 97: "Women spent their lives wrapped in veils, nameless, concealing their identity, and locked away in the dark recesses of closed in homes."
57. Segal (1981) 94.
58. Rank (1958.2) 236. Cf. also p. 246: "Woman passes into what I have called the Not-I class, which includes dangerous as well as unimportant (and neutral) things."
59. Iole's silence and her apparent lack of name assume a greater poignance in the light of the ancient Greek practise, noted by Keuls, of depriving women of personal names to the fullest extent possible. See Keuls (1985) 90: "Greek citizen women were largely doomed to anonymity."
60. Sophocles, *WT* 375–79.
61. Sophocles, *WT* 756–71.
62. Sophocles, *WT* 1071–72.
63. Sophocles, *WT* 1074–75.

64. Euripides, *Herakles* 1353–56.

65. The male fear of being feminized is a persistent theme in Greek literature. See McCary (1982), 152, on the treatment of this theme in the *Iliad;* Zeitlin (1985) 69ff. One of Plato's principal objections to tragedy is that it represents heroic men weeping, or in other ways demonstrating the weakness that is more appropriate to women. See his *Republic* 387e–388a; 605d–e; and Zeitlin (1985) 84–88.

66. Sophocles, *WT* 1159–61.

67. Fontenrose (1959), 108, equates Omphale with Echidna the viper; at 109 he identifies her with Ge—"i.e. with the Lydian earth goddess who would be called Ge in Greek." At 110 he identifies Omphale as "a regional name of the great dragoness of the combat myth." At 109 he discusses Deianeira's "demonic origin." At 322 he speculates that the origin of the name "Herakles" may be "dimly seen in such a legend as that of the hero's servitude to Omphale."

68. Homer, *Odyssey* 11.601–12.

69. See Hesiod, *fr.* 25.25–28MW; and Homer, *Odyssey* 11.601–12.

70. Nagy (1979) 208. The bifurcation of Herakles' postmortem being, into a celestial and a chthonic form, is the heroizing process shaping all heroes' lives, but most fully articulated in the myth of Herakles.

71. Hegel (1907), 470, writes of the Greeks reaching "simple universality," beyond chance and change, only in death. The apotheosis of Herakles is evidence that the Greeks themselves intuited the structural flaw in Elysium, which, though it surpasses the regions assigned to ordinary mortals in the afterlife, still falls short of Olympian godhood, being at best a mimesis of universal Being.

Chapter 5: The Divine Presence in the *Iliad*

1. Dewey (1934) 18–19.

2. My knowledge of the life cycle of the sockeye salmon is derived largely from a program in the "Nature" series on PBS. I trust that my memory recalls the facts accurately.

3. Cf. Bergson (1911) 99: "Life had to enter thus into the habits of inert matter, in order to draw it little by little, magnetized, as it were, to another track."

4. Cf. Bergson (1911), 264, on biology's impetus "to use the determinism of nature to pass through the meshes of the net which this very determinism had spread."

5. Bergson (1911) 145: *"the consciousness of a living being may be defined as an arithmetical difference between potential and real activity. It measures the interval between representation and action."*

6. Bergson (1911) 151.

7. Plato, *Phaedrus 247a–c*. See Hackforth's translation and commentary on this passage.

8. *Phaedrus* 247b.

9. See Worthen (1988) for brief remarks to this point; he makes a fuller exposition in his work in progress. I am grateful to him for our conversations on this subject.

10. Dodds (1951), 17–18, first applied the anthropological distinction between shame and guilt cultures to the ancient Greeks. Since Dodds, Homer's projection of the values of a shame culture onto his gods is an inescapable given.

11. Wilson (1949) 57. Cf. Frankfort in the same volume, 21: "The survival of the dead and their continued relationship with man were assumed as a matter of course, for the dead were involved in the indubitable reality of man's own anguish, expectation, or resentment. 'To be effective' to the mythopoeic mind means the same as 'to be.'"

12. *Odyssey* 11.216–22.

13. *Odyssey* 11.488–91.

14. Hillman (1977) 36.

15. *Iliad* I.206–14.

16. *Iliad* I.207–9.

17. Slater (1968), 150, gives us an insight into the nature of this tabu. People increase the mana of their leaders, Slater argues, by investing their leaders with "the primary narcissism of the infant.

18. Parry (1956) was the first modern scholar to locate Achilles' problem in his signifiers.

19. Willock (1970) makes this point explicit. When Athena deceives Hector in the final duel between him and Achilles, and returns Achilles' spear to him, Willcock reminds us (68): "There were two people, not three, standing out there on the plain under the walls of Troy." On this point, see also Russo and Simon (1968), who discuss Homer's tendency to represent "inner and (to us) internalized mental processes as 'personified exchanges.'"

20. Vivante (1982), 18ff., gives an excellent discussion of the fundamental difference between narrative and representation in Homer.

21. MacCary (1982), 32, calls Achilles "a hero de-centered in himself but in control of his poem; the poet sees the world through him and makes him the model of all other men, the focus of all the gods."

22. *Iliad* I.218.

23. See Pettazoni (1956) 5: "Divine omniscience is a visual omniscience." Note also Griffin (1978), who discusses the role of the gods as witnesses of the human action in the *Iliad*.

24. *Iliad* XVII.645–47.

25. *Iliad* XVII.648–50.

26. Plato, *Phaedrus* 255b–e.

27. MacCary (1982) 19: "The *erastes* [the lover] finds in the *eromenos* [the beloved] a mirror for his own beauty, (and) the eyes of the *eromenos* are a mirror for the reflection of himself, so that the erotic pattern is superficially homosexual but essentially narcissistic." See, however, Halperin (1986) for, in my view, a convincing expansion of MacCary's one-sided interpretation of Plato's mirror image in this passage,

and for a bibliography, for those wishing to pursue at greater length the place of desire
and self-consciousness in Plato's thought. See also Gould (1963), who discusses the
differences and convergences among the dominant concepts of love in our Western
tradition—the Platonic, Christian, Romantic, and Freudian.

28. See MacCary (1982) 14 and 254 n.23. MacCary champions, and develops, a
view first articulated by Snell (1953) and exemplified also in Fränkel (1961).

29. Vivante (1970) 67.

30. *Iliad* XIII.3–7.

31. *Iliad* XIII.10–16.

32. Lines 17–22. The Greek word for *imperishable* here is *aphthita*—not subject
to organic decay. See Nagy (1979) for the significance of this term in the *Iliad*, as a
foil for the perishable condition of Homer's warriors.

33. Lines 23–31.

34. See Puhvel (1981), 6–26, on the radiance and the vital force of the Indo-
European sky gods; cf. p. 15: "Vital force, health, youth, and beauty, are all associated with radiance, embodied especially by gold."

35. Lines 70–72.

36. Whitman (1958) 118. But cf. also p. 222, where Whitman understands the
gods' presence in the *Iliad* as reflecting "the deep-seated Hellenic association of heroic
force with absolute being."

37. Cf. Atchity (1978), 105, for his discussion of Hera's seduction of Zeus in *Iliad*
XIV: "Hera's perfidy implicates the very heart of universal Being." See Mueller
(1970) for a fuller treatment of deception and self-deception on the human plane in
the *Iliad*.

38. Cf. Girard (1977), 22, in reference to the plague in Sophocles' *Oedipus Ty-
rannus:* "the infection and the onslaught of reciprocal violence are one and the
same. . . . In tragedy, and outside it as well, plague is a symbol for the sacrificial
crisis."

39. For the connection between aggression and sexuality, see Burkert (1983), esp.
chap. 7, 58–72, "The Sexualization of Ritual Killing."

40. The overwhelming force of external agents and powers in the *Iliad* leads such
scholars as Snell (1953), Fränkel (1961), and MacCary (1982) to argue that the integrated ego lies outside Homer's frame of reference. Granted, the self, in Homer, is a
force field, as Fränkel calls it, with fluid boundaries between it and the world, but
surely it is too extreme to claim, as Fränkel does (88) that "the antithesis between the
I and the not-I, fundamental for our consciousness, does not yet exist for Homeric
consciousness." I read the *Iliad* as the attempt to reach past the ego, constellated by
its own signifiers, to transcendent Being.

41. See *Iliad* XIV.271–74 for a classic instance of the Styx and the nether gods as
witnesses of the oaths made by the Olympians. See also Puhvel (1981), 19, who
amplifies on Thieme's etymology of Greek *martur-* ("witness"), used mainly of the
gods in Homer, as "grasping death."

42. *Iliad* I.37–39. On Smintheus as the rat god, see Puhvel (1981) 285–89.

43. Chryses' prayer is the paradigm of the hymnal form, invoking the god by name
and attribute, and, through the device known to rhetoricians as *hypomnesis*—"remembrance," reminding the god of their I-Thou covenant, honored by a previous exchange

of gifts and favors, and calling upon the covenant for one new favor. I have treated the prayer from the other side, as a conjuration of Being into form and significance. Chryses is a devout worshipper, and no less a wizard.

44. *Iliad* I.43ff.

45. Slater (1968), 155, argues that the ancient Greeks not only tolerated but "demanded narcissistic self-indulgence" in their gods.

46. Freud's ideas have circulated in my mind for so long that I can hardly distinguish his theories from my applications, or point to the page and line where I borrowed from him. Freudians will easily sort the master's theories from the disciple's interpretations. Like archaeologists opening a long-sealed tomb, both Freud and Jung shed a new light onto ancient mythology, and we are all its beneficiaries.

47. In MacCary's reading of the *Iliad*, Achilles represents the male ego, which has not yet passed through the oedipal conflict and has not, therefore, created its superego. Governed by no superego, Achilles can feel no guilt for the catastrophe he brings upon himself and his comrades. If I understand MacCary's thesis correctly, Homer's point of view coincides exactly with that of Achilles. On this reading, Homer himself (whether we are considering the poet of the *Iliad* or the poet of the *Odyssey*) is as innocent of a psychic construct comparable to Freud's superego as any of his characters. This is hard to accept, since Homer's gods certainly act as moral conscience in both poems. Odysseus's encounter with the Cyclops in *Odyssey* IX seems also a strong representation of the oedipal conflict, if we need to find such a conflict to assure ourselves that Homer's consciousness has reached at least the oedipal stage of development. See my article on the Cyclops in the *Odyssey* (1983).

48. Slater (1968) 155.

49. Girard (1977) examines the rituals of sacrifice from the anthropological perspective. He takes the sacrifice of the surrogate victim, and the violence that motivates this sacrifice, as the basis of all religion.

50. *Iliad* I.1–5.

51. MacCary (1982) has done us a service in pointing to the mind of the child in the *Iliad,* but I cannot agree with him that Homer nowhere advances beyond a child's thoughts.

52. *Iliad* XXIV.505–6.

53. *Iliad* XXIV.526–27.

54. *Iliad* XXIV.592–95.

55. *Iliad* XXIV.25–63. These lines, with the only reference in the *Iliad* to the judgment of Paris, have been suspect ever since Aristarchus athetized them in antiquity. Despite the authority of Aristarchus, I cannot help sensing that, if this reference is an interpolation, it replaces some other explanation for the anger of Poseidon and Athena. It would be abrupt, in Homeric style, to mention the anger, and name the three gods, without some explanation of its cause. Though it is strange that the only direct reference to the judgment of Paris should occur at this late point in the poem, it seems implied in Hera's remarks to Athena at *Iliad* V.715–16 that the two of them are failing in their promise to Menelaus, that he would return home after sacking Troy. When would such a promise have been made, if not in connection with the judgment of Paris? The savage anger of Hera and Athena, on which Zeus comments at *Iliad* IV.7–48, certainly precedes, and far surpasses, considerations of Achilles' honor

alone. Can their anger be attributed to any other cause but the abduction of Paris?

56. *Iliad* XXIV.44–45.

57. See the dialogue between Achilles and Patroclus at *Iliad* XVI.2–45. Patroclus is the compassionate side of Achilles, without which he may be superhuman, yet incomplete; he is the compassion of the other Greek warriors as much as he is Achilles', being by far the most conspicuous personification of compassion on the Greek side.

58. *Iliad* XXIV.33–54. The word for alignment is *enaisimos*—"in accord with destiny, order"; therefore, "righteous" (line 40); *noema* (line 40) is the faculty of perception and internal conceptualizing.

59. See Monro's edition at XXIV.54, where he translates *kôphen gaian* as "senseless earth," and reads it as a reference to Hector's corpse. But "senseless" here suggests the wrong connotation: *kôphos* is "blunted," as a weapon (*Iliad* XI.390); or "mute, dumb," as the wave of the swelling sea (*Iliad* XIV.16). Given Apollo's outrage at Achilles' transgressions of the norms of religion, reason, and society (the three fields where the ego translates Being into meanings), "senseless" seems pale as the epithet, whether of earth or the corpse. The purpling waves at *Iliad* XIV.16 are "blunt"; i.e., they are a smooth, silent, inarticulate continuum, with nowhere a white-cap cresting as a visual or acoustic indicator of a break. Few looking into that eerie, roiling surface would think it senseless; it might suggest, rather, deep, internal sensing, pressing ominously against the membrane between instinct and meaning. In reference to the earth, I prefer to read the epithet as signifying "the inarticulate." If Olympos has established itself as the center of articulation, someone on Mt. Olympos must speak for the inarticulate earth, which was Being itself, in ancient mythology, before she bifurcated into earth and sky, and had her meanings blunted by the intellect.

60. Cf. Taylor (1975), 173, for his analysis of Hegel's discussion of the Greek view of death: "Death is a natural negation, something which happens to a man, a blow struck at him by nature. But we have also seen that death speculatively understood is a necessity, an expression of the true universality of the human spirit which thus cannot leave standing any external expression. The aim of the [death] rites is to raise death from this first to the second reality, to re-interpret it as it were from something that happens to man to some thing done. The rites preserve the body which otherwise would be prey to all the blind forces of nature, would be strewn over the earth by jackals and vultures, and in committing it to the earth make its departure a meaningful act. So that even death is recuperated for self-consciousness."

61. James Merrill (1988) 39, "The Parnassians." At *Iliad* XXIV.33–54, Apollo points to an imbalance threatening Olympos itself: the gods, while showing honor to Achilles, who gives them none, forget the honors due to the corpse of the man who had so richly honored them in his life. In the end, Apollo reminds the heavenly court that even gods need their human meanings.

62. Merrill (1988) 39 "The Parnassians."

63. *Iliad* XXIV.559–67.

64. For those who read the *Iliad* from this perspective, the gods' interventions are distinct liabilities. Cf. Kirk (1962) 372: "The close support and the constant intervention of the gods, whether in its Iliadic or its Odyssean form, seems once again to weaken the dramatic force of much of the action—if modern standards are applied."

65. Mueller (1970) discusses the tragedy of Achilles in the *Iliad* in the light of the mythical structure that has been called "the fortunate fall," in which the hero's career pendulates between sin and grace (in the Christian tradition), or "humiliation and exaltation."

66. I use "eucharist" in its widest psychological significance, not restricting it to the specific ritual form of ingesting a god's substance.

67. Diel (1980) 5. Apollo's criticism of Achilles' transgression (at XXIV.33–54) in desecrating Hector's corpse strongly supports Diel's thesis.

68. Diel (1980) takes "spiritualization-sublimation" as the major theme of mythological thought. See p. 4: "Myth represents 'the prime cause' in concrete form and calls it 'Creative Divinity,' conceived as an absolute spirit. The essential task of the human being is to fulfill the meaning of life, to conform as far as possible to the image of the absolute spirit. This task seems, therefore, to be set by the divinity."

69. Buber (1947) 15.

Chapter 6: Hamlet's Hungry Ghost

1. All citations are from *Hamlet,* ed. C. Hoy, Norton Critical Edition (New York: W. W. Norton, 1963).

2. Shakespeare (1963) 131.

3. Shakespeare (1963) 148–51.

4. Shakespeare (1963) 153.

5. Shakespeare (1963) 155.

6. Ibid.

7. Shakespeare (1963) 163.

8. Shakespeare (1963) 226. Jones's Freudian interpretation of Hamlet's confusion as expressing Hamlet's oedipal desire, suppressed by the incest tabu, is well known. While not discounting Jones's thesis, I shift the emphasis from the mother as the principal signifier in the play to the father, who is, in my view, by far the most dominant influence.

9. Jones and I, following separate trails, he the mother's and I the father's, reach a common conclusion. See Shakespeare (1963) 224: Hamlet "cannot kill him [Claudius] without also killing himself." I take the argument one step farther: Hamlet can escape suicide only by repudiating the law of the father.

10. I.i.82–103.

11. I.ii.91–92.

12. Ernest Jones understood this fact, though he places the emphasis largely on the

relations between the mother and son. See the excerpt from his essay in Shakespeare (1963) 218–26. A monograph would be required to do justice to the literature written on the relations between father and son since Freud's hypothesis of the oedipus complex. Freud's *Totem and Taboo* (1913) is a landmark, with its hypothesis of parricide as the primal crime. See also Burkert (1983), 74ff., for an interesting discussion of the relation of parricide to the cultural concept of "fatherhood." If Hamlet's mission is parricide, the commandment is obfuscated by the power of the father to instate the signifiers and to erase or muddle them at will. Is Claudius the father to be killed, or the ghost? Fatherhood seems to be a self-evident truth in the critical literature on Hamlet. But we cannot condemn Hamlet for his confusion without a critique of fatherhood as itself a complex of contradictory signifiers.

13. Slater (1968) 150.

14. Slater (1968) 150–51.

15. Slater (1968) 151.

16. Slater (1968) 152.

17. Shakespeare (1963) 179.

18. Curiously, critics searching for that objective correlative gravitate toward Gertrude, as Eliot himself does, even while he insists that her character, as given in the play, cannot fulfill the necessary function (180): "It is just *because* her character is so negative and insignificant that she arouses in Hamlet the feeling which she is incapable of representing." Is Eliot's implication that the play fails because Gertrude ought to be the villain, but has insufficient substance to achieve that status? It is puzzling that critical consensus, looking for the villain, hovers around Gertrude (and sometimes Ophelia), while the ghost of the father plies his trade unchecked. If Gertrude is too insignificant to serve as the desired correlative, is the ghost, with his extraordinary prominence, so significant as to be invisible?

19. I John 4:1.

20. Slater (1968) 194.

21. Slater (1968) 194–95.

22. Slater (1968) 195.

23. The oedipal implications of the conflict between Achilles and Agamemnon, if only implicit in *Iliad* I, become explicit in Book IX, where Achilles reads Agamemnon's offer as a bribe to draw him back under the sovereignty of the father. "Let him submit to me," Agamemnon says, in concluding the catalogue of gifts, which he is prepared to offer Achilles, "to the degree that I am the more kingly, and to the degree that I surpass him in birth (i.e., in age, dynastic status, or both)" (IX.160–62). Odysseus tactly omits this condition when transmitting Agamemnon's offer to Achilles, but by his response Achilles reveals that the gifts speak plainly enough: to accept Agamemnon's offer, Achilles must submit himself to the authority of Agamemnon to dispense all rewards (to be the "signifier"—*sêmantor*, to use one of Homer's terms for a chieftain). The most attractive item in Agamemnon's catalogue, at least in Agamemnon's eyes, who places it last for strategic emphasis, is his offer of one of his own daughters to be Achilles' wife. But what would be the worth of the dowry—the seven tribute-bearing cities named by Agamemnon, and the privileges shared with Orestes— if the price for such luxury is for Achilles to indenture himself as Agamemnon's son-in-law?

24. Jones, in Shakespeare (1963), 218–26, touches briefly on the ambiguity of the

father imago in *Hamlet,* but nowhere attempts a thorough treatment of its full complexity. Critics with a Freudian orientation may remark on the split of the father imago into Claudius and the deceased king, as Jones does, but none, I believe, has recognized in Yorick the third, and equally significant, aspect of the same archetype.

25. Shakespeare (1963) 156.

Chapter 7: The Empirical Stranger

1. The new translation, by Ward (Knopf, 1988), presents Meursault as less austere than he appears in Gilbert's translation, but since his translation has yet to become generally available, I have used Gilbert's translation or, occasionally, my own.

2. The sentence reads "Cela ne veut rien dire," which suggests an even stronger dismissal of the matter than the doubt expressed in Gilbert's translation.

3. Gilbert's "thrill of pleasure" is *joie* in the original.

4. See p. 141: Meursault takes to sleeping through the day and keeping watch at night for the first sign of dawn.

5. I am grateful to Andrew Rusk, who, in his term paper in a class in 1985, brought out the significance of this passage, and discussed Meursault's anger as the motive force of the novel.

6. On the theme of ego inflation as the hero's besetting temptation in Greek myths, see Diel (1980); also Edinger (1973) 3–36.

7. In the Gallimard edition, p. 138; in Gilbert's translation, p. 110.

8. Nagel (1979), 11–23, gives a philosophical critique of this position expressed by Camus's fictional Meursault, and by Camus himself in his *Myth of Sisyphus.*

9. Cf. Hillman (1977), 14, on the clinical symptoms of depersonalization: "One's conviction of oneself as a person and a sense of the reality of the world have departed. Everything and oneself become automatic, unreal, emptied out." See also his chapter 1 (1–51), for a fuller discussion of the place of personification in psychic well-being.

10. I am grateful to Carol Davis for pointing to the significance of this incident in a class discussion.

11. P. 134 in the Gallimard edition; p. 107 in Gilbert's translation.

12. See Eugene Holland's essay, in Layton and Shapiro (1986) 149–69, on the narcissism of the modern existentialist hero. "When today we reread *Nausea* or *The Stranger,*" Holland writes (150), "what we see is in fact a proto-typical narcissistic hero."

13. Hegel (1910) 250.

14. Hegel (1910) 249.

Chapter 8: The Universal Self

1. *Genesis* 1:27.
2. Bergson (1946) 107–29.
3. See Bergson (1911) 359–60, who argues for distinguishing the sensuous intuitions in Kant's metaphysics into the infra-intellectual, which can be translated into objective form; and the ultra-intellectual, which, diverging from objectivity toward more symbolic forms, introduces us to "the absolute itself."
4. *Iliad* II.485–86. The verb used of seeing here is regularly translated as "know" in its past tenses, as Lattimore translates it in this passage. I retain the connotation of sight in my translation so as not to lose Homer's implied contrast between the eternal witnesses on Olympos and blind humans, who depend on hearsay reports.

Bibliography

Alain (1934). *The Gods,* trans. R. Pevear. New York: New Directions, 1974.

Arrowsmith, William (1956). *The Complete Greek Tragedies,* ed. D. Grene and R. Lattimore, vol. 3: *Euripides.* Chicago: University of Chicago Press. Introduction to *The Heracles,* 270–76.

Atchity, Kenneth J. (1978). *Homer's Iliad.* Carbondale: Southern Illinois University Press.

Auerbach, Erich (1946). *Mimesis: The Representation of Reality in Western Literature,* trans. W. Trask. New York: Doubleday; Princeton, 1953.

Austin, Norman (1983). "Odysseus and the Cyclops: Who is Who," in *Approaches to Homer,* ed. C. A. and C. W. Schelmerdine, 3–37. Austin: University of Texas Press.

Ayer, Alfred J. (1946). *Language, Truth and Logic.* New York: Dover, 1952.

Bachofen, J. J. (1967). *Myth, Religion, and Mother Right,* trans. R. Manheim. Bollingen Series 84. Princeton: Princeton University Press.

Barfield, Owen (1977). *The Rediscovery of Meaning and Other Essays.* Middletown, CT: Wesleyan University Press.

Beauvoir, Simone de (1953). *The Second Sex,* trans. H. M. Parshley. New York: Alfred A. Knopf.

Bergson, Henri (1911). *Creative Evolution.* New York: Holt & Co.

Brown, G. Spencer (1973). *Laws of Form.* New York: Bantam Books.

Brown, Norman O. See under Hesiod.

Buber, Martin (1947). *Between Man and Man,* trans. R. G. Smith. London: Routledge & Kegan Paul.

——— (1970). *I and Thou,* trans. W. Kaufmann. New York: Scribner's.

Burkert, Walter (1983). *Homo Necans,* trans. Peter Bing. Berkeley and Los Angeles: University of California Press. Originally published in German as *Homo Necans* (Berlin: De Gruyter, 1972).

Callimachus, *Hymns and Epigrams,* trans. A. W. and G. R. Mair. Loeb Classical Library. Cambridge, MA: Harvard University Press, 1921 and 1977.

Campbell, Joseph (1949). *The Hero with a Thousand Faces,* 2d ed. Princeton: Princeton University Press, 1968.

——— (1959). *The Masks of God: Occidental Mythology.* New York: Viking, 1970.

Camus, Albert (1942). *L'étranger.* Paris: Gallimard.

——— (1955). *The Myth of Sisyphus and Other Essays,* trans. Justin O'Brien. New York: Alfred A. Knopf, 1964.

——— (1954). *The Stranger,* trans. Stuart Gilbert. New York: Vintage Books.

——— (1988). *The Stranger,* trans. M. Ward. New York: Alfred A. Knopf.

Cassirer, Ernst (1953). *The Philosophy of Symbolic Forms,* vol. 2: *Mythical Thought,* trans. Ralph Manheim. New Haven and London: Yale University Press.

Clay, Jenny Strauss (1983). *The Wrath of Athena.* Princeton: Princeton University Press.

Cook, A. B. (1914). *Zeus: A Study in Ancient Religion,* vol. 2. Cambridge: Cambridge University Press, 1925.

Day, John (1985). *God's Conflict with the Dragon and the Sea: A Study in the Origins of Western Speculation.* Cambridge: Cambridge University Press.

Detienne, Marcel, and Jean-Pierre Vernant (1978). *Cunning Intelligence in Greek Culture and Society,* trans. J. Lloyd. Atlantic Highlands, NJ: Humanities Press.

Dewey, John (1934). *A Common Faith.* New Haven: Yale University Press.

Diel, Paul (1980). *Symbolism in Greek Mythology,* trans. V. Stuart, M. Stuart, and R. Folkman. Boulder, CO: Shambhala. Originally published in French in 1952.

Dodds, E. R. (1951). *The Greek and the Irrational.* Berkeley: University of California Press.

Dumézil, George (1970). *The Destiny of the Warrior,* trans. A. Hiltebeitel. Chicago: University of Chicago Press.

Edinger, Edward F. (1973). *Ego and Archetype.* Baltimore: Penguin Books.

Eliade, Mircea (1963). *Myth and Reality,* trans. W. R. Trask. New York and Evanston: Harper Torchbooks.

——— (1954). *The Myth of the Eternal Return: Or, Cosmos and History,* trans. W. R. Trask. Bollingen Series 46. Princeton: Princeton University Press, 1965. Originally published in French in 1949.

Fontenrose, Joseph (1959). *Python: A Study of Delphic Myth and Its Origins.* Berkeley and Los Angeles: University of California Press.

——— (1974). "Work, Justice, and Hesiod's Five Ages." *Classical Philology* 69 (1974): 1–16.

Forsyth, Neil (1987). *The Old Enemy: Satan and the Combat Myth.* Princeton: Princeton University Press.

Fränkel, Hermann (1962). *Dichtung und Philosophie des frühen Griechentums.* Munich: C. H. Beck.

Frankfort, Henri (1949). *Before Philosophy: The Intellectual Adventure of Ancient Man,* co-author with H. A. Frankfort, J. A. Wilson, and T. Jacobsen. Baltimore: Penguin Books.

Freud, Sigmund (1900). *(ID). The Interpretation of Dreams,* trans. J. Strachey. New York: Basic Books, 1965.

——— (1910). *(LV). Leonardo da Vinci: A Study in Psychosexuality,* trans. A. A. Brill. New York: Random House, 1947.

——— (1939). *(MM). Moses and Monotheism,* trans. K. Jones. New York: Vintage Books, 1955.

——— (1913). *(TT). Totem and Taboo: Resemblances between the Psychic Lives of*

Savages and Neurotics, trans. A. A. Brill. New York: W. W. Norton, 1962.

———— (1914). "On Narcissism: An Introduction," in *Collected Papers,* vol. 4. London: Hogarth Press, 1953.

Galinsky, G. Karl (1972). *The Herakles Theme.* Oxford: Blackwell.

Gardner, Percy (1901). "A New Pandora Vase." *Journal of Hellenic Studies* 21 (1901): 1–9.

Gimbutas, Marija (1982). *The Goddesses and Gods of Old Europe.* Berkeley and Los Angeles: University of California Press.

Girard, René (1977). *Violence and the Sacred,* trans. P. Gregory. Baltimore: Johns Hopkins University Press.

Gonda, J. (1959). *Four Studies in the Language of the Veda.* The Hague: Mouton.

Gould, Stephen Jay (1977). *Ever Since Darwin.* New York: W. W. Norton.

Gould, Thomas (1963). *Platonic Love.* London: Routledge & Kegan Paul.

Griffin, Jasper (1978). "The Divine Audience and the Religion of the *Iliad.*" *Classical Quarterly,* n.s. 28.1 (1978): 1–22.

Halliday, W. R. (1913). *Greek Divination.* London: Macmillan.

Halperin, David M. (1986). "Plato and Erotic Reciprocity." *Classical Antiquity* 5 (1986): 60–80.

Harrison, Jane E. (1900). "Pandora's Box." *Journal of Hellenic Studies* 20 (1900): 99–114.

———— (1903). *Prolegomena to the Study of Greek Religion,* 3d ed. Cambridge: Cambridge University Press, 1922.

———— (1912). *Themis,* 2d ed. Cambridge: Cambridge University Press, 1927.

Hegel, G. W. F. (1907). *The Phenomenology of Mind,* trans. J. B. Baillie. New York and Evanston: Harper Torchbooks, 1967.

Heisenberg, Werner (1974). *Across the Frontiers.* New York: Harper Torchbooks. Originally published in German in 1971.

Henderson, Joseph L., and Maud Oakes (1963). *The Wisdom of the Serpent.* New York: Collier Books, 1971.

Heraclitus. *Fragments.* See Kirk and Raven (1957).

Hesiod. *(WD). Works and Days,* ed. T. A. Sinclair. Hildesheim: Georg Olms, 1966.

———— (1966). *Theogony,* edited with commentary by M. L. West. Oxford: Oxford University Press.

———— (1987). *Theogony,* translation and commentary by Richard S. Caldwell. Boston: Focus Classical Library.

———— (1959). *Works and Days; Theogony; The Shield of Herakles,* trans. R. Lattimore. Ann Arbor: University of Michigan Press.

Hillman, James (1972). *Pan and the Nightmare,* translated from the German by A. V. O'Brien of Roscher's *Ephialtes,* with Hillman's essay on Pan. New York: Spring Publications.

———— (1977). *Revisioning Psychology.* New York: Harper & Row.

Homer (1893). *Iliad,* ed. D. B. Monro, 4th ed., 2 vols. Oxford: Clarendon Press.

———— (1951). *Iliad,* trans. R. Lattimore. Chicago and London: University of Chicago.

Homeric Hymns, trans. T. Sargent. New York: W. W. Norton, 1973.

The Interpreter's Bible, vol. 3: *Job.* Nashville: Abingdon Press, 1954. Exegesis of *Job* by Samuel Terrien.

Jaffe, Aniela (1971). *The Myth of Meaning,* trans. R. F. C. Hull. New York: Putnam.

Jung, Carl G. (1954). *An Answer to Job,* trans. R. F. C. Hull. London: Routledge & Kegan Paul. Originally published as *Antwort auch Hiob* (Zurich, 1952).

———— (1919). *Psychology of the Unconscious,* trans. B. M. Hinkle. London: Routledge & Kegan Paul, 1922. Revised as *Symbols of Transformation*.

———— (1959.1). *The Archetypes and the Collective Unconscious,* trans. R. F. C. Hull, in *The Collected Works of C. G. Jung,* vol. 9, pt. 1. Bollingen Series 20. New York: Pantheon Books.

———— (1959.2). *Aion: Researches into the Phenomenology of the Self,* 2d ed., trans. R. F. C. Hull, in *Collected Works,* vol. 9, pt. 2. Bollingen Series 20. Princeton: Princeton University Press, 1968.

———— (1956). *Symbols of Transformation,* 2d ed., trans. R. F. C. Hull, in *Collected Works,* vol. 5. Bollingen Series 20. Princeton: Princeton University Press, 1967.

———— (1916). "The Transcendent Function," in *The Structure and Dynamics of the Psyche,* 2d ed., trans. R. F. C. Hull., in *Collected Works,* vol. 8. Bollingen Series 20. Princeton: Princeton University Press, 1969, 67–91.

Kerényi, Carl (1977). *Eleusis: Archetypal Image of Mother and Daughter.* New York: Schocken Books = reprint of Bollingen (1967).

———— (1976). *Dionysus: Archetypal Image of Indestructible Life,* trans. R. Manheim. Bollingen Series 65.2. Princeton: Princeton University Press.

———— (1967). "The Problem of Evil in Mythology," in *Evil,* trans. R. Manheim and H. Nagel, 3–17. Evanston, IL: Northwestern University Press.

Keuls, Eva C. (1985). *The Reign of the Phallus: Sexual Politics in Ancient Athens.* New York: Harper & Row.

Kirk, G. S., and J. E. Raven (1957). *The Presocratic Philosophers: A Critical History with a Selection of Texts.* Cambridge: Cambridge University Press.

Kirk, Geoffrey S. (1962). *The Songs of Homer.* Cambridge: Cambridge University Press.

Kirkwood, G. M. (1958). *A Study of Sophoclean Drama.* Ithaca: Cornell University Press.

Kluger, Rivkah S. (1948). *Satan in the Old Testament,* trans. H. Nagel. Evanston, IL: Northwestern University Press, 1967.

Köhler, Wolfgang (1972). *The Task of Gestalt Psychology.* Princeton: Princeton University Press.

Lacan, Jacques (1982). *Feminine Sexuality,* trans. J. Rose, ed. J. Mitchell and J. Rose. New York: W. W. Norton.

———— (1973). *The Four Fundamental Concepts of Psycho-Analysis,* trans. A. Sheridan. New York: W. W. Norton, 1978.

Lang, Mabel L. (1983). "Reverberation and Mythology in the *Iliad,*" in *Approaches to Homer,* ed. C. A. Rubino and C. W. Schelmerdine, 140–64. Austin: University of Texas Press.

Langer, Susanne K. (1953). *Feeling and Form.* New York: Scribner's.

———— (1942). *Philosophy in a New Key,* 3d. ed. Cambridge, MA: Harvard University Press, 1957.

Layton, Lynne, and Barbara Ann Shapiro, eds. (1986). *Narcissism and the Text: Studies in Literature and the Psychology of the Self.* New York and London: New York University Press.

Lévy-Bruhl, Lucien (1923). *Primitive Mentality,* trans. L. A. Clare. Boston: Beacon Press, 1966.

MacCary, W. Thomas (1982). *Childlike Achilles.* New York: Columbia University Press.

MacLean, Paul D. (1973). *A Triune Concept of the Brain and Behavior.* Toronto: University of Toronto Press.

Merrill, James (1988). *The Inner Room.* New York: Alfred A. Knopf.

Mueller, Martin (1970). "Knowledge and Delusion in the *Iliad,*" *Mosaic* 3.2 (1970): 86–103. Citations are from Wright (1978) 105–23.

Nagel, Thomas (1979). *Mortal Questions.* Cambridge: Cambridge University Press.

Nagy, Gregory (1979). *The Best of the Achaeans.* Baltimore: Johns Hopkins University Press.

Neumann, Erich (1949). *The Origins and History of Consciousness,* trans. R. F. C. Hull, Bollingen Series 42. Princeton: Princeton University Press, 1954.

Nietzsche, Friedrich (1872). *The Birth of Tragedy and the Genealogy of Morals,* trans. F. Golfing. Garden City, NY: Doubleday Anchor Books, 1956.

Nilsson, Martin P. (1925). *A History of Greek Religion.* Oxford: Clarendon Press, 1949.

Nonnus. *Dionysiaca,* trans. W. H. D. Rouse. Loeb Classical Library. Cambridge: Harvard University Press, 1940.

Otto, Rudolf (1910). *The Idea of the Holy: An Inquiry into the Non-Rational Factor in the Idea of the Divine and Its Relation to the Rational,* trans. John W. Harvey. Oxford: Oxford University Press, 1969.

Ovid. *Fasti,* ed. and trans. J. G. Frazer. Loeb Classical Library. Cambridge, MA: Harvard University Press, 1951.

———. *Metamorphoses,* ed. and trans. F. J. Miller. Loeb Classical Library. Cambridge, MA: Harvard University Press, 1916.

Owen, William H. (1968). "Commonplace and Dramatic Symbol in Seneca's Tragedies." *Transactions of the American Philological Association* 99 (1968): 291–313.

Parry, Adam (1956). "The Language of Achilles." *Transactions of the American Philological Association* 87 (1956): 1–18.

Pauli, Wolfgang (1952). "The Influence of Archetypal Ideas on the Scientific Theories of Kepler," C. G. Jung and W. Pauli, *The Interpretation of Nature and the Psyche.* Bollingen Series 51. New York: Pantheon Books, 1955.

Pettazoni, R. (1956). *The All-Knowing God: Researches into Early Religion and Culture,* trans. H. J. Rose. London: Methuen, 1978.

Pharr, Clyde (1920). *Homeric Greek,* revised by J. Wright. Norman: University of Oklahoma Press, 1985.

Plato, *Phaedrus,* trans. R. Hackforth. Cambridge: Cambridge University Press, 1952.

Plotinus (n.d.). *The Enneads,* trans. MacKenna and Page, 3d ed. New York: Pantheon Books.

Pucci, Pietro (1977). *Hesiod and the Language of Poetry.* Baltimore: Johns Hopkins University Press.

Puhvel, Jaan (1981). *Analecta indoeuropaea.* Innsbruck: Innsbrucker Beiträge zur Sprachwissenschaft.

Radin, Paul (1956). *The Trickster: A Study in American Indian Mythology.* New York: Schocken Books, 1972.

Rank, Otto (1958.1) "The Double as the Immortal Self," in *Beyond Psychology,* 62–101. New York: Dover, 1958.

——— (1958.2). "Feminine Psychology and Masculine Ideology," in *Beyond Psychology,* 235–70. New York: Dover, 1958.

——— (1914). *The Myth of the Birth of the Hero,* trans. Robbins and Jelliffe. New York: Robert Brunner, 1952.

Reyna, Ruth (1962). *The Concept of Māyā from the Vedas to the Twentieth Century.* Bombay: Asia Publishing House.

Rohde, Erwin (1894). *Psyche: The Cult of Souls and Belief in Immortality Among the Greeks,* vols. 1 and 2, 8th ed., trans. W. B. Hillis. New York: Harcourt Brace, 1925.

Róheim, Géza (1930). *Animism, Magic, and the Divine King.* New York: Alfred A. Knopf.

——— (1934). *The Riddle of the Sphinx or Human Origins,* trans. R. Money-Kyrle. London: Hogarth Press.

Russo, Joseph, and Bennett Simon (1968). "Homeric Psychology and the Oral Epic Tradition." *Journal of the History of Ideas* 29 (1968): 483–98. Citations are from Wright (1970) 41–57.

Sagan, Carl (1977). *The Dragons of Eden.* New York: Random House.

Schelling (1856). *Einleitung in die philosophie der mythologie. Collected Works,* pt. II, 1.

Schweitzer, Bernard (1922). *Herakles: Aufsätze zur griechischen Religions und Sagengeschichte.* Tübingen: Mohr.

Segal, Charles (1977). "Sophocles' *Trachiniae:* Myth, Poetry, and Heroic Values." *Yale Classical Studies* 25 (1977): 99–158.

——— (1981). *Tragedy and Civilization.* Cambridge, MA: Harvard University Press. (Chapter on *Trachiniae,* pp. 60–108.)

Seneca. (*HF*). *Hercules Furens.*

———. (*HO*). *Hercules Oetaeus.*

Shakespeare, William (1963). *Hamlet,* ed. C. Hoy, Norton Critical Edition. New York: W. W. Norton.

Simon, Bennett (1978). *Mind and Madness in Ancient Greece.* Ithaca: Cornell University Press.

Slater, Philip (1968). *The Glory of Hera.* Boston: Beacon Press.

Smith, A. H. (1890). "The Making of Pandora." *Journal of Hellenic Studies* 11 (1890): 278–83.

Snell, Bruno (1953). *The Discovery of the Mind,* trans. T. Rosenmeyer. Oxford: Oxford University Press.

Soleri, Paolo (1981). *The Omega Seed: An Eschatological Hypothesis.* Garden City, NY: Doubleday.

Sophocles. (*WT*). *The Women of Trachis* (= *Trachiniae*), ed. R. C. Jebb. Amsterdam: Servio; 1962 reprint.

Steiner, Franz (1956). *Taboo.* Baltimore: Penguin Books, 1967.

Taylor, Charles (1975). *Hegel.* Cambridge: Cambridge University Press.

Vernant, Jean-Paul (1977). "Sacrificial and Alimentary Codes in Hesiod's Myth of Prometheus," in *Myth, Religion and Society,* ed. R. L. Gordon, 57–79. Cambridge: Cambridge University Press, 1981.

——— (1980). "The Myth of Prometheus in Hesiod," in *Myth and Society in Ancient Greece,* trans. J. Lloyd. Atlantic Highlands, NJ: Humanities Press.

Vivante, Paolo (1970). *The Homeric Imagination.* Bloomington: Indiana University Press.

——— (1982). *The Epithets in Homer.* New Haven and London: Yale University Press.

von Fritz, Kurt (1947). "Pandora, Prometheus, and the Myth of the Ages." *Review of Religion* 11 (1947): 227–60.

West, M. L. (1966). See Hesiod, *Theogony.*

Whitehead, Alfred North (1926). *Religion in the Making.* New York: Macmillan.

——— (1929). *Process and Reality: An Essay in Cosmology.* New York: Macmillan.

Whitman, Cedric H. (1958). *Homer and the Heroic Tradition.* Cambridge, MA: Harvard University Press.

Widengren, Geo (1967). "The Principle of Evil in the Eastern Religions," in *Evil,* trans. R. Manheim and Hildegard Nagel. Evanston, IL: Northwestern University Press 21–55.

Willcock, M. M. (1970). "Some Aspects of the Gods in the *Iliad.*" *Bulletin of the Institute of Classical Studies* 17 (1970): 1–10. Citations are from Wright (1978) 58–69.

Wilson, John A. (1949). *Before Philosophy,* co-author with H. and H. A. Frankfort and Thorkild Jacobsen. Baltimore: Penguin Books.

Worthen, Thomas W. (1988). "The Idea of 'Sky' in Archaic Greek Poetry." *Glotta* 68 (1988): 50–62.

Wright, John, ed. (1978). *Essays on the* Iliad: *Selected Modern Criticism,* Bloomington: Indiana University Press.

Zeitlin, Froma I. (1985). "Playing the Other: Theater, Theatricality, and the Feminine in Greek Drama." *Representation* 11 (1985): 63–94.

Zimmer, Heinrich (1938). "The Indian World Mother," in *The Mystic Vision: Papers from the Eranos Yearbooks,* vol. 6, trans. R. Manheim, Bollingen Series 30. Princeton: Princeton University Press, 1968, pp. 70–102.

———— (1936). *Maya: Der indische mythos.* Stuttgart and Berlin: Deutsche Verlags-Anstalt.

Index